SO-AZQ-202

A World Bank-UNICEF Glossary
*Glossaire édité conjointement par
la Banque mondiale et l'UNICEF*

Terminology of Water Supply
and Environmental Sanitation
*Terminologie de l'approvisionnement
en eau et de l'assainissement du milieu*

English—French
Français—anglais

Paul J. Biron

**The World Bank
Washington, D.C.**

Copyright © 1987

UNICEF (United Nations Childrens Fund)
(Fonds des Nations Unies pour l'enfance)

International Bank for Reconstruction
and Development / The World Bank

Banque internationale pour la reconstruction
et le développement / Banque mondiale

1818 H Street, N.W.
Washington, D.C. 20433, U.S.A.

Library of Congress Cataloging in Publication Data

Biron, Paul J.
    Terminology of water supply and environmental
sanitation

    (A World Bank-UNICEF glossary)
    English and French
    1. Water supply engineering—Dictionaries.
2. Sanitary engineering—Dictionaries.   3. English
language—Dictionaries—French.   4. Water supply
engineering—Dictionaries—French.   5. Sanitary
engineering—Dictionaries—French.   6. French
language—Dictionaries—English.   I. Title.
II. Series.
TD9.B57   1985   628'.03'21   85-16863

ISBN 0-8213-0585-9

Contents—*Table des matières*

MATERIEL ET FOURNITURES DES PROJETS D'HYDRAULIQUE ET D'ASSAINISSEMENT DU MILIEU

EQUIPMENT AND SUPPLIES FOR WATER SUPPLY AND ENVIRONMENTAL SANITATION PROJECTS

GLOSSAIRE ABRÉGÉ FRANÇAIS/ANGLAIS

ABRIDGED GLOSSARY ENGLISH/FRENCH

Par

Paul J. Biron
Ingénieur A & M
UNICEF–PDPD/WET–HQ

By

Paul J. Biron
Ingénieur A & M
UNICEF–PDPD/WET–HQ

Note de Présentation

La liste suivante ne prétend ni être complète, ni épuiser le sujet. Des dictionnaires existent à cet effet. Toutefois ceux-ci peuvent ne pas être à portée immédiate de l'utilisateur.

Ce qui suit tend à fournir un glossaire d'accès facile en français et en anglais, des termes les plus fréquemment employés en matière d'hydraulique et d'assainissement du milieu.

Il emprunte abondamment aux descriptions et terminologies retenues par les constructeurs de matériel et fournisseurs.

La présentation repose sur les principes suivants:

(a) *Lorsque plusieurs traductions sont possibles ou doivent être envisagées, les équivalent sont séparés par le signe /.*

   Ex : exhaure — pumping/water lifting

(b) *Lorsque plusieurs traductions ont des acceptions différentes, elles sont séparées par ; .*

   Ex : agent — agent/facteur; assistant

(c) *Lorsque l'article reprend un nom clé précédemment cité, ce dernier est remplacé par (-).*

   Ex : Sous la rubrique Sondeuse, sondeuse au battage apparaît en (-) au battage

(d) *Lorsque l'article est une variante d'un article précédent, ce dernier est désigné par (-id-).*

   Ex : Après Forage á la boue, le forage á la boue en circulation inverse est rendue par (-id-) en circulation inverse.

L'utilisation des mots cités dans la liste présuppose une connaissance suffisante des règles grammaticales d'accord en genre et en nombre.

L'annexe 1 regroupe, selon un classement de leur origine et de leur transmission, les maladies attribuables aux insuffisances de l'approvisionnement.

L'annexe 2 regroupe un certain nombre de facteurs de conversion d'usage courant et de correspondance entre unités.

Introductory Note

The following list does not pretend to be exhaustive or complete. Dictionaries exist already for this purpose. However, they may not be readily available when needed.

What follows merely attempts to provide the user with a handy *French*/English glossary of the terms more frequently used in connection with water supply and environmental sanitation.

It is largely based on the descriptions and terminologies used by equipment manufacturers and suppliers.

The following presentation has been adopted:

(a) Whenever several equivalent translations exist or should be considered, the words are separated by the sign /.

   i.e., drilling rig—*atelier de forage/sondeuse*

(b) Whenever the translations have different meanings, they are separated by ;.

   i.e., agent—*agent/facteur; assistant*

(c) Whenever the entry refers to a key word quoted earlier, the latter is replaced by the sign (-).

   i.e., Under Jack, leveling jack is rendered by leveling (-)

(d) Whenever the item represents a variation on a previously quoted entry, the latter is replaced by the sign (-id-).

   i.e., After leveling jack, hydraulic, a screw type leveling jack appears as (-id-) screw type.

Use of the listed words presupposes a basic knowledge of grammatical rules of concordance in gender and number.

In Annex 1 are listed diseases related to deficiencies in water supply and/or sanitation, classified according to their origin and transmission.

Annex 2 compiles conversion factors of frequent use and equivalents between units.

Terminology of Water Supply and Environmental Sanitation

English—French

A

to abandon a well	abandonner un puits
abnormal	anormal
(-) dip	pendage (-)
abrasion	abrasion/ érosion
abrasive	abrasif
(-) cloth/paper	toile/papier émeri/papier de verre
ABS	acrylonitrile-butadiène-styrène
abutment	culée
abutting joint	assemblage en about
accretion	accroissement par dépôt d'alluvions
acreage	superficie
activity	activité
respiratory (-)	(-) respiratoire
adjustable	réglable
adjusting rod	tige de rallonge
adsorption	adsorption
(-) by activated carbon	(-) sur charbon actif
advantage	avantage
mechanical (-)	bras de levier/effet multiplicateur d'un bras de levier
aeration of water supplies	aération des eaux de consommation
(-) of waste water	(-) des eaux résiduaires
aerator	aérateur
surface (-)	(-) de surface
aerial	antenne; aérien
ageing	vieillissement
agent	agent
wetting (-)	(-) mouillant
aggregate	agrégat
open graded (-)	(-) grossier/poreux
unindurated (-)	agglomérats non consolidés
aggressivity of carbonic acid	aggressivité carbonique
air	air
intake (-)	(-) aspiré
compressed (-)	(-) comprimé
discharge (-)	(-) de refoulement
(-) lift	gazosiphon
alkaline	alcalin
alluvium	alluvion/ terre d'alluvion

alternative energy	énergie de substitution
amount	montant; teneur/proportion
analysis of water	analyses de contrôle
bacteriological (-)	(-) bactériologique
anchor	ancre
guy (-)	ancrage du haubannage
anchorage	ancrage
annular	annulaire
angle	angle
deviation (-)	(-) de déviation
(-) of dip	(-) d'inclinaison ou de pendage
anticlinal ridge	arête anticlinale
anticline	anticlinal
arrested (-)	(-) tronqué
asymmetric (-)	(-) asymétrique
composite (-)	(-) complexe
elongated (-)	(-) allongé
erect (-)	(-) droit
exposed (-)	(-) affleurant
overturned (-)	(-) déversé
recumbent (-)	(-) renversé
apron	tablier
aquifer	aquifère/ nappe/ eau(x) souterraine(s)
confined (-)	nappe captive
unconfined (-)	nappe libre
arch	voûte
area	aire/ surface
continental (-)	(-) continentale
(-) of truncation	(-) d'érosion
arm	bras
rocker (-)	brinqueballe
assistant	adjoint/ agent
technical (-)	(-) technique
auger/ground (-)	tarière
axis	axe
anticlinal (-)	(-) anticlinal
(-) of crystal	(-) d'un crystal
fold (-)	(-) de plissement
plunging/ pitching (-)	(-) plongeant
trough (-)	(-) synclinal
axle	arbre

B

back axle	pont arrière
back digger	rétro caveuse

backfill	*terre de remblayage/ remblai*	balance (-) beam (-) bob mud (-) (-) weight	*balance* *fléau* *balancier à contrepoids* *(-) à boue* *contrepoids*
backfilling	*remblayage/remblaiement/ rebouchage*	balancing	*équilibrage/compensation*
backfiring	*retour d'allumage*	balk	*poutre/solive*
backflow	*refoulement/reflux*	ball	*bille/boule*
backfolding	*plissement en retour*	(-) bearing	*roulement/palier*
background	*arrière-plan; données de base; soubassement*	(-id-) cage (-id-) cup (-) clay	*cage de (-)* *cuvette de (-)* *argile plastique*
(-) noise	*bruit de fond*	(-) cock	*robinet/soupape à flotteur*
backhoe	*pelle rétrocaveuse mécanique*	(-) joint/(-) and socket joint	*joint à rotule/joint sphérique*
(-) loader	*chargeuse-pelleteuse/ rétro-chargeuse*	(-) peen hammer (-) thrust bearing	*marteau à panne bombée* *palier de butée/de crapaudine à billes*
backing (-) pass (welding) (-) weld	*renforcement/soutien* *passe de soutien (soudure)* *soudure de (-)*	ballast	*ballast/lest/empierrement*
backlash	*contre-coup; jeu*	balling/balling up	*bourrage/embourbage*
backlath	*palplanche*	balloon	*ballon/réservoir*
backloader	*rétro-chargeuse*	ball stone	*calcaire concrétionné*
back-off (-) tool	*dévissage* *coulisse de battage*	band	*bande/ruban/courroie; intercalation de roches*
back pass (welding)	*passe sur l'envers (soudure)*	(-) brake (-) clamp (-) conveyor (-) pulley/(-) wheel	*frein à bande/à collier* *collier d'obturation* *convoyeur à bande* *poulie à courroie*
back pressure (-) valve	*contre pression* *soupape de retenue*	banded	*rubané/strié*
back slope	*surface structurale*	banding	*frettage*
back surge	*pression de retour*	bank	*banc/levée de terre/ remblai*
back thrusting	*rétrocharriage/ chevauchement en retour*	banking	*remblayage/remblai*
back twist (of a cable)	*contre-torsion (d'un câble)*	bar	*barre/banc*
backups/back-up tongs	*clés de blocage des tiges/ clés de dévissage*	barbed wire	*fil de fer barbelé*
to back up	*renforcer/soutenir*	barrel pump (-)	*baril* *corps de pompe*
backward (-) erosion (-) folding	*rétrograde* *érosion régressive* *plissement en retour*	barren (-) well	*stérile/aride* *sondage stérile*
baffle (-) collar	*chicane/déflecteur* *manchon de cimentation*	barrier fluid (-)	*barrière/clôture/barrage* *(-) de perméabilité*
to bail out	*curer/puiser*	basal (-) cleavage (-) conglomerate	*fondamental/de base* *clivage principal* *conglomérat de base*
bailer	*cuiller/soupape ou tube à clapet*	base	*base/assise/pied/socle; bas/pauvre; base (alcali)*
clean out (-) (-) valve	*(-) de curage* *vanne de (-)*	(-) frame (-) line data (-)	*chassis* *base (topographique)* *(-) de données*
bailing (-) drum (-) line or rope	*curage/puisage* *tambour de (-)* *câble de (-)*	base exchanger	*échangeur de cations*

base metal	métal commun
(-) ore	minerai pauvre
baseplate	embase
basement	socle/ soubassement
(-) rock	roche de base/ roche du socle
basin	réservoir/ cuve/ cuvette/ bassin/ fosse
drainage (-)	bassin hydrographique
(-) folds	cuvette synclinale
groundwater (-)	bassin hydrogéologique
basket	panier de repêchage/ benne/ godet/ cuiller
(-)grapple	coin agrippeur
cement (-) reservoir	réservoir à paroi de vannerie enduite de ciment
(-) sub	tube à sédiments
bath	bain/ cuve
(-) lubrication	graissage par barbotage
(-) tub	baignoire
battery	accumulateur (electr.)
bead	grain/ perle
weld (-)	cordon de soudure
weave (-)	passe large (de soudure)
welding (-)	perle de soudure
beading	dépôt d'un cordon de soudure
(-) hand tool	matoir à tubes
beam	balancier/ fléau/ poutre; faisceau/ rayon
(-) caliper	pied à coulisse
(-) compass	compas à verge/ compas à trusquin
(-) drive	commande/ transmission par balancier
(-) hook	crochet de balancier
(-) pump	pompe à balancier
walking (-)	balancier de pompe
bearer	cadre porteur/ sommier
(-) plates of an engine	berceau de moteur
bearing	palier/ coussinet/ roulement; porteur/ soutien
antifriction (-)	(-) à garniture antifriction
ball (-)	roulement à billes
ball thrust (-)	(-) de butée à billes
big end (-)	palier/ coussinet de tête de bielle
(-) bracket	plateau de (-)
(-) bush/(-) bushing	douille
bush (-)	(-) lisse
(-) cap	chapeau de (-)
crankshaft (-)	(-) de vilebrequin
floating-ring (-)	(-) à coussinet flottant
journal (-)	(-) lisse
(-) liners	douilles de (-)
needle (-)	roulement à aiguilles
roller (-)	roulement à rouleaux
taper (-id-)	(-id-) coniques
sealed (-)	(-) étanche
self-aligning (-)	(-) à rotule
(-) shell	coquille de (-)
small end (-)	palier/ coussinet de pied de bielle
thrust (-)	butée/ palier de butée
wrist pin (-)	coussinet d'axe de piston
(-) axle	essieu porteur
(-) surface	surface portante
(-) wall	mur de soutènement
water (-)	aquifère
beater	batteur
beating	battage
bedding	stratification
(-) angle	angle de (-)
(-) fault	faille parallèle aux strates
bell	cloche/ sonnette
(-) guide	cloche de guidage
(-) socket	arrache-tube
bellows	soufflet
expansion (-)	(-) de dilatation
belly	bombement
belt	courroie/ bande; zone/ ceinture
(-) clamp	agrafe de (-)
(-) drive	commande par (-)
(-) sling	élingue
(-) of weathering	zone d'altération
bench	banc/ banquette; établi
(-) gravel	gravier de terrasse
laboratory (-)	paillasse
work (-)	établi
benchmark	repère; point géodésique
bend	coude/ courbe
expansion (-)	lyre de dilatation
bender	cintreuse/ machine à cintrer
bent	courbé/ plié
(-) rod	tige faussée
(-) sub	raccord coudé
bevel	biseau/ chanfrein
(-) cutter	fraise d'angle
(-) gear/(-) spur gear	engrenages à roues coniques
(-) pinion	pignon d'angle
(-) shears	cisaille d'angle
(-) weld	soudure sur chanfrein

BHN (Brinell hardness number)	*indice de dureté Brinell*
BHP (brake horse power)	*puissance en chevaux au frein*
bickern (of an anvil)	*bigorne (d'une enclume)*
big end	*tête de bielle*
bin	*récipient/ silo/ soute/ trémie*
bind	*schiste argileux*
bed	*banc/ couche/ dépôt/ gîte/ lit/ socle/ strate*
(-) joint	*fracture horizontale*
(-) load	*charriage de fond*
(-) pinchout	*lit biseauté*
(-) plate	*bâti/ chassis (d'une machine)/ plaque d'assise ou de fondation*
(-) rock	*socle/ roche de fond*
(-) thickness	*épaisseur de couche*
bottomset (-)	*feuillet basal*
filter (-)	*couche filtrante*
foreset (-)	*feuillet frontal*
reservoir (-)	*couche réservoir*
shifting (-)	*lit divagant*
topset (-)	*feuillet sommital*
water bearing (-)	*lit aquifère*
bedded	*en couche/ stratifié/ lité*
binder/binding agent	*agglomérant/ liant*
binding	*liaison/ attache/ grippage*
(-) posts	*bornes d'appareillage électrique*
(-) screw	*borne à vis*
biscuit cutter	*coupe-carotte (forage au câble)*
bit (binary digit)	*unité de mémorisation (codage base 2 d'un ordinateur)*
bit	*trépan/ taillant/ outil de forage*
(-) breaker	*débloqueur de (-)*
(-id-) plate	*plaque de dévissage*
(-) gauge	*cercle de contrôle du calibre*
(-id-) surface	*front de taille du (-)/ de l'outil*
(-) hook	*caracole de repêchage*
(-) nose	*nez de l'outil*
(-) puller	*outil de démontage du (-)*
(-) shank	*filetage de l'outil*
blade (-)/drag (-)	*(-) à lames*
blank (-)	*couronne*
button (-)	*outil à pastilles*
carbide (-)	*outil à carbure de tungstène*
collapsible (-)	*outil/ trépan à effacement*

cone (-)/rock (-)/ roller (-)/rock roller (-)	*(-) à cones/ outil à molettes*
diamond (-)	*(-) au diamant*
drag (-)	*(-) à lames*
fish tail (-)	*(-) à 2 lames*
four-way (-)/four-wing (-)	*(-) à lames/ à 2 taillants croisés*
Mother Hubbard (-)	*(-) Mère Hubbard (au câble, à largeur constante, avec redans coupants)*
rathole (-)	*(-) d'avant-trou*
reamer (-)	*(-) aléseur/ (-) élargisseur*
removable core (-)	*carottier remontable*
roller (-)	*(-) à rouleaux*
semi-dressed	*à taillant ébauché*
spudding (-)	*(-) bêche*
star (-)	*(-) en croix*
three-way (-)	*(-) à 3 lames*
blade	*lame/ aube/ palette*
(-) grader	*niveleuse*
dozer (-)	*lame de bulldozer*
blank	*obturateur/ bouchon; normal/ ordinaire; factice/ essai à blanc*
(-) cover	*couvercle plein*
(-) flange	*bride pleine/ bride aveugle*
(-) pipe/(-) casing	*tube/ cuvelage à paroi pleine, sans crépinage*
(-) test	*essai à blanc/ essai à vide*
blanket	*couche/ entablement/ filon/ nappe/ strate*
blast	*déflagration/ jet d'air/ soufflerie*
blasting	*explosion/ abattage; décapage*
(-) charge	*charge explosive*
grit (-)/sand (-)	*décapage au sable*
shot (-)	*décapage à la grenaille*
bleaching powder	*chlorure de chaux*
bleeding	*prise/ purge/ vidange*
blender	*mélangeur*
block	*bloc/ bloquage; massif; moufle/ palan*
(-) chain	*chaîne à roulement*
(-) valve	*vanne de sectionnement*
(-) fields	*chaos/ champs de pierres/ de blocs*
(-) clusters	*amas de blocs*
(-) streams	*coulées de pierres*
fault (-)	*bloc faillé*
(-) and falls/ (-) and tackle	*palan*
(-) line	*mouflage*
(-) pulley	*moufle/ poulie mouflée*
crown (-)	*moufle fixe*

multi-sheave (-)	*moufle à poulies multiples*
traveling (-)	*moufle mobile*
blow	*affleurement*
(-) cock	*robinet d'extraction*
(-) down	*purge/chasse*
(-) hole	*soufflure/cavité; soufflard*
blow-off cock	*purgeur*
blower	*soufflante/ventilateur*
blowout	*éruption/jaillissement*
blowpipe	*chalumeau*
(-) welding	*soudure au (-)*
blow torch	*chalumeau/lampe à souder*
blunt	*émoussé*
board	*planche/passerelle*
monkey/racking (-)	*passerelle d'accrochage*
bob	*plomb (d'un fil à plomb)*
BOD (biochemical oxygen demand)	*DBO (demande biochimique en oxygène)*
body	*carrosserie/corps; consistance*
bog	*tourbière/marais*
bolt	*boulon/cheville/goupille*
(-) anchor	*(-) d'ancrage*
holding down (-)	*(-) de fixation*
U (-)	*(-) étrier fileté*
bond	*liaison/lien/joint*
bonnet	*capuchon/capot (de moteur d'un véhicle)*
boom	*flèche (d'une grue)/mât de charge*
(-) cat	*tracteur grutier à chenilles*
(-) jack	*pince à loquet*
side (-)	*pose tube à flèche latérale*
booster	*surpresseur/survolteur*
(-) pump	*surpresseur/pompe à relai*
boot	*botte; vidange d'une citerne*
(-) jack	*fourche à cliquet/outil de repêchage*
(-) socket	*accroche-coulisse*
bore	*sondage/trou de sonde; alésage*
borebit	*mèche/fleuret/tranchant; trépan*
bore hole	*trou de sonde/sondage*
boring	*percement/forage/sondage*
(-) by percussion	*sondage par battage*
deep (-)	*sondage profond*

bottom	*fond/base/socle/ soubassement*
fanning (-)	*affleurement du fond*
(-) hole	*(-) du sondage*
(-) joint	*diaclase horizontale*
(-) rake	*angle d'incidence d'un outil*
boulder	*bloc de pierre roulé*
(-) clay	*argile à blocaux*
(-) stream	*coulée de blocs*
bouldery	*caillouteux*
boundary	*limite/borne*
(-) fault	*faille limite*
bow area	*zone plissée*
bowl	*cloche de guidage; entonnoir/cuvette (géol.)*
toilet (-)	*cuvette de W.C.*
box	*boîte/caisse; raccord femelle*
(-) coupling	*manchon d'accouplement*
(-) both ends	*manchon double*
(-) girder	*poutre caisson/poutre tubulaire*
(-) and pin	*raccords femelle et mâle*
(-) spanner	*clé à douille*
(-) sub	*raccord à souder, femelle*
branching (-)	*boîte de dérivation (électr.)*
stuffing (-)	*presse-étoupe*
brace	*contre fiche/croisillon/ entretoise*
(-) head	*tourne-à-gauche; manche de manoeuvre*
bracket	*potence/console/support*
brackish	*saumâtre*
brake	*frein*
(-) band	*collier de (-)*
(-) block	*patin de (-)*
(-) drum	*tambour de (-)*
(-) lining	*garniture de (-)*
(-) shoe	*sabot de (-)*
branch	*branche/bifurcation/ embranchement*
(-) circuit	*circuit dérivé*
(-) connection	*piquage*
(-) pipe	*tuyau de dérivation*
brass	*laiton*
(-) bearing	*coussinet en (-)*
(-) soldering	*brasure*
braze	*brasure*
brazing	*brasage*

break	*cassure/ rupture*
(-) joint	*joint en chicane*
(-) out	*dévissage*
(-id-) tongs	*clé de (-)*
(-) of slope	*rupture de pente*
(-) in the succession	*lacune stratigraphique*
(-) thrust	*plan de chevauchement*
breaker	*interrupteur*
circuit (-)/(-id-) switch	*disjoncteur*
bit (-)/(-id-) plate	*plaque de dévissage*
breakdown	*avarie/ panne*
breakthrough	*percée*
breast	*front de taille*
(-) derrick	*chèvre de forage*
(-) drill	*chignole/ vilebrequin*
breccia	*brèche*
brecciated	*bréchiforme/ bréchoïde*
bridle	*bride*
(-) irons	*tendeurs*
brim	*bord/ rebord*
brush	*broussaille; balai (électr.); brosse/ pinceau*
(-) gang	*équipe de débroussaillement*
tube (-)	*écouvillon*
bucket	*godet/ bac/ seau/ benne*
(-) chain	*chaine à (-)*
(-) excavator	*excavateur à (-)*
(-) grab	*benne preneuse*
(-) trap	*purgeur à cloche*
(-) wheel	*roue à augets/ roue-pelle*
(-) latrines	*tinettes*
buckle	*gauchissement/ flambement; boucle*
buffer	*amortisseur; tampon*
buildup	*augmentation de la déviation d'un forage*
rate of (-)	*gradient d'inclinaison*
bulge	*renflement*
bulk	*masse/ chargement/ vrac*
(-) density	*densité apparente*
in (-)	*en vrac*
bulldozer	*bouteur*
bull reel	*treuil de manoeuvre*
bull rope	*câble de sondage*
bull spear	*arrache-tube*
bull wheel	*tambour de forage*
bumper	*butoir/ pare choc; amortisseur/ tampon*
(-) sub	*coulisse de battage*
crown block (-)	*amortisseur de moufle fixe*

traveling block (-)	*amortisseur de moufle mobile*
bung	*bouchon/ bonde/ obturateur*
buried	*enterré/ ensouillé*
(-) outcrop	*affleurement masqué*
bushing	*bague/ coussinet/ douille/ manchon mâle-femelle/ fourrure*
(also bush)	
kelly (-)/drive (-)	*fourrure d'entraînement de la tige carrée*
split (-)	*douille en deux parties*
spacing bush	*bague d'écartement*
butt	*about/ aboutement*
(-) joint	*join bout à bout*
(-) strap	*couvre-joint*
(-) welding	*soudure par rapprochement*

C

cab	*abri/ cabine/ poste de conduite*
cabinet	*coffret*
cable	*câble/ corde; canalisation*
armored (-)	*(-) armé*
(-) bearer/hanger	*porte câble*
(-) box	*boîte de jonction*
(-) clamp/clip	*serre-câble*
(-) crab	*porte-palan*
(-) drilling	*forage au câble/ forage par percussion*
(-) drum/(-) reel	*tambour de (-)/ dévidoir de (-)*
(-) release	*déclencheur automatique*
(-) rig	*appareil/ atelier de forage au câble*
(-) ring	*bague de suspension*
(-) sheath	*gaine*
(-) shoe	*cosse de (-)*
(-) splice	*épissure*
(-) strand	*toron d'un (-)*
(-) thimble	*raccord de (-)*
(-) tool	*outillage de forage au câble*
cage	*cage*
valve (-)	*corbeille de soupape*
cake	*dépôt/ incrustation/ croûte/ agglutination*
calculation chart	*abaque*

calf line	câble de manoeuvre du tubage	casing	tubage/cuvelage
calf wheel	tambour de levage/de manoeuvre (forage au câble)	(-) adaptor	réducteur/pièce de réduction pour (-)
(-id-) arms	bras d'un (-id-)	(-) bowl	cloche de repêchage à coins
(-id-) brake	frein pour (-id-)	(-) clamp	collier/anneau de retenue
calibrated	gradué/étalonné	(-) collar/(-) coupling	raccord/joint entre éléments de (-)
caliper	calibre/gabarit: micromètre	(-) cutter/(-) knife	coupe-tube
(-) gauge	jauge à coulisse	(-) dog	arrache-tube
(-) log	log de diamétrage	(-) grab	accroche-tube
(-) rule	calibre à vis	(-) head	tête de sonde/tête de tubage
inside (-)	diamétreur	(-) hook	crochet à tube
outside (-)	compas d'épaisseur	(-) line	câble de levage/de treuil de manoeuvre
shaft (-)	calibre à mâchoires	(-) rack	râtelier à tubage
slide (-)	pied à coulisse	(-) racker head	tête d'aggripage
cam	came/taquet	(-) ripper/(-) splitter	fendeur de tubage
(-) and followers	excentrique à galets	(-) shoe	sabot de cuvelage
(-) follower/roller	galet de la came	(-) spear	poire de repêchage
(-) and yoke	excentrique à cadre	(-) spider	support de tubage à coins
exhaust (-)/outlet (-)	(-) d'échappement	(-) string	colonne de tubage/de cuvelage
inlet (-)	(-) d'admission	(-) tongs	clés de tubage
camshaft	arbre à came	cast	coulée/moulée
(-) sprocket	pignon d'(-)	casting	moulage/pièce moulée
can (oil)	burette à huile	castor	roulette pivotante
canister	cartouche filtrante	(-) oil	huile de ricin
cap	bouchon/couvercle/ chapeau/calotte/cloche; terrains de recouvrement/ roche couverture	cat (= caterpillar)	véhicule chenillé
casing head (-)	tête de tubage	cat's eye	catadioptre
filler (-)	bouchon de remplissage	catch	cliquet/taquet
capping	terrain de recouvrement mort-terrain	(-) hook	crochet de sauvetage
		(-) wrench	clé de retenue
capstan	treuil/cabestan	caterpillar	chenille
(-) drive	commande par manège	cathead	cabestan
(-) drum head	tête de cabestan	catline	câble de cabestan
(-) lathe	tour revolver	(-) sheave	poulie de (-id-)
(-) winch	treuil à moufle	catwalk	passerelle
captor	cours d'eau capteur/ pirate	catworks	treuil auxiliaire
carburetor	carburateur	caulking	imperméabilisation/ calfatage
carrier	transporteur/véhicule porteur	cave	caverne/grotte; foudroyage
cascade	cascade	caverne	calcaire caverneux
(-) connection (electr.)	montage en série (électr.)	caving	éboulement
case	boîte/caisse/coffret	(-) formation	terrain boulant
case hardening	cementation/trempe superficielle	cavy well	puits boulant/qui ne tient pas
cased well	sondage tubé		

cell | cellule
battery (-) | élément d'accumulateur/de pile
dry (-) | pile sèche
solar (-) | cellule/pile solaire
(-) texture | texture alvéolaire/poreuse

cellular | alvéolaire/cellulaire
(-) lava | lave boueuse

cement | ciment/mortier
(-) basket reservoir | réservoir à paroi de vannerie enduite de (-)
(-) bin | silo à ciment
(-) grout | coulis de (-)
(-) mixer | mélangeur de (-)
(-) plug | bouchon de (-)
quick setting (-) | (-) à prise rapide

center | centre
(-) mark | coup de pointeau
(-) punch | pointeau
(-) spear | harpon/outil de repêchage

centrifugal | centrifuge
(-) casting | coulée centrifuge
(-) clutch | embrayage (-)
(-) compressor | compresseur (-)
(-) governor | régulateur (-)
(-) pump | pompe (-)

centrocline | cuvette

centroclinal dip | pendage périclinal

cesspool | fosse d'aisance/cloaque

chafing ring | bague de protection

chain | chaîne
(-) adjuster/(-) tightener | tendeur de (-)
(-) case/(-) guard | carter couvre-chaîne
(-) drive | commande par chaîne
(-) hoist | palan à (-)
(-) hook | crochet de (-)/croc
(-) pump | noria/pompe à chapelet
(-) tongs | serre-tubes à (-)/pince/clé à (-)
roller (-) | (-) à galets
sprocket (-) | (-) galle

chamber pot | vase de nuit/bourdalou (old)

chart | diagramme/abaque

chasm | abîme/gouffre

chassis | chassis/frame

chatter | cliquetis/vibration/broutement

check | contrôle/vérification
(-) bolt | boulon d'arrêt
(-) mark | trait de repère
(-) nut | écrou de blocage
(-) valve | clapet de retenue/clapet de pied
ball (-id-) | clapet à bille

checker | carroyage
(-) board | plaque striée/plaque antidérapante

cheesehead | tête cylindrique (de vis)

cherry picker | tube de repêchage fendu; bras élévateur/télescopique à nacelle

chilled | refroidi; coulé en coquille

chink | lézardé/fissure

chip | copeau/éclat/fragment
(-) of rock | esquilles de roches

chisel | ciseau/burin
(-) bit | trépan tranchant/trépan à biseau

chloride | chlorure

chlorinated | chloré

chlorination | chlorination

chock | cale/coin
(-) block | étai/contrefort

choke | étranglement/duse/rétrécissement
(-) coil | bobine d'impédance
(-) nipple | duse calibrée

chocking | bourrage/colmatage/engorgement

chuck | mandrin/plateau

churn | malaxeur
(-) drilling | sondage par percussion

chute | couloir/goulotte

cinder | cendre/scories/laitier

circuit | circuit
(-) breaker | coupe circuit/disjoncteur

circulation | circulation/injection
mud (-) | (-) des boues
forced (-) | (-) forcée
loss (-)/of returns | perte de (-)
reverse (-) | (-) inverse

cistern | réservoir/citerne/bâche

clack | clapet
(-) valve | soupape à (-)

clam
  (-) shell
  (-id-) bucket
  (-id-) excavator
	coquille/ crampon
	  pelle à benne preneuse
	  benne preneuse
	  excavator à (-id-)

clamp
  (-) bolt/clamping bolt
  (-) screw
  connector (-)
	collier/ bride
	  boulon de support
	  vis de blocage
	  collier d'assemblage

clamping device	*système de serrage*
clapboarding	*revêtement de bardeaux*
clarification bed	*lit filtrant*

clarifying
  (-) agent
  (-) basin
	clarificateur
	  clarifiant
	  bassin de clarification

clasp	*agrafe/ fermeture*
classification	*classification/ tri/ triage/* *tamisage*

claw
  (-) bar
 	
  (-) clutch/(-) coupling
  (-) hammer
	griffe/ crochet
	  pied de biche/ pied de
	  chèvre
	  embrayage à griffe
	  marteau à panne fendue

clay
  (-) base mud
  (-) bed/(-) layer
  boulder (-)
  bedded (-)
  burned (-)
  colloid (-)
  flint (-)
  (-) loam/silty (-)
  marl (-)
  swelling (-)
	argile
	  boue à l'(-)
	  lit/ banc/ couche d'(-)
	  (-) à blocaux
	  (-) litée
	  (-) calcinée
	  (-) colloïdale
	  (-) à silex
	  (-) limoneuse
	  (-) marneuse
	  (-) gonflante

clearance	*jeu/ intervalle*
cleat	*clivage/ tasseau/ taquet*
cleavage	*clivage/ coupure/ scission*
cleft	*crevasse/ fissure*
clevis	*manille d'assemblage*
cliff	*falaise/ escarpement à pic*

clinometer
  bead (-)
	clinomètre/ eclimètre
	  (-) à bulle

clip
  wire rope (-)
	pince/ étrier de serrage
	  serre câble

clippers	*pinces-coupantes*

clockwise
 	
  counter/anti (-)
	dans le sens des aiguilles
	  d'une montre/ sens
	  rétrograde
	  dans le sens contraire
	  des aiguilles d'une
	  montre/ sens direct

clod	*motte*
clogged	*bouché/ encrassé/ engorgé*

close
  (-) fault
  (-) fold
  (-) meshed
	clos/ épais/ fermé/ serré
	  faille fermée
	  pli reserré
	  à mailles fines

clot	*caillot/ flocon/ grumeau*
clotting	*coagulation*
clough	*ravin/ gorge*
clump	*bloc/ massif/ motte*

cluster
  (-) of gear wheels
	amas/ grappe/ groupe
	  train d'engrenage

clutch
  (-) disc
  (-) lining
  (-) plate
	embrayage/ accouplement
	  plateau d'(-)
	  garniture d'(-)
	  plateau d'(-)

coarse
  (-) aggregate
  (-) grained
	gros/ grossier
	  agrégat grossier
	  à gros grains

to coast	*marcher en roue libre*
coat	*couche/ enduit*

coating
 	
  cement (-)
  spray (-)
	couche/ croûte/ enduit/
	  revêtement/ application
	  enduit de ciment
	  étendage au pistolet/
	  au jet

cob	*pisé/ torchis*
cobble/cobblestone	*caillou/ galet/ moellon/* *pavé*

cock
  (-) key
  ball (-)
  bib (-)
  drain (-)/drip (-)
 	
  feed (-)
  gauge (-)
  pet (-)
  plug (-)
  relief (-)
 	
  sludge (-)
  stop (-)
	robinet
	  clé de (-)
	  (-) à flotteur
	  (-) à vis
	  (-) de purge/(-) de
	  vidange
	  (-) d'alimentation
	  (-) de jauge
	  (-) de purge
	  (-) à boisseau
	  décompresseur
	  (-) à boues
	  (-) d'arrêt

coffer
 	
  (-) dam
	coffrage/ revêtement de
	  paroi
	  cuvelage

cog
  (-) rack/(-) rail
  (-) wheel
	pile/ pilier; dyke; cran
	  crémaillère
	  roue dentée

cohade	*pendage*

coil	*serpentin/ bobine*	composition metal	*alliage*
	enroulement/ spire/	compound	*mélange/ composé*
	rouleau	(-) fault	*faille composée*
(-) spring	*ressort à boudin/ en*	compressed air	*air comprimé*
	spirale	(-id-) drill	*forage à l'(-)*
choke (-)	*bobine d'induction*		
cold	*froid*	compressor	*compresseur*
(-) chisel	*ciseau/ burin*	axial (-)	*(-) axial*
(-) drawn steel	*acier étiré à froid*	centrifugal (-)	*(-) centrifuge*
collapse/collapsing	*affaissement/*	compound (-)/	*(-) bi-étagé*
	éboulement/	two-stage (-)	
	effondrement	multistage (-)	*(-) à plusieurs étages*
		rotary (-)	*(-) rotatif*
collar	*bague/ collerette/*	screw (-)	*(-) à vis*
	manchon	concealed	*caché/ dissimulé/ masqué*
stop (-)	*collier d'arrêt*	(-) fault	*faille masquée*
thrust (-)	*collet de butée*	(-) outcrop	*affleurement (-)*
collection	*rassemblement/*	concentrating	*concentration/*
	récupération;		*enrichissement*
	ensemble	(-) percussion table	*table à secousses*
collector	*capteur/ collecteur*	concrete	*bêton*
brush (-)/(-) ring	*commutateur à*	(-) bed	*croûte concrétionnée*
(also) slip ring	*balai*	(-) lining	*revêtement en (-)*
collet	*douille de serrage*	ballast (-)	*(-) à base de pierraille*
		prestressed (-)	*(-) précontraint*
column	*colonne/ pilier/ poteau*	reinforced (-)	*(-) armé*
(-) adaptor	*cloche à tubulures*	vibrated (-)	*(-) vibré*
(-) drill	*perceuse à (-)*	conduit	*conduit/ tuyau/*
(-) hoist	*treuil à (-)*		*souplisseau*
(-) jib crane	*grue pivotante à (-)*		*tube/ canal*
geological (-)	*log/ échelle géologique*	(-) box	*boîte de dérivation*
stratigraphical (-)/	*profil/ coupe*	cone	*cone*
columnar section	*stratigraphique*	(-) delta	*(-) de déjection*
columnar	*en forme de colonne*	(-) pulley	*poulie étagée*
(-) jointing	*division prismatique*	(-) rock bit	*trépan conique*
(-) structure	*structure prismatique*	(-) shell (of a bit)	*coquille (d'outil de*
comfort station	*latrines/ wc/ toilettes*		*forage)*
	publiques	confining bed/layer	*toît imperméable (d'un*
comminution	*fragmentation/*	(of an aquifer)	*aquifère)*
	pulvérisation	congealing	*prise en masse*
commutator	*commutateur/ collecteur/*	conglomerate	*conglomérat*
	pulseur	conical	*conique*
compact	*compact/ serré/ tassé*	(-) drum	*tambour conique*
(-) sandstone	*grès (-)*	connecting	*groupage/ liaison/*
compaction	*compacité/ tassement*		*association*
compass	*boussole/ compas*	(-) box	*boîte de raccordement de*
(-) dial	*(-) de poche*		*câbles (électr.)*
(-) saw	*scie égoïne/(-) passe-*	(-) piece	*pièce de jonction*
	partout	(-) pipe	*tuyau de jonction*
(-) survey	*levé à la boussole*	(-) rod	*bielle/ tringle; barre de*
compliance	*conformité/ souplesse*		*connection*
component	*constituant/ composante*	(-) wire	*fil de connection*
composite	*mixed/ composé/*		
	composite		
(-) sample	*échantillon moyen*		

connection	*branchement/ assemblage/ raccord*
(-) layout/(-) drawing	*schéma de montage*
branch (-)	*piquage (sur une conduite)*
delta (-)	*montage en triangle*
earth (-)	*prise de terre*
parallel (-)	*couplage en parallèle*
(-) plug	*fiche de raccordement*
series (-)	*couplage en série*
star (-)	*montage en étoile*
consistency	*consistance*
consolidated	*consolidé/ stabilisé*
(-) formation	*formation (-)*
constant	*constant; constante*
(-) level	*niveau constant*
(-) displacement pump	*pompe à débit constant*
time (-)	*constante de temps*
constituent	*constituant*
contact	*contact*
(-) breaker	*interrupteur*
(-) maker/contactor	*contacteur*
containment	*confinement*
contaminant	*impureté*
contaminated	*contaminé*
content	*teneur/ proportion; contenu*
continental	*continental*
(-) block	*bloc (-)*
(-) shelf	*plateau (-)*
continuous	*continu*
contour	*contour/ tracé; courbe de niveau; profil équidistance*
(-) intervals	*équidistance*
(-) line	*courbe de niveau*
(-) map	*carte en courbes de niveau*
contract	*contrat/ marché; pacte/ convention*
(-) drilling	*forage sur contrat*
(-) price	*prix à forfait*
(-) purchase	*marché forfaitaire*
conditions of (-)/ (-) specifications	*cahier des charges*
turnkey (-)	*contrat clé en mains*
contraction	*contraction/ abaissement/ retrait*
(-) of metals	*retrait des métaux*
contractor	*entrepreneur*

control	*commande/ contrôle/ régulation/ réglage*
(-) battery	*batterie d'excitation*
(-) board	*tableau de commande/ de contrôle*
(-) device/ (-) instrument	*appareil/ instrument de contrôle*
(-) knob	*bouton de réglage*
(-) light	*lampe témoin*
(-) panel	*pupitre de commande*
controller	*appareil de contrôle automatique*
controls	*commandes*
converter	*convertisseur*
rotary (-)	*commutatrice*
cooling	*refroidissement/ réfrigérant*
(-) of the bit	*(-) du trépan*
(-) system	*système de (-)*
(-) water	*eau de (-)*
core	*carotte; noyau; âme*
(-) barrel	*carottier/ tube carottier*
cable tool (-id-)	*(-id-) pour forage au câble*
wire line (-id-)	*carottier remontable par l'intérieur des tiges*
(-) bit	*trépan découpeur*
(-) breaker	*arrache-carotte*
(-) catcher	*dispositif de blocage (de la carotte dans le carrottier)*
(-) drilling/coring	*carottage*
(-) extractor/(-) lifter	*extracteur de carotte*
(-) shell	*enveloppe de (-)*
(-) of anticline	*coeur d'un anticlinal*
(-) of the earth	*noyau terrestre*
cable (-)	*âme d'un câble*
coring	*carottage; noyautage*
(-) tool	*carottier*
sidewall (-)	*carottage latéral*
correction	*correction*
elevation (-)	*(-) d'altitude*
corrosion	*corrosion/ oxydation*
(-) inhibitor/ (-) preventive	*inhibiteur de (-)*
soil (-)	*(-) tellurique*
corrugated	*ondulé/ plissé/ ridé*
(-) friction socket	*tube de repêchage à frottement*
(-) iron/(-) iron sheet	*tôle ondulée*
cotter	*goupille/ clavette*
(-) driver	*chasse clavette*
(-) pin	*goupille fendue*
(-) puller	*arrache-clavette*

counter · *contre/opposé*
  (-) balance · *balancier*
  (-) bore · *épaulement interne/ contre-alésage*
  (-) current/(-) flow · *contre-courant*
  (-) flange · *contre bride*
  (-) nut · *contre-écrou*
  (-) sunk · *fraisé*
  (-id-) screw · *vis à tête fraisée*
  (-) weight · *contre-poids*

coupling · *manchon/raccord*
  (-) box/sleeve · *(-) d'accouplement*
  (-) make-up · *serrage des (-)*

course · *direction*
  (-) of outcrop · *(-) de l'affleurement*

cove · *petite baie*

cover · *couverture/couvercle/ mort-terrain*

covering · *recouvrement/couverture/ enrobage*

cowl/cowling · *capuchon/capot*

crab · *chèvre/treuil/chariot de pont-roulant*

crack · *craquelure/fissure/lézarde*

cradle · *bâti/berceau/collier*

crane · *grue/treuil*
  (-) boom · *flèche de (-)*
  (-) crab · *chariot de pont-roulant*
  overhead (-) · *pont-roulant*
  pedestal (-) · *grue rotative sur fût/ sur colonne*

crank · *manivelle/bras/vilebrequin*
  (-) shaft · *vilebrequin*

crash helmet · *casque protecteur*

crawler · *chenilles/porteur à chenilles*
  (-) loader · *chargeuse sur (-)*

creasing · *pli/plissement*
  (-) stake · *bigorne de pliage*

creek · *ruisseau*

creep · *allongement/fluage/ boursouflement/ cheminement*

crest · *crête/arête*

crevice · *crevasse/fissure*
  (-) water · *eau de diaclases*

crooked · *courbé/crochu*
  (-) hole · *sondage dévié*

cross · *croix*
  (-) beam/(-) girder · *poutre transversale*
  (-) bed · *couche oblique*

crossover sub · *réduction*
  (-) tee · *Té double*

crown · *sommet/couronne*
  (-) bit · *trépan à couronne*
  (-) block · *moufle fixe*
  (-) pulley/(-) sheave · *poulie de forage/ poulie de tête*

crumbling · *écaillement/effritement*

crusher · *broyeur/concasseur*

cubicle · *cabine*

cull · *déchet/rebut*

cup · *coupelle/cuvette*

current · *courant*

curtailment · *réduction/diminution*

curve · *courbe/courbure*

cusec · *pied cube par seconde*

cut · *coupe*

cutover land · *terrain déboisé*

cutter · *lame; haveuse*

cutting · *coupe/déblai*
  (-) edge · *tranchant de l'outil*
  (-) nippers · *pinces coupantes*
  (-) torch · *chalumeau oxycoupeur*

cuttings · *déblais de forage*

cylinder · *bouteille pour gaz; cylindre*
  (-) bloc · *bloc cylindre (d'un moteur)*
  (-) liner · *chemise de cylindre*

D

damage · *dégât/détérioration/ endommagement*
  fatigue (-) · *(-) par fatigue*

damp proof · *hydrofuge/étanche à l'eau*

damper · *amortisseur*
  surge (-) · *amortisseur de sautes de pression*

damping · *amortissement*

dampness · *humidité*

dart · *clapet*
  (-) bailer · *cuiller de curage à (-)*

dash	*tiret; petite quantité*
(-) board	*tableau de bord*
(-) pot	*amortisseur*
data	*données/ information/ références*
(-) bank	*banque de (-)*
(-) base	*base de (-)*
(-) processing	*traitement des (-)*
dating	*datation*
datum	*renseignement/ plan de référence/ donnée*
(-) horizon	*niveau de repère*
(-) level	*plan de niveau/ de référence*
(-) plane	*surface de référence*
(-) point	*point de repère*
low water (-)	*niveau de basses-eaux*
dauber	*soudeur*
dead	*stérile/ mort*
(-) center	*point mort*
bottom (-id-)	*(-id-) bas*
top (-id-)	*(-id-) haut*
(-) end/(-) line	*brin mort*
(-id-) anchor	*réa*
(-) well	*puits stérile*
debris	*débris/ éboulis*
decantation	*décantation/ séparation*
(-) tank	*bac de (-)*
decanting basin/ (-) pond	*bassin de (-)*
decay	*dégradation/ décomposition*
deceleration	*ralentissement*
decline	*baisse/ diminution*
declivity	*déclivité/ inclinaison/ pente*
deep	*profond; foncé*
(-) drilling	*forage à grande profondeur*
(-) hole	*forage profond*
(-) seated	*profond/ enraciné*
(-id-) fold	*pli (-)*
(-id-) rocks	*roches d'intrusion*
defect	*défaut*
defective	*défectueux*
deficiency	*insuffisance/ déficit*
deflected well	*sondage/ forage dévié*
deflecting	*déviation/ déclenchement*
(-) cone	*cône déflecteur*
(-) tools	*outils de déviation*
deflecteur	*chicane/ déflecteur*
defluorination	*défluoration*

defoamer	*additif antimousse*
defoaming agent	*antimoussant*
degaussing	*démagnétisation*
degradation	*décomposition/ dégradation*
degree	*degré*
(-) of hardness	*coefficient/ indice de dureté*
dehydration	*déshydratation*
deionization	*désionisation*
delay	*retard/ délai*
(-) angle	*(-) angulaire*
ignition (-)	*(-) à l'allumage*
delivery	*débit/ livraison/ décharge/ distribution*
(-) hose	*tuyau de distribution*
(-) pipe	*conduite de refoulement/ de décharge*
(-) port	*sortie de refoulement*
dell	*creux/ vallon*
delta	*delta*
(-) connection (electr.)	*montage en triangle (électr.)*
demagnetizing/ demagnetization	*démagnétisation*
demineralization	*déminéralisation*
demisting	*désembuage*
demulsifier	*désémulsifiant/ agent désémulsionnant*
dense	*compact/ dense*
(-) shale	*argile schisteuse compacte*
density	*masse volumique/ densité/ opacité/ intensité*
(-) log	*diagraphie de densité*
absolute (-)	*densité absolue*
apparent (-)	*(-) apparente*
bulk (-)	*(-) globale*
dent	*bosselement/ creux/ enfoncement*
denudation	*érosion/ mise à nu; dénudation (d'un fil isolé)*
dependability	*sécurité/ assurance*
dependable	*sûr/ précis/ assuré*
depletion	*épuisement*
(-) curve	*courbe de tarissement*
deposit	*dépôt/ sédiment/ précipité; gisement*
(-) of scale	*entartrage*
alluvial (-)	*dépôt alluvial*
eolian (-)/wind (-)	*(-) éolien*

deposition	*dépôt*	development	*développement/ extension/*
(-) of sediments	*(-) de sédiments*		*mise au point*
depot	*entrepôt/ dépôt/ magasin*	well (-)	*préparation à*
			l'exploitation d'un puits
depressant	*abaisseur*	deviation	*déviation/ écart*
depressed	*diminué/ abaissé*	(-) angle	*angle de (-)*
depression	*dépression*	device	*dispositif/ appareillage*
structural (-)	*zone d'affaissement*	clamping (-)	*(-) de serrage*
depth	*profondeur*	control (-)	*(-) de contrôle*
(-) curve	*courbe bathymétrique*	recording (-)	*(-) enregistreur*
(-) finder	*sondeur*	safety (-)	*(-) de sécurité*
(-) gauge	*jauge de (-)*	devolution	*éboulement; dévolution/*
geothermic (-)	*degré/ gradient*		*transfert (de*
	géothermique		*responsabilités)*
(-) mark	*repère de (-)*	dew	*rosée*
mean (-)	*(-) moyenne*	(-) point	*point de (-)*
derelict	*épave; abandonné*	dewatering	*assèchement*
derrick	*tour de sondage/ derrick*	(-) pump	*pompe d' (-)*
guyed (-)	*derrick haubanné*	diagram	*diagramme/ graphique/*
desalination	*dessalement*		*schéma*
desalting	*dessalage*	dial	*cadran/ limbe*
(-) plant	*unité/ installation de (-)*	(-) gauge	*jauge à (-)*
(-) process	*procédé de (-)*	(-) lock	*serrure à secret*
desander	*dessableur*	(-) manometre	*manomètre à cadran*
descaling	*détartrage/ décalaminage/*	diametre	*diamètre*
	décapage	(-) of a borehole circle	*(-) de perçage*
desert	*désert*	(-) of the grains	*(-) des particules*
(-) belt	*ceinture désertique*	diamond	*diamant*
gravel (-)	*reg*	(-) core drill	*carottage au (-)*
rock (-)	*hamada*	(-) drill	*foret au (-)/ foreuse au (-)*
sand (-)	*erg*	diaphragm	*diaphragme/ membrane*
dessicated	*deshydraté/ desséché*	(-) pump	*pompe à membrane*
design	*conception/ dessin/ étude/*	(-) valve	*vanne à (-)*
	plan/ projet	diastem	*lacune de sédimentation*
(-) power	*puissance nominale*	diatomaceous earth	*terre d'infusoires/ terre*
(-) speed	*vitesse nominale*		*à diatomées*
desilting	*dévasement*	diatomite	*kieselguhr*
desludging	*débourbage/ élimination*	dichromate	*bichromate*
	des boues	die	*filière/ matrice/ peigne;*
destructive	*destructif/ destructeur*		*poinçon/ étampe/ matrice*
(-) examination	*contrôle (-)*	(-) cast	*coulée en coquilles*
(-) wear	*usure excessive*	(-id-) alloy	*alliage coulé sous*
detachable	*amovible/ démontable*		*pression*
(-) bit	*taillant à vis*	(-) collar	*cloche taraudée (pour*
detergent	*détersif/ dispersant/*		*repêchage)*
	produit tensio-actif	(-) coupling	*cloche/ filière de*
determination	*dosage/ mesure/*		*repêchage*
	détermination	(-) nipple	*taraud de repêchage*
deterrent	*inhibiteur*	(-) stamping	*matriçage/ marque au*
detrital	*détritique*		*poinçon*
(-) deposits	*dépôts (-)*	(-) stocks	*porte filière*
		diesel engine	*moteur diésel/ diésel*
		air cooled (-)	*(-) à refroidissement*
			par air

(-) fuel	fuel/fioul/combustible pour (-)
(-) knock	cognement diésel
to dig	creuser/fouiller
digester (sludge)	digesteur (boues)
digestion sludge (-)/anaerobic (-)	digestion/décomposition décomposition anaérobique
digger back (-) mechanical (-)	terrassier/excavateur pelle rétrocaveuse pelle mécanique
digit	chiffre
digital (-) display	numérique affichage (-)
dyke	digue/fossé/intrusion
diluent	diluant
diluvial (-) sands	diluvial/diluvient sables diluvients
dim	terne/faible/trouble
dimension overall/external (-)	dimension (-) d'encombrement
dimensional (-) map (-) sketch	dimensionnel carte en relief croquis coté
dimmer	régulateur de tension
dimming	mise en veilleuse
dimple (of a bit)	épaulement (d'un outil de forage)
dip	creux/inclinaison/pendage; trempe/immersion
(-) arrow map (-) circle/(-) compass (-) fault (-) fold (-) map (-) valley	carte schématique boussole d'inclinaison faille transversale pli plongeant carte de pendage vallée inclinée
dip brazing (-) plating (-) gauge/(-) stick	brasage au bain dépôt au trempé jauge/pige de niveau
dipper (-) dredge	godet de pelle mécanique pelle mécanique
dipping (-) fault	incliné/plongeant faille inclinée
direct (-) coupled (-) current (-) drive	direct en prise directe courant continu commande directe
direction (-) of dip	direction/orientation/sens; instruction/directive (-) du pendage
(-) of flow	sens du débit
directory	répertoire/annuaire
dirt (-) road	saleté/crasse/impuretés chemin en terre
dirty	sale/souillé/encrassé
disc (also disk) (-) clutch	disque/rond/rondelle embrayage à (-)
discharge (-) air (-) curve battery (-) rate electric (-) pump (-) end	refoulement/évacuation/décharge/déversement/rejet air de refoulement d'un compresseur courbe de débits régime de décharge d'accumulateurs décharge électrique (-) d'une pompe
disconnection	débranchement/mise hors circuit/débrayage
discrepancy	différence
disengagement	débrayage/dégagement/séparation
dish Petri (-)	cuvette/récipient/coupelle boîte de Pétri
dished (-) bottom/(-) head of a storage tank	en cuvette/bombé/embouti fonds embouti (d'une cuve, d'un réservoir)
disincrustant	désincrustant
disintegration	désagrégation/effritement/désintégration
disjunction	disjonction/interruption/séparation
dislocated (-) deposit	disloqué gîte (-)
dismantling/dismounting	démontage
disparity	différence/écart
dispersion (-) agent	dispersion agent de (-)
displacement piston (-)	déplacement/décalage/volume déplacé cylindrée
display	affichage; exposition
disposal waste (-)	élimination/évacuation/rejet évacuation des déchets/mise à l'égout
disrupted (-) fold	disloqué/démembré pli faillé

dissolved	*dissous*	dot	*point*
dissolvent	*dissolvant*	(-) and dash line	*trait mixte*
distance	*distance/ écart*	dotted line	*pointillés (dessin)*
(-) piece	*entretoise*	double	*double*
distortion	*distortion/ déformation*	(-) acting	*à double effet*
distributary	*bras de rivière/ de delta*	(-) arc bit	*fleuret à taillant (-)*
distribution	*distribution/ répartition*	(-) block	*poulie/ mouffle (-)*
(-) losses	*pertes de (-)*	(-) core barrel	*carottier (-)*
(-) network	*réseau de (-)*	(-) drum winch	*treuil à deux tambours*
load (-)	*répartition de la charge*	(-) walled	*à double paroi*
disturbance	*dislocation/ pertubation*	dough	*masse pâteuse*
ditch	*fossé/ tranchée/ canal/*	dovetail	*(assemblage) en*
	caniveau/ rigole/ goulotte	(assembly)	*queue d'aronde*
(-) excavator	*trancheuse/ pelle*	dowel	*cheville/ ergot/ cale*
	fouilleuse	(-) pin	*goujon*
drainage (-)	*fossé/ rigole de*	downcreep	*glissement*
	drainage, d'assèchement	downdip	*aval-pendage*
mud (-)	*rigole à boue*	downfall	*éboulement/ chute*
divergent	*divergent*	downpipe	*tuyau de descente*
(-) dip	*pendage (-)*	downspout	*trop plein/ déversoir*
(-) unconformity	*discordance*	downstream	*aval*
	angulaire	downthrow	*rejet/ affaissement*
diversion	*dérivation/*	dowser	*sourcier/ radiesthésiste*
	détournement	draft	*avant-projet/ brouillon/*
diverter	*déflecteur*		*esquisse; courant d'air/*
divide	*ligne de partage des*		*tirage*
	eaux	drafting/drawing	*dessin/ croquis; étirage*
divining rod	*baguette de sourcier*	(-) instruments	*instruments de dessin*
division	*graduation/ repère de*	(-) machine	*appareil à dessiner*
	graduation; séparation/	(-) board	*planche à dessin*
	cloison	draftsman/draughtsman	*dessinateur*
dog	*crampon/ cliquet/ butée/*	drag	*rebroussement; drague;*
	ergot		*résistance/ traînée*
casing (-)	*arrache-tube*	(-) coefficient	*coefficient de trainée/*
(-) hook	*griffe de serrage*		*coefficient de frottement*
(-) house	*abri sur la tour de forage*	drain	*purge/ puisard/ vidange*
(-) iron	*crochet/ crampon*	(-) cock	*robinet de (-)/ de vidange*
	d'assemblage	(-) oil	*huile de vidange*
(-) nail	*clou à crochet*	(-) pipe	*tuyau de vidange*
(-) stop	*cliquet d'arrêt*	(-) pit	*puisard*
(-) wheel	*roue à rochet/ à cliquet*	drainage/draining	*drainage*
D-I-Y (do it yourself)	*à faire soi-même/ à*	(-) ditch	*fossé de (-)*
	bricoler	(-) line	*thalweg/ ligne de plus*
dolly	*chariot de manutention*		*grande pente*
dome	*dôme/ coupole/ calotte*	(-) pattern	*réseau hydrographique*
dominant	*dominant*	draw	*tirage/ étirage; petit*
(-) fault	*faille principale*		*vallon*
dope	*additif; enduit/*	(-) back	*inconvénient/ obstacle*
	enrobage/ revêtement		

(-) bar	*barre d'attelage*
(-) down	*rabattement*
(-) hook	*crochet d'attelage*
(-) off	*prélèvement/ soutirage*
(-) works	*treuil de forage*
(-id-) drum	*tambour de (-id-)*
to draw	*allonger/ étirer; dessiner;*
	soutirer
drawing	*dessin/ plan;*
	emboutissage/
	étirage
(-) paper	*papier à (-)*
(-) pen	*tire-lignes*
(-) pin	*punaise*
drawn	*étiré; épuisé*
cold (-)	*(-) à froid*
dredger/dredging machine	*drague*
dressing (of a tool)	*taille/ affûtage (d'un*
	outil)
drift	*dérive/ décalage*
(-) boulder	*bloc erratique*
(-) deposit	*dépôt glaciaire*
(-) sand/drifting sand	*sable mouvant*
sand (-)	*vent de sable*
driftage	*charriage*
drill	*perceuse/perforatrice;*
	fleuret/ foret/ mèche
(-) bit	*outil de forage/ trépan*
(-) collar	*masse-tige*
(-id-) spear	*arrache-tube*
(-) core	*carotte*
(-) cuttings	*déblais de forage*
(-) log	*coupe d'un sondage/*
	rapport de forage/ sondage
(-) pipe/(-)column/	*tiges de forage*
(-) rods	
(-id-) cutter	*coupe tige*
(-id-) pressure	*pression sur tiges de*
	forage
(-id-) strings	*train de tiges*
(-) rope	*câble de forage*
(-) stem	*masse-tige*
(-) string	*garniture/ ensemble du*
	train de sonde
driller	*foreur/ sondeur*
master (-)/(-) foreman	*chef/ maître (-)*
(-)'s log	*rapport de forage*
drilling	*forage/ perçage/*
	perforation
(-) bit	*trépan*
(-) cable	*câble de (-)*
cable (-)	*forage au câble/ forage*
	au battage

(-) clamp	*serre câble*
(-) core	*carotte*
(-) crew/(-)gang	*équipe de (-)*
(-) frame	*chevalet de (-)*
(-) jar	*coulisse de (-)*
(-) journal/	
(-) log/(-) record	*rapport de (-)*
(-) mud	*boue de (-)*
(-) rate	*vitesse d'avancement*
(-) rig	*appareil/ atelier de*
	forage/ sonde
(-) rotary	*(-) rotary*
(-) shaft	*corps de sonde*
(-) spool	*raccord de (-) à brides*
(-) tools	*outils de (-)*
drillings	*débris de forage*
drinking water	*eau potable/ eau de boisson*
drip	*goutte à goutte/ larmier;*
	tuyau de purge
(-) cock	*purgeur*
drive	*commande/ entraînement/*
	transmission
(-) axle	*essieu moteur*
(-) bushing	*coussinet pour tige*
	d'entraînement
(-) clamps	*serre-joints*
(-) head	*tête d'entraînement/*
	manchon de battage/
	mouton
(-) pipe	*colonne de tubage*
(-) shoe	*sabot*
belt (-)	*commande par courroie*
chain (-)	*commande par chaine*
fluid/hydraulic (·)	*commande hydraulique*
hand (-)	*commande manuelle*
driven	*commandé/ entraîné*
driving	*avance/ transmission*
(-) belt	*courroie de commande*
(-) chain	*chaîne de commande*
(-) kelly bushing	*fourrure d'entraînement*
(-) shaft	*arbre moteur*
(-) wheel	*roue motrice*
drop	*chute/ tombée; goutte*
(-) feed lubricator	*graisseur goutte-à-*
	goutte
(-) forged	*forgé/ façonné au*
	marteau-pilon
(-) hammer	*marteau-pilon*
pressure (-)	*perte de charge/*
	chute de pression
drought	*sécheresse*
droppings	*crotte/ fiente*
dropping pipe	*colonne d'aspiration*

drum | tambour/fût métallique
brake (-) | (-) de frein
cable (-) | (-) de câble/touret
sinking (-) | trousse coupante
winch (-) | (-) de treuil
(-) dryer | séchoir/essoreuse à (-)

dual | double

duct | conduit/gaine/
 | canalisation

dug | creusé/foncé
(-) well | puits (-)

dull | mat/terne; émoussé

dump | décharge/dépôt
(-) bailer | cuiller de cimentation
(-) cable | câble de basculement

dumping | déversement/déchargement
 | en vrac

dune | dune
wandering (-) | (-) mouvante

dung | crotte/fiente
cow (-) | bouse de vache
horse (-) | crottin de cheval
pig (-) | lisier

dust | poussière/poudre
(-) storm | tempête de (-)
(-) proof | étanche à la (-)
saw (-)/wood (-) | sciure de bois

duty | service/rendement/
 | travail
heavy (-) | renforcé/apte à un
 | service sévère

DVC/double vaulted batch | latrine à compost
 composting latrine | alternante à double voûte
 | (CCDV) à double
 | compartiment

dwindling | rétrécissement/diminution

dye | teinture/colorant

dyke | digue; filon

E

ear | ouie d'aspiration d'un
 | ventilateur; languette

earth | terre
(-) auger/(-) borer/ | tarrière
(-) boring bit |
(-) connection | contact/mise à la terre
(-) creep/(-) flow | glissement de terrain
(-) current | courant tellurique
(-) fall | éboulement
(-) grab | benne drague/ cuiller
 | d'excavation

(-) load/ | poussée de terres
(-) pressure |
(-) slide | éboulement/glissement
 | de terrain

earthen reservoir | réservoir en terre

earthquake | tremblement de terre/
 | séisme

earth works | terrassement/transport
 | de terre

easement | droit de passage/servitude

eccentric | excentrique
(-) bit | trépan (-)
(-) load | charge décentrée
(-) rod/(-) shaft | arbre (-)
(-) sheave | plateau d' (-)
(-) strap | coilier d' (-)

échelon | échelon
(-) faults | failles en (-)
(-) folds | plis en (-)

eddy | tourbillon/remous

edge | arête/tranchant/biseau/
 | taillant/fil
cutting (-) | taillant/bord coupant

eduction | sortie/décharge/
 | évacuation
(-) port | orifice d'émission/
 | de décharge

effect | action/effet/résultat
mechanical (-) | (-) mécanique

effective | effectif/efficace/réel
(-) output | production effective
(-) permeability | perméabilité réelle
(-) power | puissance (-)

efficiency | rendement/efficacité
mechanical (-) | (-) mécanique
overall (-) | (-) global

effluence | dégagement/émanation

effluent | effluent/eaux usées/
 | eaux d'égouts

ejection | projection/expulsion/
 | rejet

elastic | élastique/flexible/souple

elasticity | élasticité/souplesse
modulus of (-) | module d' (-)

elbow | coude

electric | électrique
(-) arc welding/ | soudure à l'arc
electrode welding |
(-) pump | électropompe
(-) shock | commotion
(-) soldering | brasure électrique

(-) varnish	*vernis isolant*	enclosed (-)	*(-) blindé*
(-) winder	*treuil électrique*	(-) flywheel	*volant (-)*
		(-) frame	*bâti de machine*
electrode	*électrode*	(-) hood	*capot de (-)*
		(-) lathe	*tour parallèle*
electro-deposit	*dépôt galvano plastique*	(-) load	*charge du (-)*
(-) coating	*revêtement galvano*	rated (-id-)	*charge de régime du (-)*
	plastique	(-) shaft	*arbre (-)*
		outboard (-)	*(-) hors bord*
electromagnetic	*électromagnétique*		
(-) field	*champ (-)*	entrapment	*piègeage/ empiègement*
(-) separator	*séparateur (-)*		
		environment	*milieu/ environnement*
electroplating	*électroplacage/*		
	galvanoplastie	equalizing	*égalisation*
		(-) gear	*engrenage différentiel*
elevation	*élévation/ altitude/*	(-) sub	*raccord d' (-)*
	hauteur; soulèvement/		
	surhaussement	equipment	*matériel/ appareillage/*
(-) angle	*angle de site*		*équipement*
(-) of the well	*cote de sondage*		
(-) drawing	*vue en élévation*	erection	*montage/ assemblage/*
side (-)	*vue de côté*		*dressage d'un mât*
elevator	*harnais/ élévateur*	EROS (earth resources	*EROS (satellite*
(-) bucket	*godet d'élévateur/ auget*	observation satellite)	*d'observation des*
	de noria		*ressources terrestres)*
(-) link	*bras d'élévateur*		
		erosion	*érosion/ usure/*
elongation	*allongement*		*affouillement*
		gully (-)	*ravinement*
elutriation	*décantation/ élution*	wind (-)	*(-) éolienne*
elutriator	*séparateur*	erratic	*variable/ irrégulier/*
			intermittent
emery	*émeri*		
(-) cloth	*toile d' (-)*	error	*erreur*
(-) paper	*papier d' (-)*	accidental (-)/random (-)	*(-) aléatoire*
(-) stick	*rodoir/ polissoir*		
		etching	*décapage/ attaque/*
empire cloth	*toile huilée*		*corrosion*
		(-) reagent	*décapant*
emulsifying	*émulsionnant/ émulsifiant*		
(-) agent	*agent (-)*	even	*lisse/ uni/ plat; pair*
		(-) fracture	*cassure plane*
enclosure	*inclusion/ enclave/*	(-) grained	*à grain régulier*
	enceinte	(-) number	*nombre pair*
encroachment	*empiètement/*	excavating bucket	*benne piocheuse*
	envahissement		
		excavation	*fouille/ fosse/*
end	*fin/ aboutissement; bout/*		*excavation*
	extrêmité/ bec		
(-) play	*jeu en bout*	excavator	*excavateur/ drague*
(-) thrust	*poussée axiale*		
big (-)	*tête de bielle*	excess	*excédent/ surplus/ excès*
small (-)	*pied de bielle*	(-) pressure	*surpression/ surtension*
		(-) weight	*excédent de poids*
endurance	*endurance/ fatigue*		
(-) failure	*rupture par fatigue*	exchangeur	*échangeur*
(-) limit	*limite d' (-)*		
(-) test	*essai d' (-)*	excitator	*excitatrice*
engagement	*engrènement/ accrochage/*	excreta	*excréments*
	prise		
		exhaust	*échappement/ évacuation/*
engine	*moteur/ machine*		*épuisement*
auxiliary (-)	*(-) auxiliaire*	(-) pot/chamber	*pot d' (-)*
(-) bloc	*bloc (-)*	(-) manifold	*collecteur d' (-)*

exhaust (con't)	*échappement/ évacuation/ épuisement (suite)*
(-) pipe	*tuyau d' (-)*
(-) silencer	*silencieux d' (-)*
expandable	*extensible*
expanded	*dilaté/ expansé/ développé*
(-) joint	*joint (-)*
(-) metal	*métal déployé*
(-) pipe	*tube expansé*
expanding pin tap	*taraud extensible de repêchage*
expansion	*dilatation/ expansion/ détente/ croissance*
(-) adaptor	*joint réglable*
(-) bit	*trépan réglable*
(-) joint	*joint de dilatation*
(-) loop	*lyre de dilatation*
(-) ratio	*taux de dilatation*
(-) ring	*anneau de dilatation*
(-) vessel	*vase d'expansion*
exploitation	*exploitation/ production*
exploration	*exploration*
(-) boring/borehole	*sondage d' (-)*
(-) well	*puits d' (-)*
exposure	*affleurement/ exposition*
extension	*rallonge/ extension/ élargissement*
(-) rod	*allonge de tige*
(-) shaft	*rallonge d'arbre*
(-) stem	*tige rallongée*
extent	*étendue/ degré/ amplitude*
external	*externe*
extinguisher	*extincteur*
extractable	*extractible*
extraction	*extraction*
extractor	*extracteur*
extraneous	*étranger/ en excès*
extruder	*extrudeuse/ boudineuse*
extrusion	*extrusion/ épanchement*
extrusive	*extrusif, extrusive*
(-) rock	*roche extrusive*
exudation	*exsudation/ suintement*
eye	*oeil/ oeillet/ chas/ anneau*
(-) bolt	*tirefond*
(-) let	*oeillet*
(-) piece	*oculaire*
lifting (-)	*boucle de suspension/ anneau de levage*

F

fabric	*structure/ texture; construction/ bâtiment; tissu/ toile*
oil (-)	*toile huilée*
face	*front de taille; tranchant; plateau*
(-) hardened	*cémenté*
(-) plate (of a lathe)	*plateau (de tour)*
bearing (-)	*surface d'appui*
facet	*facette*
facies	*faciès*
facilities	*moyens/ installations/ équipement*
facing	*revêtement/ garniture*
(-) ring	*garniture d'embrayage*
leather/rubber (-)	*joint en cuir/ en caoutchouc*
factor	*facteur/ agent; diviseur*
conversion (-)	*(-) de conversion*
fading	*disparition progressive/ fondu/ chute d'intensité*
failsafe	*dispositif de sécurité automatique*
failure	*panne/ échec/ défaut*
engine (-)	*panne de moteur*
metal fatigue (-)	*rupture par fatigue (d'une pièce métallique)*
fairway	*passage*
fall/fall of ground	*éboulement/ chute/ descente*
(-) block	*poulie*
fallow	*en friche/ jachère*
false	*faux/ pseudo*
(-) cleavage	*pseudo-clivage*
(-) dip	*(-) pendage*
(-) movement	*fausse manoeuvre*
fan	*ventilateur/ éventail*
(-) belt	*courroie de (-)*
(-) delta	*cône de déjection*
alluvial (-)/	*cône d'alluvions*
(-) structure	
fast	*rapide; attaché/ stable/ fixe*
(-) on nut	*écrou de blocage/ écrou indesserrable*
fastener	*attache/ agrafe*
fastening	*fixation/ attache*
fat	*graisse/ corps gras*

fatigue — *fatigue (d'un métal)*
  (-) crack — *félure par fatigue*

fatty — *gras*

faucet — *robinet*

fault — *faille/dislocation; défaut/imperfection*
  (-) block valley — *vallée d'effondrement*
  (-) line — *ligne de faille*
  (-) heave — *rejet horizontal*
  (-) throw — *rejet de (-)*
  slip (-) — *(-) d'effondrement*
  trough (-) — *massif effondré*
  upthrow (-) — *chevauchement*

faulted — *disloqué/faillé*

faulty — *défectueux*

feature — *caractéristique/trait*

feed — *alimentation/avance*
  (-) back — *rétroaction/communication en retour*
  (-) box — *boîte d'(-)*
  (-) cock — *robinet d'(-)*
  (-) hopper — *trémie d'(-)*
  (-) inlet — *admission*
  (-) line/pipe — *conduite/tuyauterie d'(-)/d'admission*
  (-) pump — *pompe alimentaire/pompe d'(-)*
  (-) screw — *vis d'(-)/vis de commande d'avance*
  (-) tank — *bâche/nourrice/réservoir d'(-)*
  gravity (-) — *(-) gravitaire*
  pressure (-) — *(-) sous pression*

feeder — *conduite/canalisation/câble (élect.) d'arrivée/d'amenée; affluent d'une rivière; distributeur*

felt — *feutre*

fen — *marais*

fence/fencing — *barrière/clôture/palissade*
  wire (-) — *treillage métallique*

fender — *pare-chocs*

ferritic — *ferritique*

ferrous — *ferreux*

ferrule — *embout/bague/virole*

fiber — *fibre*
  (-) glass — *(-) de verre*

field — *champ/terrain; gisement*
  electromagnetic (-) — *(-) électromagnétique*

file — *lime; dossier/classeur*
  coarse (-) — *(-) grossière/râpe*
  round (-) — *(-) demi-ronde/(-) queue de rat*
  smooth (-) — *(-) douce*
  three square (-)/triangular (-) — *tiers point*

filing — *limaille; classement*
  (-) machine — *machine à limer*
  (-) box — *fichier*

fill — *remblai; plein/charge*
  (-) up — *remplissage/remblayage/hauteur de remblayage*
  to (-id-) — *faire le plein/emplir à ras bord*

filler — *charge/additif*
  (-) cup/(-) plug — *bouchon de remplissage*
  back (-) — *remblayeuse*

fillet — *filet/bande; cordon de soudure*

filling — *remplissage/remblai; âme d'un câble/d'un cordage*

film — *pellicule/film/couche mince/clinquant*

filter/filtering — *filtre*
  (-) basin — *bassin de filtration*
  (-) bed/(-) layer — *couche filtrante/lit filtrant*
  (-) cake — *gâteau de filtration/de sédiments*
  (-) cartridge — *cartouche filtrante*
  cartridge (-) — *(-) à cartouche*
  (-) cloth — *toile filtrante*
  coal (-) — *(-) à charbon*
  (-) drum — *tambour filtrant*
  drum (-) — *(-) à tambour*
  (-) medium — *milieu filtrant*
  oil bath (-) — *(-) à bain d'huile*
  (-) plant — *filtre/installation de filtration*
  (-) screen — *crible à grille filtrante*
  (-) sieve — *tamis filtrant*
  sand (-) — *(-) à sable*
  slow (-id-) — *(-) lent à sable*

fin — *ailette*
  (-) tube — *tube à (-)*

fine — *fin/précis/pur; amende*
  (-) adjustment — *réglage de précision*
  (-) edge — *arête/tranchant affilé*
  (-) grained sand — *sable à grain fin*
  (-) gravel — *gravillon*

finger — *doigt/ergot*
  (-) board — *râtelier à tiges creuses*
  (-) grip — *extracteur*

finish — *fini/finissage*

fins	*ailerons*
fire	*feu/ incendie*
(-) proof	*ignifugé/ incombustible*
firing	*mise à feu; allumage; tir (de mine)*
back (-)	*retour d'allumage*
fishing	*repêchage; éclissage*
(-) basket	*panier de (-)*
(-) grab	*accrocheur de (-)*
(-) hook	*crochet/ harpon/ caracole de (-)*
(-) jar	*coulisse de (-)*
(-) socket	*souricière*
(-) string	*garniture de (-)*
(-) tap	*taraud de (-)*
(-) tool	*outil de (-)*
fissure	*fente/ fissure/ crevasse*
fit	*ajustage/ emmanchement/ emboîtement*
exact (-)	*(-) sans tolérance*
tight (-)	*(-) serré/ dur/ à force*
fitter	*ajusteur*
fitting	*ajustage/ montage/ raccord*
fittings	*accessoires de tuyauterie/ raccords de tuyauterie/ garnitures*
flagstones	*roches en dalles/ en plaques*
flake	*paillette/ flocon/ écaille*
(-) structure	*structure en gruau*
flammable	*inflammable*
flange	*bride/ collet/ collerette/ bord rabattu*
(-) coupling	*joint/ manchon à (-)*
blank (-)/blind (-)	*(-) pleine/ (-) d'obturation*
coupling (-)/mating (-)	*(-) d'accouplement*
counter (-)	*contre bride*
discharge (-)	*(-) de refoulement*
drum (-)	*joue d'un tambour*
hanger (-)	*(-) de suspension*
mounting (-)	*(-) de montage*
studded (-)	*(-) goujonnée*
threaded (-)	*(-) filetée*
wheel (-)	*jante d'une roue*
flanged	*à bride/ à boudin/ à bourrelet*
(-) ends	*extrêmités à brides*
(-) fittings	*raccords (-)*
(-) wheel	*roue à boudin*

flank	*flanc/ côté*
(-) dip	*pendage latéral*
leading (-)	*bord d'attaque d'un outil*
trailing (-)	*bord de fuite d'un outil*
flap	*abattant/ clapet/ trappe*
(-) valve	*soupape à clapet/ soupape antiretour*
check (-)	*clapet de retenue*
flare	*collet rabattu/ évasement*
flash	*éclair/ étincelle*
(-) weld/(-) welding	*soudure par étincelage*
flat	*plat/ plan; bas fond/ replat*
(-) bed truck	*camion à plateforme surbaissée (ex : porte-char)*
mud (-)	*replat boueux*
sand (-)	*replat sableux*
flaw	*défaut/ paille (dans le métal); fissure*
flexible	*flexible/ souple*
(-) coupling	*accouplement élastique*
(-) drive	*commande élastique*
(-) hose	*tuyau flexible*
flexure	*courbure/ flexion*
(-) fault	*pli-faille*
(-) point	*point de flexion*
flint	*silex*
(-) clay	*argile à (-)*
flinty	*caillouteux*
float	*flotteur*
(-) operated valve	*soupape/ valve à (-)*
floating	*flottant/ flottement*
(-) axle	*essieu (-)*
(-) earth	*terrain boulant*
floc	*floc/ flocon*
(-) point	*point de floculation*
flocculation	*floculation*
flocky	*floconneux*
flooding	*inondation/ engorgement*
floor	*plancher*
(-) block	*moufle de (-)*
(-) stand	*colonne de manoeuvre*
flotation	*flottation*
flow	*courant/ débit/ écoulement; fluage*
(-) bean	*duse*
(-) control	*réglage/ contrôle de débit*
(-) fold	*pli de fluage*

(-) meter	*débitmètre*
(-) rate	*débit*
(-) sheet	*schéma de fonctionnement*
counter (-)	*à contre-courant*
eddy (-)	*régime turbulent*
viscous (-)	*régime laminaire*
reverse (-)	*débit inverse/circulation inverse*
trickle (-)	*ruissellement/suintement*
fluid	*fluide*
brake (-)	*(-) pour frein hydraulique*
flume	*gorge/ravin; canal d'amenée*
fluometer	*appareil de dosage du fluor*
fluoride	*fluorure*
fluorination	*fluoration*
fluorine	*fluor*
flush	*affleurant; chasse d'eau*
(-) joint	*joint lisse*
(-) mounting	*montage encastré*
(-) pipe	*tige lisse*
(-) valve	*soupape/vanne de vidange*
back (-)/counter (-)	*circulation inverse*
to (-) out	*rincer*
flute	*cannelure*
fluted	*plissé/cannelé*
flutter	*turbulence*
flux	*courant/flux/marée montante; décapant/ fondant (de soudure)*
fly nut	*écrou à oreilles*
foam	*mousse/écume*
foaming agent	*agent moussant*
foil	*clinquant/feuille mince*
fold	*pli*
box (-)	*(-) coffré*
dipping (-)	*(-) plongeant*
inclined (-)	*(-) déjeté*
overturned (-)	*(-) déversé*
folia	*feuillets des schistes (ex : ardoises)*
foliated	*lamellaire*
foliation	*foliation*
(-) structure	*structure feuilletée*
follow-up	*rappel/relance/suite/ suivi*
foolproof	*indéréglable/à l'abri des fausses manoeuvres*
foot	*pied*
(-) brake	*frein à pied*
(-) bridge	*passerelle*
(-) operated	*à commande au pied*
(-) shoe	*sabot-guide*
(-) valve	*clapet de pied*
footage	*avancement du forage (en pieds)*
foothill	*contre fort de montagnes/ piémont/colline*
force	*force/contrainte*
(-) pump	*pompe refoulante*
centrifugal (-)	*(-) centrifuge*
gravity (-)	*(-) de gravité/pesanteur*
(-) feed	*alimentation sous pression*
(-id-) lubrication	*graissage forcé*
fore	*avant*
(-) man	*chef d'équipe/contre maître*
(-) runner	*précurseur*
(-) set beds	*couches frontales*
forge	*forge*
portable (-)	*(-) portative/(-) de chantier*
fork	*bifurcation/fourchette*
(-) lift truck/(-) truck	*chariot élévateur à fourche*
(-) wrench	*clé à fourche*
form	*coffrage*
(-) steel	*(-) métallique*
formation	*formation/terrain/ couches*
(-) lines	*plans de stratification*
caving (-)	*(-) boulante*
intermediate (-)	*(-) intermédiaire*
fosse	*fossé/fouille*
fossil	*fossile*
fouling	*encrassement; accumulation de dépôts; salissures*
foundation	*fondation;assise*
(-) bolt	*boulon de (-)*
(-) raft	*radier*

foundry	fonderie
(-) air furnace	four à réverbère
(-) bucket/(-) ladle/	poche de coulée
(-) cupola	cubilot de (-)
(-) flask	chassis de moulage
(-) furnace	four de (-)
(-) pattern	modèle de (-)
(-) pit	fosse de coulée
fracture	fracture/rupture/ cassure
(-) line	ligne de (-)
(-) pattern	structure de (-)
(-) plane	plan de (-)
fragmental	clastique/détritique
frame	bâti/cadre/chassis/ structure/charpente
(-) work	bâti/charpente; coffrage
free	libre/débarrassé de/avec jeu
(-) alkali	alcali libre
(-) end of a rope	brin libre d'une corde/ d'un câble
(-) exhaust	échappement (-)
(-) fall	chute (-)
(-id-) boring	forage à (-id-)
(-) point indicator	indicateur de coincement (des tiges)
(-) stone	pierre de taille
(-) wheel	roue libre
freehold	propriété foncière perpétuelle
fresh	frais/neuf/nouveau/ pur
(-) air	air pur
(-) bit	trépan neuf
(-) food supply	vivres frais
(-) water	eau douce
fretting	corrosion/usure par frottement
friable	friable
friction	frottement/friction
(-) angle	angle de (-)
(-) breccia	brèche de friction/de dislocation
(-) clutch/(-) gear	embrayage à friction
(-) plate	disque d'embrayage
(-) socket	tube de repêchage à frottement
fringe	bordure/frange
fritted	fritté
(-) rock	roche vitrifiée/roche recuite

front	front/antérieur/ avant
(-) axle	essieu avant
(-) of a thrust	(-) de charriage
(-) view	vue de face
(-) wheel	roue avant
(-id-) drive	traction avant
frontal layer	couche frontale
frost	gelée/givre
(-) crack	crevasse/craquelure de gel
(-) cracking/ (-) splitting	gélifraction
(-) blasting/(-) prying/ (-) wedging	éclatement par le gel
hoar (-)	givre
(-) glass	verre dépoli
froth	écume/mousse
frother/frothing agent	agent moussant
frozen	gelé/congelé/coincé/ immobilisé
(-) casing	tubage coincé
(-) pipe/(-) drill pipe	tube coincé
(-) string	garniture (de forage) coincée
fuel	carburant/combustible/ fioul
(-) can nozzle	bec verseur de bidon à carburant
(-) feed	alimentation en (-)
(-) filter	filtre à (-)
(-) gauge	jauge de (-)
(-) injector	injecteur de combustible
(-) pump	pompe d'alimentation en (-)
diesel (-)	gas-oil/gasoil/gazole
(-) oil	fuel oil/fioul/mazout/ huile lourde/huile combustible
fulcrum	pivot/articulation support de levier
full	plein/rempli/complet
(-) dip	pendage vrai/plongement réel
(-) line	trait plein (dessin)
(-) load	pleine charge
(-) scale/(-) size	à l'échelle grandeur
fundamental	fondamental/primitif
(-) rocks	roches du socle
funnel	entonnoir
guide (-)	(-) de guidage

furnace	four
(-) flue	carneau d'un (-)
(-) hearth	creuset/ sole d'un (-)
(-) mouth	gueulard
(-) slag	scorie de (-)
air (-)	(-) à réverbère
crucible (-)	(-) à creusets
solar (-)	(-) solaire
furrow	strié/ cannelure/ rayure
fuse	fusible; détonateur; coupecircuit
fusion	fusion
(-) welding	soudage par (-)

G

gage/gauge	jauge/ mesure/ calibre; manomètre/ indicateur de pression
(-) glass	tube de niveau
(-) hole	orifice de jaugeage
(-) pressure	pression manométrique
(-) rod	tige de (-)
bit (-) surface	front de taille de l'outil/ du trépan
float (-)	(-) à flotteur
level (-)	indicateur de niveau
plate (-)	calibre pour tôles
pressure (-)	manomètre
rain (-)	pluviomètre
thickness (-)	(-) d'épaisseur
thread (-)	calibre pour filetage
wire (-)	(-id-) pour fils
galling	éraillure
galvanised	galvanisé
gang	équipe
gantry	portique; pont roulant
(-) crane	grue à (-)/ chèvre
gangway	passerelle de service/ voie de circulation
gap	intervalle/ trou; hiatus/ cluse/ écart; faille
(-) fault	faille ouverte
(-) lathe	tour à banc rompu
air (-)	entre-fer (engine)
dry/wind (-)	cluse sèche
erosional (-)	lacune d'érosion
water (-)	cluse active/ cluse vive
garbage	ordures
gas, gasoline (US)/ petrol (UK)	essence
gash	coupure/ entaille

gasket	joint/ garniture
cylinderhead (-)	(-) de culasse
metallic-abestos (-)	(-) métalloplastique
gate	passage/ porte/ ouverture/ vanne
(-) valve	robinet vanne
gauge, gage (see gage)	jauge/ calibre (voir gage)
gauze	gaze/ toile métallique
gear	engrenage/ roue dentée; mécanisme
(-) box	boîte de vitesse
(-) case	carter d' (-)
(-) change	changement de vitesse
(-) motor	motoréducteur/ moteur avec réducteur
(-) pump	pompe à (-)
(-) wheel	roue d' (-)/ roue dentée
bevel (-)/bevel spur (-)	(-) conique/(-) à roue conique
driven (-)	roue menée
driving (-)	roue menante
helical (-)	(-) hélicoïdale
high (-)	pignon de grande vitesse/ à grande vitesse
low (-)	pignon de petite vitesse
mating (-)	roues conjuguées
meshing (-)/sliding (-)	pignon baladeur/ pignon glissant
gearing	engrenage
friction (-)	embrayage à friction
gel	gel
gelling agent	agent gélifiant
generating set	groupe électrogène
generator	générateur/ génératrice/ dynamo
welding (-)	poste de soudage
geologic/geological	géologique
(-) clock	tableau chronologique
(-) column	échelle/ coupe (-)
(-) survey	étude (-)/ service (-)
(-) window	fenêtre tectonique
geology	géologie
field (-)	(-) de surface
stratigraphic (-)	(-) stratigraphique
geophone	géophone/ sismographe
geophysical survey	étude géophysique
geosuture	géofracture
geosyncline	géosynclinal
geothermal	géothermique
(-) gradient/ geothermic depth	gradient (-)/ degré (-)

gib	*contre-clavette*
gimlet	*vrille/ foret*
gin	*chèvre*
(-) pole	*chevalement/ flèche de levage*
(-id-) truck	*camion-grue*
girder	*poutre/ poutrelle/ longeron*
box (-)	*(-) caisson*
girt	*entretoise*
glacis	*glacis*
gland	*presse-étoupe*
(-) nut	*chapeau de (-)*
(-) packing	*garniture d'étanchéité*
(-) ring	*bague d'étanchéité*
glen	*ravin/ vallée étroite*
gliding	*glissement*
(-) plane	*plan de (-)*
glow plug	*bougie de réchauffage*
go-devil	*ramoneur/ râcleur (de pipe line)*
goggles	*lunettes protectrices*
gooseneck	*col de cygne/ col de tête d'injection*
gorge	*ravin/ gorge*
gouge	*gouge*
(-) bit	*mèche à cuiller/ tarière*
(-) zone	*zone broyée*
governor	*régulateur*
flow (-)	*(-) de débit*
speed (-)	*(-) de vitesse*
grab	*accrocheur/ benne preneuse/ grappin/ pelle automatique*
(-) bucket	*benne preneuse*
(-) crane	*grue à benne*
(-) iron	*accrocheur*
rope (-)	*grappin pour câbles*
graben	*graben/ fossé tectonique*
grade	*grade/ degré/ pente/ rampe; qualité/ nuance/ teneur*
down (-)	*déclivité/ pente descendante*
high (-)	*de bonne qualité/ à grande teneur*
up (-)	*montée/ rampe/ pente ascendante*
graded	*classé/ gradué*
(-) profile	*profil régularisé*

grader	*trieur/ appareil à trier*
road (-)	*niveleuse/ profileuse*
gradient	*gradient/ pente/ plan incliné/ rampe*
angle of (-)	*angle de déclivité*
reverse (-)	*contre pente*
grading	*classement/ triage*
(-) screen	*crible classeur*
graduated	*gradué*
(-) scale	*échelle (-)*
(-) screw	*vis micrométrique/ vis (-)*
grain	*grain*
(-) size distri-bution	*granulométrie*
(-) volume deter-mination	*mesure de porosité des roches*
coarse (-)	*gros (-)*
close (-)	*(-) serré/ faible porosité*
fine (-)	*(-) fin*
granite	*granit*
(-) wash	*arkose/ roche granitique remaniée*
granule	*granule/ grain*
(-) roundstone	*gravier fin*
granulose/granulous	*granuleux*
graphite	*graphite*
(-) grease	*graisse graphitée*
grapple	*grappin/ harpon*
basket (-)	*coin agrippeur (de repêchage)*
wireline (-)	*(-) pour câbles*
grappling	*accrochage (repêchage)*
grate	*grille/ tamis*
(-) bar	*barreau de (-)*
grating	*caillebotis/ grillage/ treillis*
gratuity	*gratification/ indemnité/ prime*
gravel	*gravier*
(-) packing	*gravillonnage des crépines*
(-) soil	*sol graveleux*
pea (-)	*gravillon*
gravimetry	*gravimétrie*
gravity	*pesanteur/ gravité; densité (Baumé, API, etc.)*
(-) feed	*alimentation par gravité*
(-) flow	*écoulement par gravité*
specific (-)	*densité/ poids spécifique*

gray iron/gray pig iron	*fonte grise*
grazing angle	*angle d'incidence rasante*
grease	*graisse*
(-) cup	*graisseur*
(-) gun	*pompe à (-)*
cup (-)/heavy (-)	*(-) consistante*
rope (-)	*(-) pour câbles*
tacky (-)	*(-) filante*
grey waters	*"eaux grises"/eaux grasses (essentiellement eaux de vaisselle et d'ustensiles de cuisine domestiques)*
grid	*grille/tamis; quadrillage/ réseau*
griefstem	*kelly/tige carrée d'entraînement*
grinder	*meuleuse/affûteuse/ rectifieuse*
grinding	*meulage/rodage*
(-) compound/(-) paste	*pâte à roder*
(-) stone	*pierre à aiguiser/meule à aiguiser*
(-) wheel	*meule/roue à meuler*
grip	*prise/pince d'accrochage/ serrage*
bulldog (-)	*serre câble*
grips	*mâchoires d'un étau*
grit	*abrasif/particule abrasive; sable grossier/gravillon*
groove	*cannelure/gorge/rainure*
grooved pulley	*poulie à gorge*
grooved shaft	*arbre cannelé*
ground	*sol/terre/terrain*
(-) cable	*câble de mise à la terre*
(-) clearance	*garde au sol*
(-) feature/	*accident/détail*
(-) irregularity	*de terrain*
(-) level	*niveau du sol*
(-) pipe	*canalisation enterrée*
(-) survey	*levé terrestre*
(-) water	*eau souterraine*
(-id-) basin	*bassin hydrogéologique*
(-id-) level	*niveau hydrostatique*
dead (-)	*mort-terrain*
grounding	*mise à la terre*
grouting	*jointement du tubage/ cimentation/injection de coulis/de boue*
grove	*bocage/plantation d'arbres*
growth	*augmentation/croissance/ gonflement*
grubbing	*dessouchage*
guard	*gardien; dispositif de sécurité/capot/carter*
(-) rail	*garde-corps/garde-fou rampe de protection*
mud (-)	*garde boue*
gudgeon	*goujon/tourillon*
(-) pin	*axe*
guesstimate (guess + estimate)	*estimation approchée*
guide	*guide/guidage*
(-) arm	*bras de (-)*
(-) bearing	*palier (-)*
(-) casing shoe	*sabot de (-)*
(-) line	*câble ou ligne de (-); directive générale*
(-) post	*colonne de (-)*
(-) roller	*galet de (-)*
(-) shoe	*sabot de (-)*
bell (-)	*cloche de (-)*
overshot (-)	*sabot de (-id-)*
gulch	*ravin/gorge*
gully	*rigole*
(-) erosion	*ravinement*
gummy	*gommeux/gluant*
gun metal	*bronze industriel*
gun	*canon/arme*
jet (-)	*giflard*
spray (-)	*pistolet à peindre*
gunk	*déchets graisseux/ cambouis*
gush	*jaillissement*
gusset	*gousset (de jonction de poutrelles)*
gust	*rafale de vent*
gutter	*caniveau/goulotte/ gouttière*
guy/guy wire	*hauban/haubannage*
(-) anchor	*ancrage du haubannage*
guyed	*haubanné*
guying	*haubannage*

H

hack	*pic/ pioche; brèche/ entaille*
(-) saw	*scie à métaux*
hade	*écart de la verticale/ angle du pendage avec la verticale*
(-) of fault	*angle du plan de faille avec la verticale*
half	*demi/ semi/ moitié*
(-) round	*semi-circulaire*
(-) turn socket	*cloche à demi-tour (pour repêchage)*
hallmark	*poinçon de garantie/ de contrôle*
hammada	*désert rocheux/ hammada*
hammer	*marteau/ pilon*
(-) drill	*(-) perforateur*
(-) face/(-) peen	*panne de (-)*
(-) grab	*trépan-benne*
(-) hardening	*écrouissage/ martelage à froid*
(-) mill/(-) crusher	*broyeur à (-)*
air (-)/pneumatic (-)	*(-) pneumatique*
ball peen (-)	*(-) à panne sphérique*
claw (-)	*(-) à panne fendue*
geologist (-)	*(-) de géologue*
pile (-)	*mouton/(-) pour battage de palplanches*
riveting (-)	*rivoir/(-) rivoir*
sledge (-)	*(-) à devant/ masse*
steam (-)	*(-) pilon*
water (-)	*coups de bélier*
hammering	*battage/ martelage*
hand	*main; aiguille de cadran*
(-) dog	*clé à tige*
(-) drill	*perceuse à main/ chignole*
(-) drilling of well	*forage à bras*
(-) drive	*commande manuelle*
(-) hoist	*palan à bras*
(-) hole	*trou de poing/ trou de visite*
(-) pump	*pompe à main*
(-) rail	*garde-corps/ main courante/ rambarde*
(-) saw	*scie égoïne/ scie à main*
(-) tight coupling	*raccord serré à la main*
(-) wheel	*volant*
(-) winch	*treuil à bras*

handbook	*manuel/ formulaire/ précis*
handle	*poignée/ manette/ levier/ bras*
hang	*inclinaison/ pendage/ pente*
hanger	*bride support/ collier, ou crochet de suspension/ olive, tige de suspension*
casing (-)	*coins, griffes de suspension du tubage*
pipe (-)	*étrier de suspension d'une tuyauterie, ou canalisation*
hanging	*accrochage/ suspension*
(-) rod	*tringle de suspension*
(-) valley	*vallée suspendue*
(-) wall	*terrain de recouvrement*
hard	*dur*
(-) digging	*forage en terrain (-)*
(-) driving	*emmanché à chaud*
(-) rock	*roche dure*
(-) rubber	*ébonite*
(-) solder	*brasure*
(-) water	*eau dure*
hardened	*durci/ trempé*
case (-)	*cémenté*
(-) steel	*acier trempé*
hardening	*durcissement/ trempe*
torch (-)	*trempe au chalumeau*
hardness	*dureté*
(-) degree	*degré hydrotimétrique*
(-) number	*indice de (-)*
(-) scale	*échelle de (-)*
hardware	*quincaillerie/ ferronnerie/ matériel et équipements d'informatique*
harness	*harnais/ harnachement/ attelage*
hatch	*panneau/ trappe*
hatchet	*hachette*
haulage	*halage/ roulage/ transport/ camionnage*
hawk bill	*tenaille à souder*
hazard	*danger/ risque*

head	tête/ calotte; hauteur d'élévation/ de refoulement/ charge hydraulique	hiatus	hiatus/ lacune
(-) frame	chevalement	hide	cuir/ peau
(-) gasket	joint de culasse	hill	colline
(-) gear	superstructure/ chevalement	(-) side	versant/ pente
		(-id-) waste	éboulement
(-) lamp/ (-) light	phare/ projecteur	hillock	butte/ colline/ monticule/ tertre
(-) loss	perte de charge		
(-) of water	pression d'eau/ charge d'eau/ hauteur de chute	hind	arrière
(-) pipe	conduite d'alimentation/ d'amenée	hinge	charnière/ gond
		(-) pin	broche/ cheville/ goujon
(-) pulley	poulie de tête	hinged	articulé
(-) room	hauteur libre sous plafond/ sous voûte/ hauteur de passage	hinter land	arrière-pays
		hit-or-miss	au hasard
(-) waves	ondes de première arrivée	hoarding	palissade/ clôture en planches
(-) wind	vent debout		
casing (-)	(-) de tubage	hoag head	tête de pompe à boue
cementing (-)	(-) de cimentation	hog wallow	dépression de dimension réduite
(-) circulating	(-) de circulation		
cylinder (-)	culasse (de moteur)	hog wallowed soil	sol mamelonné
delivery/ discharge (-)	hauteur de refoulement	hoist	monte-charge/ palan/ treuil
hexagon (-)	tête à six pans		
hydraulic (-)	pression en hauteur de colonne d'eau	(-) drawworks	treuil de levage
		(-) drum	tambour de treuil
pressure (-)	hauteur piézométrique	(-) rope	câble de levage
static (-)	pression statique	(-) tackle	palan de levage
suction (-)	hauteur d'aspiration	hold	prise/ tenue
well (-)	tête de puits	(-) down bolt	boulon de retenue/ boulon de scellement
headboard	traverse d'appui (du treuil rotary)		
		holder	support/ étau
header	collecteur/ distributeur/ manifold	slip (-)	support de coins
		holdfast	crampon/ crochet
headstock	poupée de tour (fixe)	holding	fixation/ assemblage
heap	tas/ amas/ terril	hole	trou/ forage
		blow (-)	soufflard
heat	chaleur	grout (-)	trou d'injection
(-) capacity	pouvoir calorifique	hollow	cavité/ creux
(-) insulation	isolement thermique/ calorifuge	(-) rod	tige creuse
		hone	pierre à aiguiser
heave/ heaving	gonflement/ boursoufflement	hook	crochet
		(-) block	moufle-crochet combiné
heavy	dense/ lourd	(-) up	montage
height	hauteur	(-id-) nipple	raccord de montage
hoisting (-)	(-) de levage	rotary (-)	(-) de levage
		wall (-)	(-) redresseur
helical/ helicoidal	hélicoïdal	hoop	frette/ cercle
(-) gear	engrenage (-)		
helmet	casque protecteur	hopper	trémie
hemlock bark	extrait amincissant pour boue de forage (extrait d'écorce de sapin)	horizon	horizon/ zone
hemp	chanvre		
herring bone	chevrons		
(-) gear	engrenage à (-)		

horn	avertisseur/ corne/ trompe
(-) socket	tube de repêchage
horse	chevalet
(-) back	dos d'âne/ intercalation stérile
(-) cock	trépan aléseur
(-) collar	manchon de sécurité des masses-tiges
(-) head	contrepoids de pompe à balancier
(-) shoe dune	dune en fer à cheval
horsepower/hp	cheval vapeur anglo-saxon
brake (-)/bhp	puissance en chevaux au frein
nominal (-)	puissance nominale
hose	tuyau flexible/ flexible/ manche
(-) coupling	raccord de (-)
(-) reel	tambour d'enroulement/ dévidoir
canvas (-)	manche en toile
fire (-)	manche à incendie
mud/rotary (-)	flexible d'injection de boue
rubber (-)	tuyau en caoutchouc
hot	chaud
(-) drawn	étiré à (-)
(-) forging	forgeage à (-)
(-) galvanized	galvanisé à chaud/ au bain
(-) tapping	piquage d'un branchement sur une conduite en charge
(-) tinning	étamage à chaud
household connection	branchement/ raccordement particulier
household waste	ordures ménagères
housing	abri/ boitier/ cage/ carter/ enveloppe/ logement
pump (-)	carter de pompe
hub	moyeu (d'une roue); mire de nivellement; piquet
(-) brake	frein sur (-)
(-) cap	chapeau de (-)/ chapeau de roue
hue	teinte/ nuance
hum	vrombissement/ ronflement·
humidity	humidité
relative (-)	(-) relative
hump	bosse/ sommet d'une courbe

hunting	flottement/ marche oscillante/ oscillation de vitesse
hurdle	barrière/ clôture
hurricane	ouragan
hydrant	bouche d'eau/ prise d'eau
fire (-)	bouche d'incendie
hydraulic	hydraulique
(-) brake	frein (-)
(-) cement	ciment (-)
(-) clutch	embrayage (-)
(-) coupling	couplage (-)
(-) drive	commande (-)
(-) fill	remblai (-) ·
(-) fracturing	fracturation (-)
(-) head	hauteur piézométrique/ hauteur de charge
(-) jack	vérin (-)/ cric (-)
(-) jar	coulisse (-)
(-) mortar	mortier (-)
(-) ram/hydram	bélier (-)
(-) torque	
converter	convertisseur de couple (-)
hydrochloric	chlorhydrique
hydrogeology	hydrogéologie
hydrography	hydrographie
hydrology	hydrologie
hydrometre	aéromètre/ densimètre
hydrostatic	hydrostatique
hydrous	aqueux/ hydraté
hypochlorite	hypochlorite
Hertz/Hz	période (unité de fréquence)

I

I-beam	poutre/ poutrelle en I
id (inside diametre)	alésage/ diamètre intérieur
idle	ralenti/ inactif
(-) gear	roue folle/ roue de renvoi
(-) period	temps mort
(-) roll	poulie de tension
(-) running	marche au ralenti
idler	ralentisseur/ régulateur
(-) nozzle	gicleur de ralenti
idling	marche au ralenti

IDWSSD (international drinking water supply and sanitation decade) — *DIEPA (décennie internationale de l'eau potable et de l'assainissement)*

igneous — *igné*

ignition — *allumage/inflammation*
(-) circuit — *circuit d' (-)*
(-) coil — *bobine d' (-)*
(-) plug — *bougie d' (-)*

illumination — *éclairage*

imbalance — *balourd*

imbedded — *enfoncé/incrusté encastré*

imbricated — *imbriqué*

immersion — *immersion*

impact — *choc/impact résistance aux chocs*
(-) fatigue/
(-) strength

impeller — *roue à aubes/rouet/rotor*
pump (-) — *rotor de pompe*
vane (-) — *turbine à ailettes*

impervious — *étanche/imperméable*

implementation — *mise en oeuvre*

impression block — *bloc d'empreinte*

incipient — *naissant*

inclination — *inclinaison*

incline — *plan incliné*

inclinometer — *inclinomètre/inclinoscope*

inclusion — *enclave/inclusion*

increase — *augmentation/élévation/hausse*

increment — *accroissement/augmentation*

incumbrance — *servitude/charge/hypothèque*

index — *indice/repère*

indicator — *indicateur/indice*
mud flow (-) — *débitmètre à boue*
torque (-) — *(-) de couple*
tong (-id-) — *(-id-) de vissage*

inducer — *aubage d'entrée d'un compresseur centrifuge*

induration — *durcissement/endurcissement*

inert — *inerte*
(-) gas — *gaz (-)*
(-id-) welding — *soudage sous (-id-)*

infiltration — *infiltration*

inflatable — *gonflable*

inflow — *arrivée/entrée/venue*
water (-) — *venue d'eau*

ingrained — *incrusté/imprégné*

ingredient — *ingrédient*

ingress — *admission/entrée*

inlet — *admission/orifice/lumière*
(-) manifold — *tubulure d' (-)/collecteur d' (-)*
(-) valve — *soupape d' (-)*
air (-) — *prise d'air/arrivée d'air*
water (-) — *arrivée d'eau*

inlier — *fenêtre géologique*

inner — *intérieur/interne*
(-) tube — *chambre à air*

input — *apport/admission/entrée*

insert — *pièce rapportée*
(-) bit — *outil de forage à picots*

insulation — *isolant/calorifuge*
(-) chip — *crochet/bracelet/collier d'assemblage (d'éléments calorifuges)*
(-) material — *matériau (-)*
(-) strength — *résistance d'isolement*
low (-) — *mauvais isolement*
heat (-) — *isolation thermique*

insulator — *isolateur/isolant*

intake — *admission/alimentation/arrivée/prise*
(-) port — *lumière d' (-)*
(-) valve — *soupape d' (-)*

interbedding — *alternance des couches/interstratification*

interface — *interface/tranche*

interference — *interférence; brouillage/parasite (radio)*

interlock — *enclenchement/couplage/emboîtement*

interlocking device — *dispositif de verrouillage*

interstice — *intervalle/interstice/vide*

intrusive	*intrusif*
(-) breccia	*brèche intrusive*
invert	*radier*
inverted fold	*pli renversé*
iodine	*iode*
iron	*fer*
(-) casting	*fonte*
(-) filing	*limaille de (-)*
(-) sheet	*feuillard/tôle de (-)*
(-) slag	*scorie*
flat (-)	*fer plat*
pig (-)	*fonte en saumons, en gueuses*
irrigation	*irrigation*
drip (-)	*(-) au goutte à goutte*

J

jack	*cric/vérin*
(-) and circle	*(-) de serrage des joints de tige (sur crémaillère circulaire)*
(-) bit	*taillant amovible*
(-) board	*support de tige, pendant le vissage d'une nouvelle longueur*
(-) hammer	*marteau pneumatique*
(-) knife	*couteau de poche*
(-id-) derrick/mast	*mât de forage repliable*
(-) latch	*loquet à ressort*
(-) plane	*varlope*
(-) screw	*(-) à vis*
(-) tool	*vérin de serrage*
hand (-)	*(-) à main*
hydraulic (-)	*vérin hydraulique*
latch (-)	*accrocheur de repêchage*
lifting (-)	*câble de levage*
screw (-)	*vérin à vis*
jacket	*chemise/enveloppe/manchon*
jag	*pointe/dent (de scie)*
jam	*embouteillage/encombrement*
jam nut	*contre écrou*
jamb	*jambage/montant/chambranle*
jar	*coulisse de forage; battement*
(-) socket	*arrache-coulisse*
bumper (-)	*coulisse d'amortissement*
fishing (-)	*coulisse de repêchage*
jarring	*broutage d'un outil*
jaw	*mâchoire/crabot*

jenny	*grue mobile*
jerk	*secousse*
(-) line	*câble à (-)*
jet	*injection/jet*
(-) pump	*éjecteur*
jib	*bras/flèche*
(-) crane	*grue à flèche*
jig	*gabarit/calibre*
jitter	*instabilité*
job	*besogne/tâche*
jobber	*ouvrier à la tâche/tâcheron/sous-traitant*
jockey	*attelage*
(-) pulley	*pignon tendeur/galet de guidage*
(-) stick	*cravache (pièce de liaison du serre-câble au limiteur de course du balancier, dans le battage au câble)*
jog	*décrochement/ébranlement*
joining pin	*broche/goupille*
joint	*joint/assemblage/raccord; commun/coordonné*
(-) leakage	*fuite au joint/défaut d'étanchéité*
(-) make-up loss	*perte de longueur au vissage*
(-) pattern	*réseau de fractures*
(-) pin	*tourillon*
(-) plate	*couvre-joint*
(-) welding	*soudure par recouvrement*
bedding (-)	*(-) de stratification*
caulked (-)	*(-) calfaté*
dovetail (-)	*(-) à queue d'aronde*
expansion (-)	*(-) de dilatation/(-) d'expansion*
forced-in (-)	*(-) emmanché à force*
safety (-)	*(-) de sûreté*
rotary (-id-)	*embout de sûreté (rotary)*
soldered (-)	*(-) soudé*
spigot (-)	*(-) à emboîtement*
tool (-)	*(-) de tiges (de forage)*
union (-)	*raccord union/union*
welded (-)	*(-) soudé/cordon de soudure*
jointer	*varlope/machine à rainer, à rainurer*
jointers	*tubes raboutés*
jointing	*fissuration; assemblage/emboîtement*
(-) material	*liant*

joist	entretoise/ chevron/ madrier/ solive
jolt	cahot/ saccade/ secousse
jolting machine	crible laveur à secousse
journal	tourillon/ fusée d'essieu/ portée
jug	broc/ cruche
jump	saut/ accident/ discontinuité
voltage (-)	saut de tension (électr.)
jumper	shunt/ bretelle/ pontage (électr.); fleuret/ fleuret d'amorçage
(-) bar	
jumping	aplatissement/ écrasement/ refoulement
junction	branchement/ dérivation/ raccordement
(-) box	boîte de jonction
mains (-)	noeud de canalisations
junk	rebut/ déchets de ferraille/ détritus
(-) basket	panier de repêchage/ tube à sédiments
(-) bit	outil de nettoyage
(-) catcher	carottier de repêchage
(-) feeler	tâte-ferraille (pour repêchage)
(-) pipe	tube reformé
(-) racks	râtelier/ supports de transport des outils et accessoires
(-) sleeve	manchon à ferraille
(-) sub	panier à sédiment
jut	saillie
jutting	saillant/ en saillie
juvenile	juvénile/ peu évolué
(-) water	eau juvénile/ eau magmatique

K

karst	karst
covered (-)	(-) couvert
deep (-)	(-) complet/ (-) profond
(-) plain	plaine karstique
shallow (-)	(-) superficiel/ (-) incomplet
(-) valley	valley karstique
keg	barillet/ tonnelet

kelly/kelley	tige carrée d'entraînement
(-) bushing	carré d'entraînement de la tige carrée
roller (-id-)	coins d'entraînement à roulements à rouleaux
(-) drive bushing	coins d'entraînement
(-) hole/rat hole	trou de la tige carrée
(-) saver sub	raccord d'usure (monté sur le filetage de la tige carrée pour réduire son usure)
(-) spinner	entraineur de la tige carrée
square (-)/hexagonal/ octogon (-)	tige carrée/ hexagonale/ octogonale
kettle	bassin/ trou glaciaire
giant's (-)	marmite de géant
key	clé/ clavette; repère; légende d'une carte/ d'un plan
(-) bed	niveau/ couche repère
(-) seat/(-) hole	excentrement d'un sondage en forme de trou de serrure
(-id-) reamer	aléseur pour corriger l'excentrement en trou de serrure
(-) seating	coincement dû à l'excentrement du trou de sonde
(-) way	logement/ rainure de clavette
keying	calage/ coinçage
kick	cahot/ recul/ secousse
(-) back	retour en arrière
(-) over tool	outil de décentrage
(-) starter	démarreur au pied
kieselguhr	kieselguhr/ diatomite
kill line	conduite de sécurité
kinematics/kinematic	cinématique
kinetics/kinetic	cinétique
king pin	axe de pivotement/ pivot central/ pivot d'accouplement tracteur-semi remorque
kink	coque d'un câble/ noeud/ tortillement
kinking of a cable	vrillage d'un câble
kit	trousse/ jeu de petits outils; jeu de pièces nécessaire au montage d'un appareil complet
kitten	petit tracteur à chenilles
klaxon	avertisseur

knife	*couteau*
(-) casing mill	*coupe-tube*
(-) edge	*(-) de balance*
(-) switch	*interrupteur*
knob	*bouton; bosse de terrain*
knock	*cliquetis/ cognement/ détonation*
(-) down	*démontable*
engine (-)	*cliquetis*
knoll	*monticule/ tertre*
know how	*savoir-faire*
knuckle	*articulation/ rotule*
(-) joint	*joint universel/ genouillère*
knurled	*moleté*
(-) nut	*écrou (-)*
knurling wheel	*molette/ roue moletée*

L

lab	*labo*
(laboratory)	*(laboratoire)*
label	*étiquette/ désignation*
labeled	*étiqueté/ marqué*
laboratory	*laboratoire*
labour/labor	*main d'oeuvre*
lacquer	*lacque/ vernis*
lacuna	*lacune/ hiatus*
lacustrine	*lacustre*
ladder	*échelle*
(-) ditcher	*excavateur à godets*
(-) lode	*filon en échelons/ en gradins*
folding (-)	*(-) pliante*
ladle	*poche de coulée*
lag	*retard/ décalage*
angle of (-)	*angle de (-)*
ignition (-)	*délai d'allumage*
lagging	*retard/ ralentissement; calorifugeage/ revêtement*
lagoon	*lagon*
(-) deposits	*dépôts lagunaires*
lahar	*avalanche/ coulée boueuse*
lake	*lac*
(-) bed	*couche lacustre*
(-) deposit	*dépôt lacustre*
crater (-)	*(-) cratère/ (-) de cratère*

laminar	*lamellaire/ laminaire*
(-) flow	*écoulement laminaire*
laminated	*laminé/ feuilleté*
(-) shale	*schiste/ argile stratifiée*
lamp	*lampe/ ampoule électrique*
arc (-)	*(-) à arc*
hurricane (-)	*(-) tempête*
incandescent (-)	*(-) à incandescence*
(-) socket	*douille de (-)*
land	*terrain/ parcelle/ aire*
(-) area	*aire continentale*
(-) chain	*chaîne d'arpenteur*
(-) fall	*éboulement*
(-) leveling	*nivellement*
(-) measuring/	*arpentage*
(-) surveying	
(-) register	*cadastre*
(-) waste	*matériaux détritiques*
landing	*atterrissage/ débarquement*
(-) nipple	*raccord à portée intérieure*
(-) sub	*raccord de pose*
landlocked	*enclavé/ sans bordure maritime*
landmark	*borne/ repère/ élément topographique*
landslide	*glissement de terrain*
lap	*chevauchement/ recouvrement/ plissement*
(-) joint	*joint à recouvrement/ assemblage à clin*
(-) weld/(-) welding	*soudure à recouvrement*
lapping	*rodage*
(-) compound	*pâte à roder*
(-) of rings	*(-) des segments (d'un moteur)*
lapse	*espace/ écart de temps; erreur/ faute*
lashing	*fouettement des tiges; amarrage*
latch	*clenche/ loquet/ verrou*
(-) jack	*accrocheur (de repêchage)*
(-) key	*passe-partout*
(-) pin	*mentonnet*
latching	*accrochage/ enclenchement/ verrouillage*
late	*en retard*
(-) admission	*retard à l'admission*
lateritic	*latéritique*
lath	*latte*
lathe	*tour*

latrine	latrine/ cabinet/ cabinet d'aisance
bucket (-)	(-) à tinette
composting (-)	(-) à compostage
batch (-id-)	(-id-) alternante
continuous (-id-)	(-id-) permanente
double vault (-id-)/ DVC (-)	(-id-) à double compartiment ou voûte/ (-) CCDV
flush (-)	(-) à réservoir de chasse
pit(-)/dry pit (-)	(-) à fosse/(-)à fosse sèche
improved (-id-)	(-id-) améliorée
(ROEC) Reed odorless	(-) inodore système Reed (LIR)
earth (-)/ permanent (-id-)	(-) à fosse permanente améliorée (CFPA)
VIP (ventilated improved pit) (-)	(-) amélioré à fosse autoventilée (LAA)
pour-flush (-)	(-) à chasse d'eau
squat plate (-)	(-) à la turque
multrum (-) (Swedish design of an anaerobic improved permanent double vaulted latrine)	(-) multrum (conception suédoise d'une latrine anaérobique permanente à deux compartiments)
UTAFIFI (-) (Tanzanian adaptation of above)	latrine UTAFIFI (évolution en Tanzanie du modèle précédent)
lattice	treillis/ lattis/ toile métallique
(-) girder	poutre en (-)
(-) plane	plan réticulaire
(-) structure	structure fenestrée
launcher	lanceur
slip (-)	support de coins à déclenchement
launder	caniveau/ rigole
lava	lave
(-) ash	cendre volcanique
(-) shield	bouclier de (-)
lay	configuration/ disposition
(-) out	plan/ tracé/ agencement/ disposition
(-) tongs	clé de vissage/ dévissage des tiges
layer	couche/ horizon géologique
water (-)	(-) d'eau/ zone aqueuse
weathered (-)	zone altérée
laying	pose
(-) down/(-) out	dégerbage (des tiges/ tubage, etc.)
leaching	lessivage; filtration
lead	plomb; avance/ amenée
(-) screw	vis mère
(-) time	délai de démarrage
(-) tongs/breakout tongs	clé de déblocage
leaf	feuille

leak	fuite
(-) detector	détecteur de (-)
(-) free/(-) proof	étanche
leakage	fuite/ perte/ coulage
lean-to	appentis
leap	saut/ dislocation/ rejet
leather	cuir
(-) packing	garniture de (-)
oiled (-)	(-) chamoisé
ledge	rebord/ saillie
fault (-)	escarpement de faille
lee side/leeward	face aval coté sous le vent
left hand	à gauche
(-) drill pipe	tige de forage à filets à gauche
left lay cable	câble toronné à gauche
leg	montant/ jambe/ pied; branchement
(-) of angle	aile de cornière
length	longueur de tube/ de tige
(-) of drill pipe	longueur d'assemblage des tiges
lengthening	allongement
(-) rod	rallonge
lens	lentille; objectif
(-) shaped	lenticulé/ lenticulaire
lenticular	lenticulaire
(-) reservoir	réservoir (-)
(-) sands	sables (-)
(-) structure	structure (-)
levee	levée de terre/ digue/ bourrelet alluvial
level	niveau/ surface; teneur
(-) gauge/(-) indicator	indicateur de (-)
(-) of reference	(-) de référence
(-) screw	vis de calage/ de mise à (-)
(-) seam	couche horizontale
(-) surface	surface de (-)
ground water (-)	(-) phréatique
hydrostatic (-)/water table (-)	(-) hydrostatique
mean sea level/msl	niveau moyen de la mer
spirit (-)	niveau à bulle
leveling/leveling survey	nivellement
(-) pole/(-) rule/ (-) staff	mire de (-)/ mire graduée

lever | levier/balancier/manette
(-) arm | bras de (-)
balance (-) | (-) à contrepoids
(-) safety valve | soupape de sûreté à (-)
clutch/coupling (-) | (-) d'embrayage
gear (-) | (-) de changement de vitesse
pawl (-) | (-) à cliquet
sand-reel (-) | (-) du tambour de curage

lid | couvercle; clapet

lie key | clé/fourche de retenue

life | vie/durée/longévité;

lift | élévation/levée/levage; ascenseur/monte-charge
(-) hook | crochet de levage
(-) pump | pompe élévatoire
(-) of a pump | hauteur de refoulement
(-) truck | chariot élévateur
(-) winch | treuil
air (-) | remontée pneumatique/gazosiphon
suction (-) | hauteur d'aspiration

lifting | levage/relevage/soulèvement/élévation
(-) arm | bras élévateur
(-) capacity | force portante/puissance de levée
(-) device/(-) gear | appareil de (-)
(-) hook | crochet de (-)
(-) jack | vérin de (-)/cric
(-) speed | vitesse de (-)
(-) sub | tête de (-)

light | léger; clair; facile; lumière
(-) alloy | alliage (-)
(-) switch | commutateur/interrupteur
flashing (-) | feu à éclats
warning (-) | lampe témoin

lighting | éclairage/allumage
(-) fixture | appareil d' (-)
emergency (-) | (-) de secours

lightning | éclair/foudre

limb | flanc d'un anticlinal

lime | chaux
(-) milk/(-) water | lait de (-)
(-) mortar | mortier de (-)
(-) mud | boue carbonatée
(-) treatment | traitement (des eaux) à la chaux
hydrated (-) | (-) éteinte
quick (-) | (-) vive

limestone | calcaire
argillaceous (-) | (-) argileux
banded (-) | (-) rubanné
chalky (-) | (-) crayeux

cherty (-) | (-) à silex
crumbly (-) | (-) grumeleux/pulvérulent
crystalline (-) | (-) cristallin
dolomitic (-) | (-) dolomitique
oolitic (-) | (-) oolithique
pellet (-) | (-) graveleux
sandy (-) | (-) sableux
shell (-) | (-) coquillier

limit | limite
(-) gauge | calibre de tolérance

line | ligne/câble/trait
(-) breaker | conjoncteur-disjoncteur (électr.)
(-) losses | pertes en (-)
(-) of dip | (-) de pente/direction du pendage
(-) of outcrop | (-) d'affleurement
(-) pressure | pression de (-)
(-) shaft | arbre principal (de transmission)
(-) up | alignement/mise en ligne
(-) wire | fil/conducteur sous tension (électr.)
back up (-) | câble de la clé de blocage (tiges de forages)
bailing (-) | câble de curage
blowing (-) | conduite d'évacuation d'air
cable-tool (-) | câble de battage
cathead (-) | câble de cabestan
drilling (-) | câble de forage
guy (-) | hauban
pressure (-) | circuit de refoulement de la boue
swabbing (-) | câble de curage
through (-) | arête synclinale

linear | linéaire

lined | chemisé/doublé/enduit/garni
Babbit (-) bushing | coussinet garni d'antifriction

liner | chemise/manchon/garniture; crépine
(-) clamp | butée de (-)
(-) collar | collerette de (-)
cylinder (-) | (-) de cylindre
gravel packed (-)/gravel pack screen | crépine à gravillonnage incorporé

link | maillon/chaînon/biellette/étrier/lien/tringle
(-) block | bielle d'accouplement/coulisse
chain (-) | maillon d'une chaîne
elevator (-) | bras d'élévateur

lint | charpie

lintel	*linteau*
lip	*rebord/ bec/ lèvre*
pouring (-)	*bec verseur*
liquid	*liquide*
(-) head	*charge hydrostatique*
lisier	*pig droppings/ pig manure*
litmus	*tournesol*
live	*vivant/ en vie; en charge;*
	sous tension
(-) load	*poids roulant*
(-) pipe	*conduite en charge*
(-) weight	*charge utile*
(-) wire	*fil sous tension*
load	*charge/ débit/ effort/*
	poussée/ puissance
(-) capacity	*charge utile*
(-) indicator	*indicateur de charge/*
	drillomètre
axle (-)	*(-) par essieu*
bed (-)	*charriage de fond*
breaking (-)	*(-) de rupture*
dead (-)	*(-) statique/ poids mort*
live (-)	*(-) utile/ poids roulant*
pullout (-)	*(-) d'arrachement*
thrust (-)	*poussée/ pression*
loader	*chargeuse-pelleteuse*
back (-)	*rétro-chargeuse*
frontend (-)	*tracto chargeur*
loading	*chargement/ en charge*
loam	*limon/ vase*
location	*position/ emplacement*
well (-)	*emplacement d'un forage*
locator	*localiseur/ détecteur*
underground line (-)	*détecteur de canalisations*
	enterrées
tool joint (-)	*détecteur de joints*
lock	*serrure/ verrou/ attache*
(-) angle	*angle de braquage*
(-) nut	*contre-écrou/ écrou de*
	verrouillage
(-) screw	*vis de blocage*
vapor (-)	*tampon de vapeur*
locking	*verrouillage*
log	*coupe géologique/ enregis-*
	trement; diagraphie;
	bûche/ grume
(-) book	*journal de sonde*
dip (-)	*enregistrement du*
	pendage
driller's (-)	*diagraphie du sondeur*

logging	*diagraphie/ diagramme;*
	carottage
electric (-)	*enregistrement des*
	résistivités
lithologic (-)	*diagraphie électrique/*
	coupe/ diagramme
	lithologique
mud (-)	*diagraphie de boue*
well (-)	*diagramme des*
	connaissances d'un puits
long	*long*
(-) clay	*argile plastique*
(-) run	*production/ essai*
	prolongé
(-) ton (2,249 lbs)	*tonne anglaise (1,016 kg)*
longitudinal	*longitudinal*
(-) fault	*faille (-)*
(-) seam	*couche (-)*
(-) section	*(-id-)/ profil (-)*
loop	*boucle/ ceinture/*
	doublement/ maille
feedback (-)	*(-) de régulation*
ground (-)	*circuit de masse*
loose	*amovible/ desserré/*
	fou/ lâche/ libre/ mou
(-) circulation	*circulation libre*
(-) fit	*ajustage libre*
(-) ground	*terrain ébouleux*
(-) pulley	*poulie folle*
(-) rope	*câble mou*
(-) sand	*sable boulant*
(-) stuff/material	*terrain meuble*
(-) textured	*spongieux*
loosening	*déblocage/ desserage*
lopsided	*déversé*
lorry	*camion*
loss	*perte*
(-) of circulation	*(-) de circulation*
dead (-)	*(-) sèche*
frictional (-)	*(-) par frottement*
heat (-)	*(-) thermique*
power (-)	*(-) d'énergie*
(-) of pressure	*(-) de charge*
lost	*perdu*
(-) hole	*trou (-)*
(-) record	*lacune stratigraphique*
lot	*quantité; lot de terrain/*
	parcelle
low	*bas; faille*
(-) angle fault	*faille plate*
(-) carbon steel	*acier à basse teneur en*
	carbone
(-) dip	*pendage faible*
(-) grade	*à faible teneur*
(-) pressure	*basse pression*
structural (-)	*dépression/ ensellement*

lower	*inférieur*
(-) block	*moufle (-)*
(-) heating valve	*pouvoir calorifique inférieur*
(-) wall of a fault	*lèvre inférieure d'une faille*
lubricant/lube/ lubricating fluid	*lubrifiant*
lubricating nipple	*graisseur*
force and splash lubricating/bath lubrication	*graissage par barbottage*
lubrication	*graissage*
drop feed (-)	*(-) goutte à goutte*
force feed (-)	*(-) forcé*
ring (-)	*(-) par bague*
wick feed (-)	*(-) par mèche*
lug	*cosse/oreille/patte*
lukewarm	*tiède*
lumber	*bois de charpente/de construction*
lump	*morceau/motte*
lumpy	*grumeleux*
lute	*mastic/calfat*
lye	*lessive*
sludge (-)	*boue alcaline*

M

machine	*machine*
(-) shop	*atelier de mécanique*
(-) tools	*machines-outils*
machining	*usinage*
(-) allowance	*surépaisseur pour croissance et friction*
macrometer	*macromètre*
macroscopic	*macroscopique*
maculose	*tacheté*
(-) rock	*roche (-)*
made	*fabriqué*
(-) ground	*remblai*
magnesian limestone	*dolomie/dolomite*
magnet	*aimant/magnétique*
(-) coil	*bobine magnétique*
(-) separator	*séparateur magnétique*
electro (-)	*électro (-)*
fishing (-)	*(-) de repêchage*

magnetic	*magnétique*
(-) attraction	*attraction (-)*
(-) bearing	*direction (-)*
(-) clutch	*embrayage (-)*
(-) declination	*déclinaison (-)*
(-) dip	*inclinaison*
(-) field	*champ (-)*
(-) needle	*aiguille aimantée*
(-) pole	*pôle (-)*
magnetization	*aimantation*
magnetometer	*magnétomètre*
magnification	*agrandissement/ grossissement/ amplification*
magnifying glass	*verre grossissant/loupe*
magnitude	*grandeur*
order of (-)	*ordre de (-)*
main	*principal; canalisation/ conduite/câble*
(-) bearing	*palier (-)*
(-) bottom	*roche de fond/bedrock*
(-) current	*courant de secteur*
(-) fault	*faille (-)*
(-) pulley	*poulie motrice*
(-) rope	*câble de tête*
distribution (-)	*conduite de distribution*
electric (-)	*canalisation électrique*
live (-id-)	*(-id-) sous tension*
live (-)	*conduite en charge*
maintenance	*entretien*
(-) crew	*équipe d' (-)*
make	*construction/montage; fermeture d'un circuit électrique*
(-) and break	*autorupteur/ conjoncteur-disjoncteur*
(-) of casing	*descente de tubage*
(-) shift tooling	*outillage de fortune*
(-) up	*vissage; apport; appoint*
(-id-) length	*longueur de raccordement*
(-id-) torque	*couple de serrage/ couple de vissage*
male	*mâle*
(-) connection/ (-) joint	*raccord (-)*
(-) fishing tap	*taraud mâle de repêchage*
malleable	*malléable/ductile*
(-) cast iron/ (-) pig iron	*fonte (-)*
man	*homme*
(-) hole	*trou d' (-)/ trou de visite/ regard de visite*
(-) power	*main d'oeuvre*

mandrel	*mandrin*
(-) socket	*(-) de repêchage/ porte outil de repêchage*
manifold	*collecteur/ distributeur*
exhaust (-)	*collecteur d'échappement/ tubulure d'échappement*
inlet (-)/intake (-)	*tubulure/ tuyauterie d'admission*
manila rope	*câble en chanvre de Manille*
manograph	*manomètre enregistreur*
manometer	*manomètre/ indicateur de pression*
manpower	*main d'oeuvre*
mantle	*enveloppe/ manchon/ manteau*
manual	*manuel/ à la main*
manure	*fumier*
manway	*trou d'homme/ trou de visite*
map	*carte*
(-) drawing	*minute cartographique/ plan*
(-) grid	*quadrillage de la (-)*
(-) making	*cartographie*
(-) sheet	*coupure/ feuille de (-)*
assessment (-)	*(-) foncière*
base (-)	*fond de (-)/(-) de base*
contour (-)	*(-) à courbes de niveau*
geological (-)	*(-) géologique*
location (-)	*plan de localisation*
structural (-)	*(-) structurale*
mapping	*cartographie*
aerial (-)	*(-) aérienne*
margin	*excédent/ jeu/ marge/ écart*
marginal	*marginal*
(-) crevasse	*crevasse (-)/ rimaye*
(-) deep	*fosse (-)*
(-) fold	*pli (-)*
(-) texture	*texture (-)*
marine	*marin, marine*
(-) denudation	*érosion (-)*
(-) deposits	*dépôts (-)*
(-) sediments	*sédiments (-)/*
mark	*repère/ marque/ ligne de jauge*
bench (-)	*repère de nivellement*
flood (-)	*laisses de crue*
ripple (-)	*ride*
setting (-)	*repère de calage*
marker	*indicateur/ niveau repère*
(-) bed	*couche repère*

marking	*marquage*
markstone	*borne/ pierre de bornage*
marl	*marne*
cherty (-)	*(-) à silex*
sandy (-)	*(-) sableuse*
marshy	*marécageux*
masonry	*maçonnerie*
mast	*mât*
free standing (-)	*(-) non haubanné*
guyed (-)	*(-) haubanné*
(-) head	*tête de (-)*
telescopic (-)	*(-) télescopique*
master	*maître/ principal*
(-) brake cylinder	*cylindre principal de frein*
(-) drive bushing (of the kelly)	*gaine d'entraînement de la tige carrée*
(-) key	*passe-partout*
(-) switch	*interrupteur (-)*
(-) tap	*taraud mère*
material	*matériau/ matière; matériel/ fournitures*
dissolved (-)	*matière dissoute/ en solution*
drifted (-)	*matériaux échoués*
matter	*matière/ substance; affaire*
foreign (-)	*corps étranger*
organic (-)	*(-) organique*
mattock	*pioche*
maximum	*maximal/ maximum*
(-) allowable working pressure	*pression de marche (-)/ timbre*
mean	*moyen, moyenne*
(-) effective pressure	*pression effective (-)*
(-) level	*niveau (-)*
(-) sea level	*(-id-) de la mer*
weighted (-)	*moyenne pondérée*
meander	*méandre*
(-) core	*mamelon central*
(-) survey	*levé topographique par cheminement*
cut off (-)	*(-) recoupé*
ingrown (-)	*(-) encaissé*
meaning	*signification*
measure/ measuring/ measurement	*mesure/ mesuration/ métrage*
(-) chain	*chaîne d'arpenteur*
(-) glass	*verre gradué*
(-) rod	*règle de jauge/ pige*
(-) rule	*règle graduée*
(-) tape	*(-) à ruban/ mitre à ruban*

mechanical
  (-) advantage
  (-) efficiency
  (-) feed
  (-) forced feed
    lubricator

mécanique
  bras de levier
  rendement (-)
  alimentation (-)

  graisseur (-) pour
  graissage sous pression

medium
  (-) sand
  porous (-)

moyen; milieu
  sable à grain (-)
  milieu poreux

megger ground tester

magnétomètre megger de
  mesure de résistivité

melting
  (-) bath
  (-) crucible/(-) pot
  (-) heat
  (-) zone

fusion/fonte
  bain de (-)
  creuset
  chaleur de (-)
  zone de (-)

membrane
  semi permeable (-)

membrane/diaphragme
  (-) semi-perméable

meniscus

ménisque

mercury
  (-) switch
  (-) vapor lamp

mercure
  interrupteur à (-)
  lampe à vapeur de (-)

mesh

  (-) sieve
  constant (-) gear

maille/trame/trémie;
  engrènement/prise
  tamis à (-)
  pignon de prise
  constante

metal
  (-) alloy
  (-) clad/(-) cladding
  (-) gauze
  (-) prop
  (-) ridge
  expanded (-)
  gun (-)
  powdered (-)

métallique/métal
  alliage (-)
  placage (-)
  gaze/toîle (-)
  étançon (-)
  massif de métal
  métal déployé
  bronze
  métal fritté

to metal

empierrer/(-) macadamiser

metalled road

route empierrée/
  macadamisée

metamorphic
  (-) grade/rank
  (-) water

métamorphique
  degré de métamorphisme
  eau (-)

metamorphism

métamorphisme

meter
  (-) prover

  (-) reading
  electric (-)
  flow (-)

compteur; mètre
  boucle d'étalonnage/
  étalon de contrôle de (-)
  relevé/lecture de (-)
  (-) électrique
  débitmètre/indicateur
  de débit

positive displacement/
positive volume (-)
rotary displacement (-)
velocity (-)
volumetric dump-
type (-)

(-) volumétrique

  (-) à pistons rotatifs
  tachymètre
  (-) volumétrique à
  bascule/ à culbuteur

metering
  (-) pump

comptage
  pompe à débit constant

micro balloons

microbilles (pour réduire
  l'évaporation)

micro filtration

microfiltration

micrometer

micromètre/palmer

micro seismogram

diagraphie acoustique

mil

millième de pouce
  (0.0254 mm)

mild
  (-) steel

doux
  acier (-)

milk of lime

lait de chaux

mill

  (-) scale
  clean out (-)
  tapered (-)

moulin; usine; broyeur/
  fraise
  calamine/ battitures
  fraise de nettoyage
  fraise conique

milled

laminé; fraisé

milling

  (-) machine
  (-) shoe

fraisage; laminage;
  broyage
  fraiseuse
  sabot de (-)

mineral

minéral

mining
  ground water (-)

exploitation des mines
  exploitation d'eau fossile/
  sur-exploitation des eaux
  souterraines

mire

boue/vase/limon

mishap

accident/panne

miter/mitre
  (-) weld
  (-) wheel

angle
  soudure d'angle
  roue d'angle

mixer
  concrete (-)
  mud (-)

malaxeur/mélangeur
  (-) de béton/bétonnière
  (-) de boue

mixing
  (-) cock/valve
  (-) drum

mélange/malaxage; mixage
  vanne/robinet mélangeur
  tambour mélangeur

mixture

mélange

moisture	*humidité*	motive	*moteur/ motrice*
(-) content	*état hygrométrique/*	motor	*moteur*
	teneur en (-)	(-) driven	*motorisé*
(-) loss	*perte d' (-)*	(-id-) pump/(-) pump	*motopompe*
(-) proof	*inaltérable par l' (-)*	(-) generating set	*groupe électrogène*
soil (-)	*(-) du sol*	(-) generator set	*groupe convertisseur*
		(-) grader	*niveleuse automotrice*
mole	*digue/ môle; taupe; poids*	(-) oil	*huile pour (-)*
	moléculaire	(-) winch	*treuil à moteur/*
(-) ratio	*rapport moléculaire*		*treuil mécanique*
		adjustable speed (-)/	*(-) à vitesse réglable*
mollusk	*mollusque*	variable speed (-)	
		sealed (-)	*(-) blindé*
moment	*moment*	series (-)	*(-) série*
bending (-)/	*(-) de flexion*	shunt wound (-)	*(-) shunt*
(-) of flexure		single phase (-)	*(-) monophasé*
		slip-ring (-)	*(-) à bagues*
momentum	*quantité de mouvement/*	synchronous (-)	*(-) synchrone*
	force vive	three-phase (-)	*(-) triphasé*
angular (-)	*moment cinétique*		
		mottled	*moucheté/ tacheté/*
monadrock	*butte-témoin/ mont isolé*		*truité*
		(-) clay	*argile bigarrée*
monitor	*appareil de contrôle/*	(-) iron/(-) pig	*fonte truitée*
	de surveillance		
		mould/mold	*moisissure; moule/*
monitoring	*contrôle/ régulation/*		*moulage*
	surveillance	vegetable (-)	*terreau/ humus*
(-) device	*dispositif/ appareillage*		
	d'écoute/ contrôle/	mouldering/moldering	*effritement/ tomber en*
	surveillance		*poussière*
monkey board	*plateforme d'accrochage*	moulding/molding	*moulage; moulure/*
			baguette/ jonc
monkey wrench	*clé anglaise/ clé à molette/*	(-) box	*chassis de (-)*
	clé universelle	(-) press	*presse à mouler*
		injection (-)	*(-) par injection*
monoclinal/monocline	*monoclinal*		
(-) fold	*pli (-)*	mouldy/moldy	*moisi*
(-) valley	*vallée (-)*		
		mound	*monticule/ bosse/ butte/*
monopod jackup	*autoélévatrice monopode*		*colline/ levée de terre*
		(-) of breakdown	*cône d'éboulis*
moor	*lande/ terrain*	cinder (-)	*cône de déjection*
	marécageux		
(-) rock	*grès à gros grain*	mount	*montagne; monture/*
dry (-)	*lande*		*support/ montage*
wet (-)	*tourbière*		
		mountain	*montagne*
moped	*mobylette*	(-) meal	*diatomite/ terre à*
			diatomées
moraine	*moraine*	(-) stream	*torrent*
		résidual (-)	*butte-témoin*
mortar	*mortier*		
hydraulic (-)	*(-) de chaux/*	mounting	*montage/ support*
	(-) hydraulique	(-) bracket	*chaise/ patte de*
			fixation
mortise	*mortaise*	(-) lug	*patte d'attache*
		(-) pad	*console*
moss	*mousse/ tourbière*		
		mousehole	*trou de manoeuvre*
mother	*mère*		
(-) rock	*roche (-)*	mouth	*orifice/ embout*
(-) water	*eau (-)*		
		muck	*déblais/ détritus/ morts-*
motion	*mouvement*		*terrains de recouvrement*
reciprocating (-)	*(-) alternatif*		

mud | boue/ limon/ vase
  (-) barrel | cuiller à (-)
  (-) bit | trépan à (-)
  (-) cake | dépôt de (-)
  (-) circulation | circulation de (-)
  (-) cracks | fissures de retrait
  (-) ditch | goulotte/ rigole à (-)
  drilling (-) | (-) de forage
  (-) fluid/(-) flush | (-) d'injection
  (-) guard | garde (-)
  (-) hose | flexible d'injection de (-)
  (-) line | conduite de (-)
  (-) loss | perte de (-)
  (-) mixer/(-) gun | mélangeur de (-)
  (-) pit | bac à (-)
  (-) pump | pompe à (-)
  (-) return line | tube dégorgeoir
  (-) socket | cuiller à clapet
  spud (-) | (-) de démarrage
  (-) thickener | épaississant pour (-)
  (-) thinner | amincissant pour (-)
  (-) weight balance | balance à (-)

mudding — envasement

muffler — pot d'échappement/ silencieux

mule head — balancier de pompe

multiple | multiple/ simultanée
  (-) fault | faille (-)
  (-) stage cementing | cimentation étagée

mute — muet

muzzle — buse/ tubulure

multrum latrine | latrine multrum
  (Swedish design of an anaerobic improved permanent double-vaulted latrine) | (anaérobique permanente à deux compartiments de conception suédoise)

N

nail | clou
  screw (-) | vis à bois/(-) fileté

naptha | essence lourde
  cleaner's (-) (dry cleaning) | solvant de nettoyage (à sec)
  painters' (-) | solvant pour peinture et vernis

nappe | nappe de charriage
  (-) inlier | fenêtre tectonique
  (-) outlier | lambeau de charriage/ témoin de chevauchement
  downsliding (-) | nappe d'écoulement
  overthrust (-) | nappe de chevauchement

native | natif/ pur
  (-) clay | argile native
  (-) rock | matrice/ roche encaissante
  (-) salt | sel gemme

natron — soude carbonatée

natural | naturel
  (-) angle of slope | pente (-)
  (-) current | courant tellurique
  (-) slope | talus (-)

natural gas | gaz naturel
  (-) liquids/ngl | (-) liquéfié

NBS (National Bureau of Standards) | office de normalisation (USA)

near | proche
  (-) face | face proximale

neck | goulot/ col/ collet;
  (-) flange | bride à rebord
  (-) of land | langue de terre/ isthme

needle | aiguille
  (-) bearing | roulement à (-)
  (-) dial | cadran à (-)
  injector (-) | (-) d'injecteur
  (-) valve | vanne à pointeau

negative | négative/ négatif
  (-) electrode | electrode (-)
  (-) terminal | borne (-)

neighbourhood/ neighborhood — environs/ voisinage

nest | nid
  (-) of tubes | faisceau de tubes
  crow's (-) | nid de pie/ passerelle du mouffle fixe

net | net; effectif; filet
  (-) caloric value | pouvoir calorifique inférieur
  (-) positive suction head | hauteur pratique d'aspiration

netted | en lacis/ en réseau
  (-) structure | structure réticulée

network | réseau
  distribution (-) | (-) de distribution

ngl (natural gas liquids) — gas liquide naturel

nib — pointe d'un outil/ d'une plume

nick — encoche/ entaille

nippers | pinces/ tenailles
  cutting (-) | (-) coupantes

nipping fork — clé de retenue

nipple | raccord droit à filetage mâle
  flow (-) | duse de fond à clapet
  grease (-) | raccord-graisseur
  injector (-) | tête d'injecteur
  lifting (-) | raccord de levage
  reducing (-) | raccord de réduction
  shoulder (-) | raccord à épaulement

nitrogen	*azote*
nodular	*noduleux*
nodule	*nodule/ rognon*
noise	*bruit*
(-) level	*niveau de (-)*
background (-)/	*(-) de fond*
wind (-)	
no-load	*à vide*
(-) voltage	*tension (-)*
nominal	*nominal*
non conformable	*discordant*
non conformity	*discordance*
no-return valve	*clapet de retenue*
non spinning rope	*câble anti-torsion*
noose	*noeud coulant*
normal	*normal*
(-) device	*sonde (-) (de diagraphie électrique)*
(-) dip	*pendage (-)/ pendage général*
(-) downthrow	*affaissement/ effondrement (-)*
(-) fault	*faille (-)*
(-) fold	*pli (-)/ pli symétrique*
(-) habitus	*faciès (-)*
(-) thread engagement	*longueur de recouvrement d'un joint de tube*
(-) throw	*projection verticale du rejet*
north	*nord*
nose	*nez; saillant anticlinal traverse d'extrêmité*
(-) sill	
bit (-)	*nez de l'outil*
cutter (-)	*nez de molette*
nozzle	*ajutage; gicleur; bec verseur*

O

oakum	*filasse/ étoupe*
oblique	*oblique*
(-) bedding/	*stratification (-)*
(-) lamination	
(-) fault	*faille diagonale*
obscured	*masqué*
observation	*observation/ contrôle*
(-) period	*période d' (-)*
(-) well	*puits d' (-)/ puits-témoin*
obsolete	*dépassé/ périmé*

obstruction	*bouchage/ engorgement/ obstruction*
occlusion	*occlusion*
occupation	*emploi/ profession/ utilization*
occurence	*manifestation/ présence/ venue*
ocean	*océan*
(-) deeps	*profondeurs océaniques*
ocker/ochre	*ocre*
octane number	*indice d'octane*
(-id-) improver	*anti détonant*
ocular	*oculaire*
odometer	*compteur kilométrique*
odd	*impair; dépareillé*
odorless/odourless	*inodore*
off	*hors service*
(-) center	*décalé/ désaxé/ excentrique*
off highway vehicle	*véhicule tous-terrains*
off lap	*régression/ retrait*
off-peak	*hors pointe*
(-) time	*heures creuses*
offset	*décalage/ décentrement; déport horizontal; impression*
(-) cones	*cônes à axes divergents*
(-) skewness	*dérapage d'un outil*
ohmmeter	*ohmmètre*
oil	*huile/ pétrole brut*
(-) bath	*bain d' (-)*
(-id-) filter	*filtre à (-id-)*
(-) can	*burette/ bidon d' (-)*
(-) cloth	*toile cirée*
(-) duct	*canalisation d' (-)*
(-) film	*pellicule lubrifiante*
(-) hole	*lumière de graissage*
(-) level gauge	*indicateur de niveau d' (-)*
(-) pump	*pompe à (-)*
(-) ring	*bague de graissage*
(-) screen	*filtre à (-)*
(-) seal	*garniture d'étanchéité/ joint d'étanchéité*
(-) stone	*pierre à aiguiser*
(-) sump	*carter d' (-)*
oiler	*graisseur*
oiling	*graissage*
ointment	*onguent/ pommade*

on-off	marche-arrêt
(-) regulation	réglage par tout ou rien
on stream	en marche
ooze	boue/ vase/ sédiment
to ooze	sourdre/ suinter
open	ouvert/ libre
(-) fault	faille ouverte
(-) hole	sondage non tubé
opening	orifice/ ouverture
operating	fonctionnement/ manoeuvre
ore	minerai
orienting	orientation
(-) sub	raccord d' (-)
(-) tool	outil d' (-)
orifice	orifice
ounce	once (avoir du poids = 28.35 grammes)
outcrop	affleurement
outer	externe/ exterieur
outfit	outillage/ équipement
outlet	orifice/ refoulement/ échappement
(-) pressure	pression de refoulement/ de sortie
outlier	avant-butte
outline	aperçu/ généralités
output	production/ rendement/ débit
outshoot	saillie
outside	extérieur
(-) diameter	diamètre (-)
outskirts	banlieue/ bord/ limite
outwash plain	plaine alluviale proglaciaire
oval socket	cloche de repêchage ovale
overall	global/ total; survêtement de travail
(-) dimensions	cotes d'encombrement
overburden	couverture/ morts-terrains/ terrains de couverture
thickness of (-)	épaisseur de la couverture
overcharge	surcharge

over current	surintensité
over deepening	surcreusement
overdrive	surmultiplication
overestimate	surestimation
overall	déversoir
overfault	faille anormale/ inverse
overflow	trop plein
overfold	pli déversé
overfolding	recouvrement
overhang	porte à faux/ surplomb
overhanging side	paroi surplombante
overhaul	révision générale/ dépose de moteur
overhead	frais généraux/ aérien/ de tête
(-) camshaft	arbre à cames en tête
(-) costs	frais généraux
(-) line/(-) power line	ligne aérienne (électr.)
(-) traveling crane	pont-roulant
over heating	échauffement anormal/ surchauffe
overland	par voie de terre
overlap	chevauchement/ recouvrement/ débordement des couches
(-) fault	faille de chevauchement
(-) welding	soudure à recouvrement
overlapping folds	plis en échelons
overload	surcharge
(-) clutch	limiteur de couple à friction
(-) relay	relais à maximum d'intensité
overlook	négligence/ omission; surveillance
overlying beds	couvertures
overmigration	surmigration
overpressure	surpression
overrun	dépassement/ débordement

overshot	*cloche de repêchage à coins/souricière à tige*
(-) guide	*cloche guide*
cattail (-)	*chaussette de repêchage*
circulating (-)	*cloche à circulation*
releasing (-)	*cloche libérable*
oversize	*refus de crible; suralésé; surépaisseur*
overspeed	*survitesse/vitesse excessive*
(-) governor	*régulation de vitesse excessive*
(-) preventer	*limiteur de vitesse*
overstep	*formation transgressive*
overthrust	*charriage/chevauchement*
(-) block	*bloc/masse charriée*
(-) fold	*pli-faille couché*
(-) line	*ligne de chevauchement*
(-) nappe/sheet	*nappe de charriage*
(-) plane	*surface de charriage*
block (-)	*charriage cisaillant*
overtight	*bloqué/trop serré*
overtilted	*renversé*
overtonging	*vissage excessif*
overturned fold	*pli renversé*
overweight	*surcharge*
oxidation	*oxydation*
oxide	*oxyde*
oxidized	*oxydé*
oxyacetylene blowpipe	*chalumeau oxyacétylénique*
oxy gas cutting	*oxy-coupage*

P

pack	*paquet; garniture/bourrage*
(-) cloth	*toile d'emballage*
package	*emballage/empaquetage*
packaging	*conditionnement*
packer	*presse étoupe/garniture d'étanchéité; packer*
anchor (-)	*packer à coins d'ancrage*
sidewall (-id-)	*packer à sabot d'ancrage dans le terrain*
casing (-)/ hook wall (-)	*packer pour tubage/ (-) pour colonne*

packing	*bourrage/garniture; tassement/compaction*
(-) box	*presse étoupe*
(-) gland	*boîte à garniture*
(-) nut	*vis de presse-étoupe*
pad	*tampon; patin*
(-) lubricator	*(-) graisseur*
mounting (-)	*bride de fixation*
padded	*rembourré*
padding	*rembourrage/remplissage*
(-) of ditch	*(-) de la fouille*
paddle	*ailette/palette*
pail	*sceau*
paint	*peinture*
(-) spraying	*(-) au pistolet*
(-) thinner	*diluant pour (-)*
paleozoic	*paléozoïque*
pallet	*palette/plateforme de manutention*
palm-nut oil	*huile de palmiste*
palm oil	*huile de palme*
paludal	*palustre*
pamphlet	*brochure/opuscule*
pan	*cuvette/cuve; bassin; horizon durci*
(-) conveyor	*chaîne/convoyeur à godets*
(-) scraper	*râcleur de pipeline*
clay (-)	*horizon argileux compact*
hard (-)	*croûte concrétionnée*
settling (-)	*bac de décantation*
water-seal (-)	*cuvette (de WC) à col de cygne*
pane	*carreau de verre; face d'une pièce*
(-) of a hammer	*panne de marteau*
panel	*panneau/tableau/pupître; jury/commission/groupe*
control (-)	*pupître de commande/ tableau de mesure/ de commande*
instrument (-)	*tableau-planche de bord/ tableau de manoeuvre*
(-) discussion	*table ronde*
paper	*papier; communication*
(-) capacitor	*condensateur au papier*
(-) chromatography	*chromatographie sur papier*
(-) strip	*bande de (-)*
litmus (-)	*(-) tournesol*
sand (-)	*(-) de verre*
scale (-)	*(-) millimétré*
paraclase	*paraclase*

paraffin	*paraffine*	paving	*pavage*
(-) oil	*pétrole lampant*	(-) breaker	*marteau piqueur*
(-) wax	*cire de paraffine*		*pneumatique*
parallax	*parallaxe*	pawl	*cliquet/ rochet/ linguet*
parallel	*parallèle*	peak	*pic/ cime/ crête/ sommet;*
(-) connection	*montage en dérivation/*		*pointe*
	en parallèle	(-) load	*charge de pointe/*
(-) faults	*failles parallèles*		*charge maximum*
(-) folds	*plis concentriques*	(-) time	*heure de pointe*
(-) transgression	*transgression*	(-) value	*valeur de crête*
	concordante	(-) voltage	*tension de crête*
(-) unconformity	*transgressivité parallèle/*	off (-)	*hors pointe*
	pseudoconcordance	peat	*tourbe*
parent	*parent*	(-) bog	*tourbière*
(-) material	*matériau d'origine*	(-) moss	*terre de bruyère*
(-) rock	*roche mère*	limnic (-)	*tourbe lacustre*
paring	*rognure*	pebble	*caillou/ galet*
parkerizing	*protection contre la*	(-) gravel	*cailloutis*
	corrosion par	(-) stone	*galet ou caillou roulé*
	phosphatation	pedal	*pédale*
ppm (parts per million)	*mg par kg (ou litre d'eau)*	pedestal	*socle/ support*
particule	*particule*	pediment/rock (-)	*glacis rocheux désertique*
(-) board	*panneau en particules*	pedometre	*compte-pas/ podomètre*
	de bois agglomérées/	peel	*peau/ écaille*
	panneau aggloméré	peen hammer	*marteau à panne*
parting	*division/ séparation*	peephole	*regard/ ouverture*
(-) line of the		cleaning (-)	*(-) de nettoyage*
waters	*ligne de séparation*	inspection (-)	*(-) de visite*
	des eaux	peg	*cheville/ fiche/ clavette/*
partition	*paroi/ cloison*		*piquet*
(-) process	*bifurcation des eaux*	(-) legging	*frappe irrégulière du*
(-) rock	*roche encaissante*		*trépan au battage*
pass	*col (montagne); passage;*	pellets	*boulettes/ granules/*
	passe; coupe-file/ permit		*pastilles*
passage	*passage/ passerelle/*	pendulum	*pendule/ balancier*
	allée/ couloir	peneplain	*pénéplaine*
passageway	*corridor/ galerie*	penetrants	*pénétrants/ mouillants/*
passivation	*passivation*		*imprégnants*
patch	*pièce rapportée/ emplâtre/*	penetration	*pénétration*
	"rustine" (réparation de	(-) recorder	*enregistreur de (-)*
	pneumatiques); morceau	depth of (-)	*profondeur de (-)*
patching	*colmatage/ raccommodement*	rate of (-)	*vitesse d'avancement*
casing (-)	*rapiècement d'un tubage*	penstock	*canal d'amenée*
patent	*brevet d'invention*	perched	*perché*
path	*chemin/ trajectoire/*	(-) block	*bloc erratique*
	trajet	(-) water	*eau supérieure*
pattern	*patron/ modèle/ gabarit*	percolating water	*eau d'infiltration*
flow (-)	*diagramme d'écoulement*	percussion	*percussion/ battage*
tooth (-)	*profil de dent*	(-) boring	*sondage par battage*
well (-)	*géométrie des puits*	(-) rig	*sondeuse par battage*
pavement	*chaussée*		
boulder (-)	*pavé désertique*		

perennial — *pérenne/ perpétuel*
  (-) spring — *source pérenne/ (-) intarissable*

perforating — *perforation*
  jet (-) — *(-) par jet abrasif*

performance — *performance/ rendement/ comportement*

permeation — *imprégnation/ pénétration*

peroxide — *peroxyde*
  (-) number — *indice de (-)*
  hydrogen (-) — *eau oxygénée*

petcock — *robinet purgeur*

petroleum — *pétrole*
  (-) jelly — *vaseline*

phacoidal — *lenticulaire*

phial — *fiole/ flacon*

photocell — *cellule photoélectrique*

phreatic — *phréatique*
  (-) surface sheet — *nappe (-)*

piano string — *corde à piano*

pick — *pic/ marteau piqueur*

pick-ups/pick-up — *pince de repêchage*
  grab
  (-id-) points — *points d'accrochage*

picket — *jalon/ piquet*

pickling — *décapage*

pig — *cochonnet/ râcleur*

pig droppings — *lisier*

pig iron — *fonte en gueuse*

pile — *pile/ tas/ pilotis*

pilot — *pilote/ modèle*
  (-) bit — *outil pilote*

pin — *broche/ cheville*
  (-) punch — *chasse-goupille*
  (-) sub — *raccord à souder male*

pinion — *pignon*

PIP latrine (permanent — *cabinet à fosse, permanent*
improved pit latrine) — *amélioré (CFPA)*

pipe — *tuyau/ tube*
  (-) bed — *lit de pose*
  (-) bender machine/ — *cintreuse/ machine à*
  (-) bending machine — *cintrer les tubes*
  (-) bracket — *cavalier*
  (-) brush — *hérisson*

  (-) clamp — *bride/ collier de serrage*
  (-) coupling — *manchon/ accouplement*
  (-) cutter — *coupe-tube/ coupetige*
  (-) cutting machine — *tronçonneuse*
  (-) dog — *arrache tuyau*
  (-) fingers — *râtelier à tiges*
  (-) fittings — *raccords de tuyauterie*
  (-) flange — *collet/ bride*
  (-) grab — *accroche-tube*
  (-) grip — *pince à griffe*
  (-) hook — *crochet de manutention des tiges*
  (-) locator — *détecteur de canalisations*
  (-) manifold — *collecteur/ répartiteur*
  (-) nipple — *manchon*
  (-) rack — *parc à tiges/ gerbage de tiges/ tubes*
  (-) rams — *mâchoires d'obturateur*
  (-) reamer — *aléseur pour tubes*
  (-) reducer — *raccord de réduction*
  (-) riser — *colonne montante*
  (-) saddle — *collier de dérivation*
  (-) scraper — *râcleur/ piston râcleur/ furet*
  (-) sleeve — *fourreau*
  (-) straightener — *redresseur de tiges*
  (-) thread protector — *manchon protecteur*
  (-) tongs — *pince à tuyaux*
  (-) vise — *étau à tubes*
  (-) wrapping — *enrobage des canalisations*
  (-) wrench — *clé à tubes*
  ball & socket (-) — *tuyau à emboitement*
  blow (-) — *chalumeau (de soudure)*
  delivery (-) — *conduite de refoulement*
  drawn (-) — *tube étiré*
  drop (-) — *colonne d'aspiration*
  feed (-) — *conduite d'alimentation*
  galvanised iron/GI (-) — *tube acier galvanisé*
  gravel (-)/sand (-) — *orgue géologique*
  inlet (-) — *(-) conduite/ tuyauterie d'admission/ d'alimentation*
  live (-) — *conduite en charge*
  overflow (-) — *tuyau de trop-plein*
  stand (-) — *colonne montante; bonne fontaine*
  suction (-) — *tuyau d'aspiration*
  tail (-) — *tuyau d'échappement*

pipefitter — *tuyauteur*

pipeline — *canalisation/ conduite/ tuyauterie/ pipeline (d'hydrocarbures)/ oléoduct*

pipette — *pipette/ compte-gouttes*

piping	*conduite/ tuyauterie*
piracy	*pillage*
stream (-)	*capture de cours d'eau*
piston	*piston/ plunger*
(-) packing	*garniture de (-)*
(-) pin	*axe de (-)*
(-id-) bushing	*coussinet de pied de bielle*
(-) ring	*segment de (-)*
(-) rod	*tige de (-)*
pit	*fosse/ puits/ puisard*
drain (-)/soak-away (-)	*puisard/ puits perdu*
mud (-)/slush (-)	*bac à boue*
settling (-)	*bassin de décantation*
pitch	*brai/ poix; inclinaison/ pente*
pitch	*pas d'un filetage*
(-) circle/(-) line	*cercle primitif (d'engrenages)*
screw/thread (-)	*pas de vis*
pitman	*bielle d'une sondeuse au battage*
pits	*piqûres (de corrosion)*
plain	*simple/ ordinaire; plaine*
outwash (-)	*plaine alluviale/ pro-glaciaire*
plan	*projet/ dessin*
plane	*plan*
(-) of cleavage	*(-) de clivage*
(-) of unconformity	*surface de discordance*
(-) table survey	*levé à la planchette*
plank	*planche/ madrier*
plant	*usine/ installation*
pumping (-)	*station de pompage*
plaster	*plâtre*
plastic	*plastique*
plate	*plateau/ plaque; tôle*
(-) clutch	*embrayage à disque*
(-) shale	*schiste en plaquettes*
anchor (-)	*plaque d'ancrage*
base/bed (-)	*socle/ embase/ semelle*
bit-breaker (-)	*plaque de vissage d'un trépan*
clutch (-)	*disque d'embrayage*
squat (-)	*cuvette à la turque (WC)*
plateau	*plateau (géologie)*
plated	*plaqué/ doublé.*
platen/ platten (machine tool)	*plateau/ table (machine outil)*
platform	*plate-forme*
(-) lift truck	*chariot élévateur*

plating	*placage/ revêtement*
platy	*tabulaire/ en plaquettes*
(-) parting/	*séparation/ division*
(-) structure	*en plaquettes*
play	*jeu*
plication	*interpénétration*
pliers	*pinces/ tenailles*
plinth	*socle/ support; plinthe*
plot	*plan/ tracé; repère; parcelle de terrain*
plotting	*levé/ relevé/ planimétrage*
(-) paper	*papier quadrillé*
(-) scale	*échelle de restitution*
(-id-) paper	*papier millimétré*
plug	*bouchon/ tampon/ obturateur; fiche de prise de courant; bougie (de moteur)*
(-) cock	*robinet à boisseau*
cementing (-)	*(-) de cimentation*
drain (-)	*(-) de vidange*
glow/heat (-)	*bougie de réchauffage*
plugging	*comblement/ bouchage/ colmatage*
plumb	*plomb*
(-) line/plummet	*fil à plomb*
plunge	*inclinaison/ plongement*
plunger	*piston*
(-) valve	*clapet de (-)*
ply	*couche; toron*
plywood	*bois contre plaqué*
multiply wick	*mèche à torons multiples*
pneumatic	*pneumatique*
(-) control	*commande (-)*
(-) drill	*marteau à air comprimé/ marteau piqueur*
pocket	*poche*
(-) compass	*boussole de (-)*
pod	*nacelle; boîtier de distributeur*
point	*point; pointe/ aiguille*
(-) of anchorage	*(-) d'ancrage*
(-) of discharge	*(-) de refoulement*
(-) welding	*soudure par points*
control (-)	*canevas de base*
deflection (-)	*point de déflection*
yield (-)	*seuil de cisaillement*
pointing	*pointage*
polder	*polder*

pole	pôle; poteau/perche/ mât
(-) drill	forage aux tiges pleines
(-) tools	outils pour (-id-)
polish/polished	poli
pollutant	polluant
pollution	pollution
poly-cycle engine	moteur polycarburant
polyethylene	polyéthylène
HDPE/high density (-)	(-) à haute densité
LDPE/low density (-)	(-) à basse densité
pond	étang/bassin/mare
decanting (-)	bassin de décantation
oxydation (-)	lagunage
pontoon	ponton/flotteur
pool	gisement; flaque; groupement/communauté
poppet valve	soupape à clapet/ soupape à tige
pore	pore
(-) pressure	pression interstitielle
(-) space	porosité/volume des pores
porosity	porosité
porous	poreux/perméable
port	lumière/orifice
exhaust (-)/outlet (-)	orifice d'échappement
intake (-)	orifice d'admission
portable	portatif
(-) lamp	lampe baladeuse
positive	positif
(-) booster	survolteur
(-) displacement meter	compteur volumétrique
(-) pump	pompe volumétrique
(-) terminal	borne positive (électr.)
post	montant/poteau/pilier/ pieu
(-) stone	grès à grain fin
back-up (-)	poteau de fixation de câble de la clé de . dévissage
guide (-)	pilier de guidage
samson (-)	support de balancier (sondeuse à battage)
posting	affichage
potential	potentiel
(-) transformer	transformateur de tension
potentiometer	potentiomètre/réducteur de tension

pothole	marmite de géant/cuvette/ nid de poule
pound	livre (0.454 kg)
pounding	cognement/martellement/ broyage
pour	coulée
powder	poudre
brazing (-)	(-) à souder
powdered	en poudre
(-) metal	métal fritté
power	puissance/force/énergie
(-) consumption	consommation d'énergie
(-) efficiency	rendement énergétique
(-) factor	facteur de puissance
(-) hammer	marteau-pilon
(-) plant	groupe propulseur
(-) stroke	course motrice
(-) takeoff	prise de force
(-) transformer	transformateur de puissance
(-) unit	groupe moteur
brake (-)	puissance au frein
calorific (-)/heating (-)	pouvoir calorifique
drilling thrust (-)	vitesse d'avancement du forage
lifting (-)	puissance ascensionnelle/ force de levage
motive (-)	force motrice
resolving (-)	pouvoir de résolution
solar (-)	énergie solaire
solvent (-)	pouvoir dissolvant
suspending (-)	pouvoir suspensif
wind (-)	énergie éolienne
ppm/parts per million	mg par kg/par litre
precipice	précipice
precipitate	précipité
precipitation	précipitation
(-) gauge	pluviomètre/udomètre
precoat	précouche (de filtration)
prefabrication	préfabrication
prefabs	objets/maisons/huttes préfabriqués
preglacial	antéglaciaire
pre ignition	préallumage
(-) knock	cliquetis par (-)
preliminary	préliminaire
(-) survey	préreconnaissance
prelubricated bearing	palier prélubrifié
preservative	préservateur
(-) coating	revêtement (-)

preset	*réglé à l'avance/ préréglage*	profile	*coupe/ profil*
		(-) of a borehole	*(-) d'un sondage*
presintering	*préfrittage*	(-) paper	*papier quadrillé*
		cross (-)	*profil en travers*
press	*presse*	longitudinal (-)	*profil en long*
(-) button	*bouton poussoir*		
(-) fitted	*emmanché à force*	projecting	*saillant*
bending (-)	*(-) à cintrer/ à plier*		
hydraulic (-)	*(-) hydraulique*	prong	*dent/ griffe/ doigt d'égalisation*
pressing	*embouti/ emboutissage*		
		proof	*preuve; à l'épreuve de/ résistant*
pressure	*pression*	(-) stress	*limite élastique*
(-) build up	*remontée/ montée en (-)*		
(-) charging	*suralimentation*	prop	*étai/ support/ poteau/ console/ boisage de soutènement*
(-) control	*régulation de la (-)*		
(-) decline	*baisse de (-)*		
(-) die casting	*coulée/ moulage en coquille*	propeller	*hélice*
(-) drop	*perte de charge*	proportion	*teneur/ dosage/ proportion*
(-) filtration	*filtration sous (-)*		
(-) gauge	*manomètre*	proportioning pump	*pompe doseuse*
(-) grease gun	*graisseur pour graissage forcé*	prospecting/prospection	*prospection/ exploration*
(-) head	*hauteur de refoulement*	protective	*protecteur/ protégeant*
(-) lubrication	*graissage sous (-)*	(-) agent	*inhibiteur*
(-) reducer	*détendeur*	(-) coating	*revêtement de protection*
(-) reducing valve	*mano-détendeur*	(-) goggles	*lunettes de protection*
(-) wave	*onde de propagation*	(-) hat/(-) helmet	*casque de sécurité*
back (-)	*contre-pression*		
discharge (-)	*(-) de refoulement*	protector	*protecteur*
feed (-)	*(-) d'alimentation*	(-) sleeve	*manchon (-)*
overburden (-)	*(-) géostatique*	thread (-)	*(-) de filetage*
rock (-)	*(-) de formation*		
		protractor	*rapporteur d'angle*
prestress	*précontrainte*		
		protusion	*protusion/ dépassement*
preventive	*préventif*		
(-) maintenance	*entretien préventif*	proving	*épreuve*
corrosion (-)	*inhibiteur de corrosion*	(-) tank	*récipient de calibrage des compteurs*
primary	*primaire*		
(-) dip	*inclinaison (-)*	pseudo anticline	*faux anticlinal*
(-) rock	*roche (-)*		
		pseudo syncline	*pseudosynclinal*
primer	*enduit/ couche d'apprêt*		
		PSI (pounds per square inch absolute)	*pression absolue en livres par pouce carré*
priming	*couche d'impression (peinture); amorçage d'une pompe*		
		PSIG (pounds per square inch gauge pressure)	*pression manométrique en livres par pouce carré*
print	*empreinte; impression*		
blue (-)	*dessin de fabrication/ plan ("bleu")*	puckering	*froncement/ plissotement*
		puddle	*flaque/ bowlier/ glaise; loupe de puddlage*
probe	*sonde*		
procedure	*mode opératoire/ déroulement*	pull	*tirage/ traction*
		(-) in cable	*câble de (-)*
proceedings	*compte rendu*	(-) in torque	*couple d'accrochage d'un moteur*
process	*procédé/ processus*	(-) out torque	*couple de décrochage d'un moteur*
processing	*traitement*	braking (-)	*effort de freinage*
data (-)	*(-) des données*	effective (-)	
producing/productive	*producteur/ productif*		
(-) well	*puits (-)*		

to pull	*tirer/extraire; remonter un train de tiges*	mud (-)	*(-) à boue*
		multistage (-)	*(-) multicellulaire*
pull rod	*tige d'entraînement/ tringle de traction/ bielle*	plunger (-)	*(-) à piston*
		positive dis-	
(-) carrier	*support de (-)*	placement (-)	*(-) volumétrique*
		reciprocating (-)	*(-) alternative*
pulley	*poulie*	rotary (-)	*(-) rotative*
(-) block	*moufle/(-) mouflée*	sand (-)	*(-) à sable*
(-) shell	*caisse de (-)*	self-priming (-)	*(-) à amorçage automatique*
(-) tackle	*palan*		
(-) wheel/groved (-)	*poulie à gorges*	stripping (-)	*(-) d'assèchement*
bailing (-)	*treuil de curage*	suction (-)	*(-) aspirante*
casing line (-)	*(-) de câble de manoeuvre du tubage*	submersible (-)	*(-) électrique immergée*
		vacuum (-)	*(-) à vide*
crown (-)	*(-) de tête*	vane (-)	*(-) à ailettes*
loose (-)	*(-) folle*	vertical	
sandline (-)	*(-) de curage*	turbine (-)	*(-) à turbine verticale*
stepped (-)	*(-) étagée*		
		pumping	*pompage/épuisement*
pulling	*décuvelage/remontée/ extraction*	(-) beam	*balancier de pompes*
		(-) jack	*chevalet de (-)*
(-) casing	*décuvelage*	(-) rod	*tige de (-)*
(-) head	*tête d'arrachage de tubage*		
		punch	*poinçon/pointeau/ bouterolle/ emporte-pièces*
(-) machine	*treuil auxiliaire*		
(-) rate	*vitesse de remontée des tiges*	(-) mark	*coup de pointeau*
		center (-)	*pointeau*
(-) tools	*outils de repêchage*	pin (-)	*chasse-goupille*
pulp	*pulpe*	punching	*poinçonnage*
(-) thickener	*épaississeur de boue*		
		pup-joint	*masse-tige courte*
pulse	*impulsion/signal/onde*		
original (-)	*impulsion de départ*	push	*poussée*
(-) train	*train d'impulsions*	(-) button	*bouton-poussoir*
pumice	*pierre ponce*	pushup	*renflement*
pump	*pompe*	putty	*mastic*
(-) barrel/(-) casing	*corps de (-)/cylindre*		
(-) brake	*brinquebale/levier de (-)*	PVC (polyvinyl chloride)	*chlorure de polyvinyle*
(-) discharge	*refoulement d'une (-)*		
(-) house	*station de pompage*	pyroclastic	*pyroclastique*
(-) impeller	*turbine de (-)*	(-) breccia	*brèche volcanique*
(-) lift	*hauteur d'aspiration*		
(-) plunger/(-) ram	*piston/plongeur de (-)*		
(-) rod/(-) tree	*tige de (-)/tringlage de (-)*		
bilge (-)	*(-) de cale*		
booster (-)	*surpresseur*		

Q

quadrant	*quart de cercle/ quadrant*

centrifugal	*(-) centrifuge*	quadravalent/	*tétra valent*
deep-well (-)	*(-) de fond*	quadrivalent	
dewatering (-)	*(-) d'assèchement*		
diaphragm (-)	*(-) à membrane*	quagmire	*marécage*
discharge (-)	*(-) de refoulement*		
donkey (-)/duplex (-)	*(-) à deux cylindres plongeurs*	quake/earthquake	*tremblement de terre/ secousse tellurique*
drainage (-)	*(-) d'exhaure*	quantization	*quantification*
exhaust (-)	*(-) d'épuisement*		
feed (-)	*(-) d'alimentation*	quaquaversal dip	*pendage rayonnant*
force (-)	*(-) refoulante*		
gear (-)	*(-) à engrenages*	quarry	*carrière*
hand (-)	*(-) manuelle*	(-) spall	*résidu/déchet de (-)*
injection (-)	*(-) d'injection*	(-) stone	*pierre de taille*
lift (-)	*(-) aspirante*		
lift and force (-)	*(-) aspirante et refoulante*		
motor (-)	*motopompe*		

quart	quart de gallon
US (-)	américain
Imp (-)	britannique
quarter	quart; cantonnement/ logement
quartz	quartz
(-) cutting	éclat/feuille de (-)
(-) grains	grains de (-)
(-) gravel	gravier de (-)
(-) reef	filon de (-)
(-) rock	quartzite
(-) sand	sable quartzeux
(-) veinlet	veinule de (-)
quartziferous	quartzifère
quartzite	quartzite
quebracho	amincissant de boue de forage (extrait du quebracho)
quenching	trempe
(-) bath	bain de (-)
(-) oil	huile de (-)
quick	rapide/boulant
(-) break switch	interrupteur instantané
(-) coupling/(-) union	raccord (-)
(-) ground	terrain boulant
(-) hardening/	ciment à prise (-)
(-) setting cement	
(-) lime	chaux vive
(-) sand	sable mouvant
(-) silver	mercure
quill	fourreau
(-) bearing	roulement à aiguilles
quinquivalent	pentavalant

R

R and D (research and development)	recherche et applications
rabbit (also pig, for pipeline cleaning)	furet (pour nettoyage de canalisation)
race	course; voie/chemin de roulement
ball (-)	roulement à billes
ball bearing (-)	gorge de roulement

rack	râtelier/support; crémaillère
casing (-)	(-) à tubage
loading (-)	rampe de chargement
pipe (-)	parc à tiges/gerbeur de tiges (de forage)
rack & pinion drive	commande par pignon et crémaillère
racker	appareil de manutention des tiges
casing (-) head	tête d'agrippage
pipe (-) arm	bras de manutention
racking	gerbage
(-) fingers	doigts d'accrochage
radial	radial; pneumatique à carcasse radiale
(-) fault	faille (-)
(-) flow	écoulement (-)
radiant	rayonnant/radiant
(-) heat	chaleur (-)
(-) intensity	intensité énergétique
radiation	rayonnement
(-) factor	facteur de (-)
(-) logging	diagraphie par (-)
scattered (-)	(-) diffus
solar (-)	(-) solaire
radiator	radiator
honeycomb type (-)	(-) nid d'abeille
radiobeacon	radiophare
radioelement	élément radioactif/ radioélément
radiography	radiographie
radio isotopes	radio-isotopes
radio prospection	prospection radiométrique
radius	rayon
(-) arm	tendeur/jambe de force/ tringle de poussée
bending (-)	(-) de courbure
radix	base de numération
raft	radeau
foundation (-)	radier/châssis de fondation
rag	chiffon/lambeau
(-) bolt	boulon de scellement
(-) line	corde en chanvre (forage au battage)
rail	rail/guide
railing	garde-fou/parapet/ main-courante
railway/railroad	chemin de fer

rain	*pluie*	**rasp**	*râpe*
(-) bow	*arc en ciel*	**ratchet**	*rochet/ cliquet*
(-) drop	*goutte de (-)*	(-) drill	*perceuse à cliquet*
(-) fall	*chute de pluie/ averse;*	(-) pipe cutter	*coupe-tubes à (-)*
	hauteur pluviométrique	(-) wheel	*roue à (-)*
(-) gauge/(-) gage	*pluviomètre/ udomètre*	(-) wrench	*clé à (-)*
(-) pillar	*pyramide coiffée*	**rate**	*allure/ vitesse/ rapport/*
(-) print	*empreinte de goutte de (-)*		*taux*
(-) rills	*rigoles*	(-) of flow/	
(-) wash	*ruissellement des eaux*	flow (-)	*débit*
	de (-)	(-) of penetration	*vitesse d'avancement*
ash (-)	*(-) de cendres*	interest (-)	*taux d'intérêt*
eruption (-)	*(-) d'éruption*	**to rate**	*classer/ étalonner/ estimer/*
raising	*extraction/ remontage/*		*régler*
	relevage	**rated**	*nominal/ calculé/ estimé*
(-) legs	*jambes de levage*	(-) capacity	*capacité*
rake	*rateau/ crochet;*	(-) power	*puissance (-)*
	inclinaison/ pendage	**rathole**	*trou de rat/ avant trou;*
(-) angle	*angle de dégagement*		*emplacement de garage*
(-) vein	*filon vertical*		*de la tige carrée (kelly)*
drill (-)	*obliquité d'arête d'un*	(-) bit	*trépan d'avant-trou*
	trépan	**rating**	*puissance/ intensité/*
ram	*bélier/ marteau-pilon;*		*rendement; évaluation/*
	piston-plongeur; mâchoire		*estimation/ classement*
blind (-)	*mâchoire à fermeture*	engine (-)	*(-) d'un moteur*
	totale	knock (-)	*intensité de cliquetis*
hydraulic (-)/	*(-) hydraulique*	performance (-)	*évaluation/ classement*
hydram			*des accomplissements*
to ram	*damer/ tasser; tamponner*	**ratings**	*caractéristiques*
ramjet	*statoréacteur*	**ratio**	*taux/ rapport*
ramp	*plan incliné/ rampe*	compression (-)	*(-) de compression*
rampart	*rempart/ levée*	drive (-)	*rapport de transmission*
boulder (-)	*(-) de blocs*	expansion (-)	*(-) de dilatation*
shingle (-)	*levée de galets*	gear (-)	*rapport de*
rancidity	*rancidité/ rancissement*		*démultiplication*
random	*aléatoire/ au hasard*		*d'engrenages*
(-) noise	*bruit (-)/ bruit de fond*	**ravine**	*ravin*
(-) sampling	*échantillonnage au hasard*	(-) stream	*torrent*
range	*amplitude/ échelle/*	**raw**	*brut/ cru/ en l'état*
	gamme/ intervalle/	(-) data	*données (-)*
	rangée/ série;cuisinière	(-) materials/	
(-) finder	*télémètre*	(-) stocks	*matières premières*
(-) of lost data	*lacune stratigraphique*	(-) water	*eau (-)/ eau non traitée*
(-) of mountains	*chaînes de montagne*	**ray**	*rayon/ trajectoire*
(-) pole	*jalon*	**reach**	*bief*
gas (-)	*cuisinière à gaz*	lower (-)	*(-) inférieur*
long (-)	*à longue échéance*	**reactant**	*réactif*
rank	*rang/ classement*	**reaction**	*réaction*
rape/rapeseed	*colza*	(-) flask	*ballon de (-)*
rapid	*rapide*	(-) stress	*tension de (-)*
(-) steel	*acier (-)*	chemical (-)	*(-) chimique*
rare	*rare*	side (-)	*(-) parasite*
(-) earths/	*terres rares*	**reactor**	*réacteur; bobine de*
(-) earth metals			*réactance*
(-) gas	*gaz rare*	**reader**	*lecteur (ordinateur)*

reagent	*réactif*
reamer	*alésoir/ élargisseur*
(-) bit	*trépan aléseur*
drill (-)	*aléseur*
rotary (-)	*aléseur à rouleaux*
reaming	*alésage/ reforage*
(-) bit	*trépan aléseur*
rear	*arrière*
(-) axle	*pont (-)*
(-) dump truck	*camion-benne déchargeant par l'arrière*
rebate	*ristourne/ rabais*
REC/revised earth closet, double vaulted	*latrine améliorée à double compartiment*
recalibration	*réétalonnage*
receiver	*récepteur*
transmitter (-)	*émetteur (-)*
receptacle	*récipient*
receptor	*géophone*
recess	*retrait/ cavité/ enfoncement/ évidement*
reciprocating	*alternatif*
(-) compressor	*compresseur à pistons*
(-) pump	*pompe alternative*
recirculation	*recirculation*
reclaiming	*régénération/ récupération; épuration; assèchement*
mud (-)	*régénération de la boue*
reconditioning	*remise en état/ rénovation/ réparation*
reconnaissance	*exploration/ reconnaissance*
record	*document/ archives/ procès verbal*
recorder	*appareil enregistreur*
recording	*enregistrement*
analog (-)	*(-) analogique*
digital (-)	*(-) numérique*
recoverable	*récupérable*
recovery	*récupération*
(-) vehicle	*camion dépanneur/ dépanneur*
recrusher	*broyeur secondaire*
rectification	*redressement/ correction; parachèvement à la meule d'une surface usinée*

rectilinear	*rectiligne*
recumbent	*renversé/ couché*
(-) anticline	*anticlinal (-)*
(-) fold	*pli couché*
recuperation	*récupération; régénération*
recycle	*recyclage; recirculation*
red	*rouge*
(-) hardness/ (-) shortness	*fragilité à chaud*
(-) hot	*chauffé au rouge*
(-) lead	*minium de plomb*
redox	*oxydation-réduction*
(-) reaction	*réaction d'oxydoréduction*
reduced	*réduit*
(-) diameter	*diamètre (-)*
(-) middle limb	*flan médian étiré*
reducer	*réducteur/ manchon de réduction*
reducing	*réduction*
(-) coupling	*manchon de (-)*
(-) flange	*bride de (-)*
(-) nipple	*(-) mâle-mâle*
(-) sub/(-) union	*raccord de (-)*
(-) valve	*détendeur/ soupape de (-)*
reducibility	*réductibilité*
reduction	*réduction*
(-) drive gear/ (-) gear	*réducteur de vitesse à engrenage*
(-) of area	*striction*
(-) of rocks	*effritement de roches*
(-) ratio	*taux de réduction*
free air (-)	*correction d'altitude*
Redwood viscosimeter	*viscosimètre Redwood*
Reed odourless earth closet/ROEC	*latrine améliorée inodore système Reed*
reef	*récif*
(-) belt	*ceinture de (-)*
(-) plate	*platier/ platier récifal*
(-) knoll	*pinacle corallien*
algal (-)	*calcaire à algues*
beach (-)/sand (-)	*banc de sable*
reel	*bobine/ tambour/ touret*
cable (-)	*dévidoir de câble*
sand (-)	*tambour de curage*
reeling	*bobinage/ dévidage*
to reeve (a wireline)	*moufler un câble*
reeving	*mouflage*
eight line (-)	*(-) à huit brins*

reference	*référence*	regulation	*réglage/régulation/*
(-) gauge	*jauge étalon/calibre*		*règlement*
	étalon	regulator	*régulateur/détendeur*
(-) plane	*plan de (-)*	regulus	*régule*
reflected	*réfléchi*	(-) metal	*plomb antimoine*
(-) wave	*onde (-)*	reinforced	*renforcé*
reflection	*réflection*	(-) concrete	*béton armé*
fake (-)	*fausse (-)*	reinforcement	*renfort/renforcement*
ghost (-)	*(-) fantôme*	(-) of weld	*surépaisseur de la*
reflector	*réflecteur*		*soudure*
corner (-)	*(-) en trièdre*	rejection	*rebut/rejection*
refolded fold	*pli replié*	(-) limits	*limites de (-)*
refolding	*replissement*	rejuvenated	*rajeuni*
reforestation	*reboisement*	(-) water	*eau remise en*
refracted wave	*onde réfractée*		*circulation*
refraction	*réfraction*	related rocks	*roches connexes*
broadside (-)	*(-) en arc/(-) à départ*	relative	*relatif*
	latéral	(-) humidity	*degré hygrométrique/*
index of (-)	*indice de (-)*		*humidité relative*
refractometer	*réfractomètre*	relaxation	*relaxation*
refractory	*produit réfractaire*	(-) time	*temps de (-)*
refrigeration	*réfrigération*	stress (-)	*(-) de contrainte*
refueling	*ravitaillement en*	relay	*relai*
	combustible	latching (-)	*(-) à enclenchement*
refund	*remboursement*	power (-)	*(-) de puissance*
refuse	*déchet/déblais/refus*	release	*dégagement/détente*
	d'un tamis	(-) valve	*soupape de décharge*
(-) dump	*terril/crassier; décharge*	quick (-id-)	*(-id-) rapide*
	publique	releasing	*libérable/décrochable*
regeneration	*régénération*	(-) spears	*arrache-tubes*
regenerator	*régénérateur/récupérateur*		*décrochables (repêchage)*
register	*registre; entrée d'air*	reliability	*fiabilité*
	réglable	reliable	*fiable*
registered	*enregistré/breveté*	relict	*résiduel*
(-) design	*modèle déposé*	(-) sediment	*relique sédimentaire*
registration	*enregistrement/*	relief	*relief; sécurité/*
	immatriculation		*sûreté/dégagement*
regression	*régression*	(-) cock	*robinet de décharge/*
(-) line	*droite de (-)*		*décompression*
(-) plane	*plan de (-)*	(-) map	*carte en relief*
linear (-)	*(-) linéaire*	(-) pipe	*évent*
weighted (-)	*(-) pondérée*	(-) valve	*vanne de détente/*
regular	*régulier*		*soupape de trop plein*
		remanence	*rémanence*
		remelting	*refonte*
		remnants	*restes*

remote	éloigné
(-) control	télécommande/commande à distance
(-id-) switch	interrupteur de télécommande
(-) sensing	télédétection
removable	amovible
(-) blade bits	trépans à lames (-)
(-) cutter bits	trépans à couteaux (-)
(-) limer	chemise/fourreau (-)
removal	élimination
renewable	renouvelable
rent	fente/déchirure; loyer/rente
rental	loyer
repair	réparation
(-) part	pièce de rechange
(-) shop	atelier de (-)
repeatable	concordant
repellent	répulsif
water (-)	hydrofuge
replacement	substitution
(-) cost	valeur de remplacement
(-) parts	pièces de rechange
replenishment	remplissage
report	procès-verbal/compte-rendu; détonation
repose	repos
angle of (-)	angle de talus naturel
reprint	tiré à part
requirement	exigence/besoin/spécification
rescue	sauvetage
research	recherche/investigation
resection	relèvement topographique
reservoir	réservoir
residual	résiduel/résiduaire
(-) magnetism	rémanence
(-) stress	tension (-)
residue	résidu/reste
weathering (-)	dépôts éluviaux
residuum	résidu
resilience	résilience
resin	résine
anion exchange (-)	(-) anionique
cation-exchange (-)	(-) cationique
epoxy (-)	(-) epoxy
urea-formal-dehyde (-)	(-) urée formol
resinous	résineux
resistance	résistance (électr.)
(-) welding	soudure par (-)
resistivity	résistivité
apparent (-)	(-) apparente
formation water (-)	(-) de l'eau de gisement
surface (-)	(-) superficielle
true (-)	(-) vraie
true formation (-)	(-) réelle de la roche
resolution	résolution; dédoublement
high (-)	haute (-)
resources	ressources
response	réponse
(-) curve	courbe de (-)
restarting	remise en marche
restriction	étranglement/diaphragme
result	résultat
resurgent	résurgent
retaining	de retenue
(-) valve	soupape (-)
(-) wall	mur de soutènement
retardant/retarder	retardateur
retarded	retardé
(-) ignition	allumage (-)
retention	rétention
reticule	réticule
reticulated	réticulé
retractor	rétracteur
block (-) mechanism	dispositif de retard du moufle
retrievable	récupérable
retrieving tool	outil de récupération
retrogressive erosion	érosion remontante
return	retour/renvoi
(-) bend	coude double
(-) spring	ressort de rappel
(-) stroke	course de (-)
mud (-)	tube dégorgeoir
reusable	réutilisable
revamping	réfection/modernisation/transformation
reversal	renversement/inversion
(-) of dip	changement de pendage
dip (-)	plongement inverse

reverse	*inverse*	**ripper**	*défonceuse*
(-) circulation	*circulation/ injection (-)*	**ripple**	*ondulation*
(-) dip	*pendage (-)*	sand (-)	*ride de plage*
(-) fault	*faille renversée*	**ripsaw**	*scie de long*
(-) osmosis	*osmose (-)*	**rise**	*remontée/ montée;*
(-) slope	*contre-pente*		*crue; exhaussement*
reversing	*renversement/ inversion*	(-) heading	*plan incliné*
(-) switch	*inverseur de marche/*	(-) of span	*flèche*
	de polarité	continental (-)	*glacis continental*
revolution	*tour/ révolution*	**riser main**	*tuyau de refoulement*
(-) per minute/rpm	*tours par minute*	**riser pipe**	*colonne montante*
revolving	*rotatif/ pivotant/*	**rising**	*remontage/ montée;*
	tournant		*rampe/ montant*
ria	*vallé inondée/ ria*	(-) pipe	*tuyau de refoulement*
rib	*nervure/ membrane/*	**risk**	*risque*
	entretoise/ support	**river**	*fleuve/ rivière*
cooling (-)	*ailette de*	(-) bank	*rive/ berge d'un (-)*
	refroidissement	(-) bed	*lit de (-)*
ribbed	*nervuré/ cannelé/ strié*	(-) drift/(-) load	*apport/ alluvions des (-)*
ribbon structure	*structure rubannée*	(-) mouth	*embouchure de (-)*
rich	*riche*	**rivet**	*rivet*
(-) clay	*argile grasse*	(-) set	*bouterolles à façonner*
(-) lime	*chaux grasse*		*les rivets*
ridge	*arête/ crête/ chaîne/*	**riveted**	*rivé*
	croupe/ dorsale	**rivulet**	*ruisseau*
anticlinal (-)	*crête anticlinale*	**road**	*route*
rift	*crevasse/ clivage/ fissure*	(-) breaker	*marteau-piqueur*
(-) valley	*fossé d'effondrement/*	(-) grader	*niveleuse*
	vallée faillée	**rock**	*roche/ rocher*
(-) zone	*zone de fracture*	(-) bar	*verrou*
rig	*atelier de forage/ tour*	(-) bench	*replat structural*
	de forage/ sondeuse	(-) bit	*tricône/ trépan à*
(-) crew	*équipe de forage*		*molettes*
rigid	*rigide/ raide*	(-) drill	*marteau pneumatique/*
rill	*sillon/ trace/ rigole*		*fleuret*
rim	*jante/ bourrelet/ lèvre/*	(-) exposure	*affleurement*
	rebord	(-) failure	*effondrement*
(-) syncline	*synclinal bordier*	(-) formation	*lithogenèse*
ring	*anneau/ couronne;*	(-) salt	*sel gemme*
	segment	(-) sample	*échantillon/ carotte*
(-) joint/(-) gasket	*joint circulaire/ joint*	(-) shelter	*roche surplombante*
	torique	(-) slide	*glissement de terrain*
(-) lubrication	*graissage à bague*	(-) weathering	*érosion/ altération*
(-) shape	*annulaire*		*des (-)*
(-) sticking	*gommage des segments*	argillaceous (-)/	*(-) argileuse*
hold-down (-)	*anneau de retenue*	clayey (-)	
locking (-)	*anneau de verrouillage*	crystalline (-)	*(-) cristalline*
scraper (-)	*segment râcleur*	intrusive	*(-) intrusive*
seal (-)	*bague d'étanchéité*	primary (-)	*(-) originelles*
starter (-)	*couronne de démarreur*	sealing (-)	*(-) couverture*
thrust (-)	*anneau de butée*	**rocker**	*berceau/ balancier*
ringed	*muni d'un anneau de*	(-) arm	*culbuteur*
	renfort	(-id-) roller	*galet de (-)*
		(-) shovel	*chargeuse mécanique*

rocking	balancement/agitation par balancement
rocky	rocheux
(-) matrix	gangue
rod	tige pleine/tringle
(-) elevator	élévateur de (-)
(-) fork	fourche de retenue
(-) holder	porte électrode
(-) man	porte-mire
(-) packing	garniture de (-)
connecting (-)	bielle
stirring (-)	agitateur
welding (-)	baguette de soudure
ROEC (Reed odorless earth closet) latrine	latrine sans odeur à fosse excavée, système Reed
roll	rouleau/cylindre
(-) mill	laminoir
rolled	laminé
(-) pipe	tube (-)
roller	rouleau/galet
(-) bearing	palier à (-)
sealed (-id-)	(-id-) étanche
(-) bit	trépan à molettes
(-) chain	chaîne à (-)
rolling	laminage
(-) dogs	coins de retenue
roof	toît/voûte
(-) rock	roche couverture
(-) subsidence	affaissement du toît
roofing	toîture/couverture
(-) material	matériel d'étanchéité
(-) slab	dalle de (-)
room	chambre/espace
root	racine
(-) drum	tambour d'enroulement
(-) of a fold	(-) d'une nappe de chariage
(-) of a weld	base de la soudure
thread (-)	racine de filet
rooting	enracinement
rope	câble/corde
(-) clip	serre-câble
(-) drilling	sondage au (-)
(-) drive	commande par (-)
(-) grab	grappin à (-)
(-) sheave	poulie à (-)
(-) socket	douille de (-)
(-) spear	harpon à (-)
(-) splice	épissure
(-) strand	toron
(-) winch	treuil à (-)
bailing (-)	(-) de curage

rotary	rotatif
(-) bit	trépan pour forage (-)
(-) boring/	sondage/forage rotary
(-) drilling	
(-) compressor	compresseur (-)
(-) drill bushing (kelly)	carré d'entrainement/ fourrure d'entrainement (tige carrée)
(-) line	câble de manoeuvre
(-) pump	pompe (-)
(-) swivel	tête d'injection de rotary
rotating	tournant/rotatif
(-) field	champ tournant
rotor	rotor/induit de motor
rotten	pourri
(-) rock	roche (-)
rough	brut/rugueux
(-) cast	brut de coulée
(-) sandstone	grès grossier
roughing	dégrossissage/ébauchage
round	round
(-) timber	rondin/bois rond
route	itinéraire/tracé
routine	routine
(-) maintenance	entretien courant
rubber	caoutchouc
rubbing	frottement/friction
(-) stone	pierre à aiguiser
(-) surface	surface de (-)
rubbish	refus/remblai/éboulis
rubble	agglomérat
(-) stone	caillou/galet roulé
rugged	accidenté/rugueux; solide
rule	règle
(-) of thumb	(-) pratique
ruling pen	tire-ligne
rumble	grondement/bruit sourd
run	essai/marche/opération/ fonctionnement
(-) off	écoulement/eau de ruisselement
test (-)	marche témoin
runner	curseur/rotor

running	marche/fonctionnement; coulant/boulant
(-) costs	frais d'exploitation
(-) fit	emboîtement tournant
(-) ground	terrain coulant
(-) in	rodage
(-) order	ordre de marche
(-) pressure	pression de marche
(-) sand	sable boulant
(-) water	eau courante
rupture	rupture
(-) load	charge de (-)
rust	rouille
(-) proof	antirouille/ inoxydable
rusty	rouillé
ruttles	brèche de faille/brèche de friction

S

sack	sac
saddle	étrier/voûte; bride pour obturation de fuite; collier de prise latérale
(-) axis	axe anticlinal
(-) bearing	palier de balancier
(-) bend	charnière anticlinale
(-) flange	bride filetée pour obturation de canalisation
(-) reef/(-) vein	gîte en selle/gîte de charnière anticlinale
pipe (-)	selle de raccordement ou collier de prise latérale
structural (-)	dépression
safe	sûr/sans danger
(-) load	charge admissible
safeguard	mesure de sécurité/ protection
(-) equipment	équipement de protection
safety	sécurité/sûreté
(-) board	passerelle d'accrochage de tiges
(-) catch	fermoir de sûreté/ cran de sûreté
(-) clamp	mâchoire de (-)/ bride de (-)
(-) coefficient/ factor	coefficient de (-)
(-) device	dispositif de (-)
(-) fuse	fusible de (-)
(-) gloves	gants de (-)
(-) margin	marge de (-)
(-) plug	bouchon fusible/ plomb de (-)
(-) shoes	chaussures de (-)

sag	affaisement/point bas/ flambage/flexion/mou d'un câble
salient	saillant/en saillie
saliferous	salifère
(-) breccia	brèche (-)
salina	lac salé
saline	saline
(-) deposit	dépôt salin
salinity	salinité
salinization	imprégnation saline
salinometer	salinomètre
salt	sel; salin
(-) brine	saumure
(-) content	teneur en (-)/salinité
(-) dome	dôme de (-)
(-) intrusion	intrusion saline
(-) marsh/(-)swamp	marais salant
(-) plug	noyau/masse de (-)
(-) water	eau salée
(-id-) flow	venue d' (-id-)
(-) works/saltern	saline
bay (-)/sea (-)	(-) marin
rock (-)	(-) gemme
salvage	sauvetage
(-) pipe	tube de récupération
salve	baume/onguent/ pommade
sample	échantillon/éprouvette
(-) bag	sachet à (-)
(-) cock	robinet d'échantillonnage
(-) examination	analyse des carottes
(-) mark	repère d' (-)
(-) through	bac de récupération des (-)
bailer (-)	(-) pris dans la cuiller de curage
bit (-)	(-) récupéré dans le trépan
core (-)	carotte
sampler	carottier/ échantillonneur
piston core (-)	(-) à piston
sidewall (-)	échantillonneur latéral
sampling	échantillonnage
samson post	support de balancier/ de levier de battage
(-) braces	entretoises du (-)

sand	*sable*	scaffold	*échafaudage;*
(-) bed	*couche de (-)*		*accrochage*
(-) blasting	*décapage au (-)*	scalant	*détartrant*
(-) bucket	*pompe à (-)/ cuiller à (-)*	scalar	*scalaire*
(-) casting	*coulée dans le (-)*	scale	*écaille/ tartre/ calamine/*
(-) drift	*vent de (-)*		*incrustation; échelle/*
(-) drum	*treuil de curage*		*graduation/ règle*
(-) dune/(-) hill	*dune de (-)*		*graduée/ étendue*
(-) heave	*poulie de curage*	(-) coated	*entartré/*
(-) hog	*poche à (-)*	(-) crust	*incrustré*
(-) line	*câble de curage*	(-) deposit	*tartre/ incrustration*
(-) packing	*bouchae au (-)*	(-) formation	*entartrage*
(-) paper	*papier de verre*	(-) inhibitor	*inhibiteur*
(-) pipe	*orgue géologique*		*d'entartrage*
(-) pit	*sablière*	(-) preventer/	*désincrustant/*
(-) pulley	*poulie de câble de*	(-) remover	*anticalcaire ·*
	curage	(-) trap	*séparateur d'impuretés*
(-) pump/(-)sucker	*pompe à (-)*	(-) drawing	*dessin á l'échelle*
(-) reel	*tambour/ treuil de*	(-) model	*maquette/ modèle à*
	curage		*l'échelle*
(-) trap	*piège à (-)*	(-) of hardness	*échelle de dureté*
closely-packed (-)	*(-) compact*	(-) unit	*division de l'échelle*
coarse-grained (-)	*(-) grossier*	(-) up	*extrapolation*
consolidated (-)	*(-) consolidé*	according to (-)	*à l'échelle*
cross bedded (-)	*intercalation de (-)*	scales	*balance*
fine-grained (-)	*(-) fin*	(-) beam	*fléau de (-)*
loose (-)	*(-) non consolidé*	mud (-)	*(-) à boue*
open (-)	*(-) très perméable*	scaling	*détartrage/ écaillage/*
running (-)	*(-) bouland (-) mouvant*		*entartrage/ piquage*
sand blasted	*décapé/ dépoli au*	scalloped surface	*suface découpée*
	jet de sable	scalping	*précriblage; enlèvement*
(-) pebble	*caillou façonné/ pierre*		*de la couche superficielle*
	à facettes	scaly structure	*structure écailleuse*
sanded up	*ensablé/ enlisé/ obstrué*	scan	*trace*
	par le (-)	scanning	*balayage/ exploration*
sandstone	*grès*		*radio-électrique*
(-) band	*intercalation de (-)*	(-) speed	*vitesse de (-)*
(-) grit	*(-) grossier*	scar	*cicatrice*
(-) lens	*lentille de (-)*	scarf	*recouvrement; assemblage*
fine grained (-)	*(-) fin*		*à mi-bois*
fossiliferous (-)		(-) weld	*soudure à (-)*
shelly (-)	*(-) coquillier*	scarfing	*aboutement/*
sandstorm	*tempête de sable*		*encastrement*
sandy	*sableux/ sablonneux/*	(-) joint	*assemblage en*
	arénacé		*sifflet*
sanitation	*assainissement/ hygiène*	scarp	*escarpement/ gradin*
sap	*sève*	fault (-)	*ressault/ gradin*
saturant	*produit imprégnant*		*de faille*
saturated	*saturé*	scarped	*abrupt/ escarpé*
saturation	*saturation*		
(-) concentration	*charge saturante*		
saw	*scie*		
(-) blade	*lame de (-)*		
(-) dust	*sciure de bois*		
(-) tooth bit	*couronne dentée*		
hack (-)	*(-) à métaux*		
scab	*écailles; tartre*		

scatter	dispersion/ éparpillement
(-) sheave crown	bloc couronne á cinq poulies
back (-)	rétrodiffusion
scattering	diffusion/ diffraction/ dispersion
scavenging	balayage/ entraînement/ évacuation
(-) air	air de (-)
(-) port	lumière de (-)
(-) stroke	course d'échappement
scent	odeur
schedule	calendrier/ indicateur/ prévision/ programme
scheduling	ordonnancement
schematic	schématique
schmidt net	projection de Lambert (cartographie)
scissor	ciseaux
(-) fault	faille en (-)
(-) tongs	pinces coupantes
scoop	godet/ pelle
scope	étendue/ portée champ d'application
score	rayure/ stries/ rainure
scoring	éraillures/ rayage
scotch	sabot de frein
scour	creusement/ érosion/ afouillement
wind (-)	érosion éolienne
scouring	affouillement
scrap/scraping	déchets/ ferraille/ fragment/ morceau/ rebut
scraper	curette/ râcleur/ grattoir
casing (-)	râcleur de tubage
scratch	strie/ rayure
scratcher	râcleur de paroi/ hérisson
scree	talus d'éboulis
screen	filtre/ tamis/ écran, cible
(-) sizing	calibrage au tamis
jigging (-)/ shaking (-)	crible à secousses
mud (-)	filtre à boue
tromel (-)	crible rotatif

screening	filtrage/ tamisage/ criblage/ classement
(-) drum	tambour de tamisage/ trommel
(-) machine	crible mécanique/ machine à tamiser
(-) test	essai éliminatoire/ essai de pré-sélection
screenings	refus de tamisage/ déchets de criblage
screw	vis
(-) bell	cloche de repêchage
(-) clamp	serre-joints
(-) connection	raccordement vissé
(-) cutting lathe	tour à fileter
(-) driver	tournevis
(-) flowmeter	compteur à moulinet
(-) head	tête de (-)
(-) jack	vérin à (-)
(-) joint	joint à (-)
(-) lag	tire-fonds
(-) pitch	pas de filetage/ pas de (-)
(-id-) gauge/gaje	jauge de pas de (-)
(-) pump	pompe à (-)
(-) spring	ressort à boudin
(-) thread	filetage de (-)
(-) with cleaved head	(-) à tête fendue
adjusting (-)	(-) de réglage
counter sunk (-)	(-) à tête fraisée
grub (-)	(-) sans tête
round head (-)/ cheese head (-)	(-) à tête ronde
slow running (-)	vis de ralenti (moteur)
screwed	vissé
(-) joint	joint (-)
scriber	pointe à tracer
to scrub	épurer/ nettoyer
scrubbing	épuration/ nettoyage
SCUBA (self-contained underwater breathing apparatus)	appareil respiratoire autonome de plongée sous-marine
scuffed bearing	palier usé
scuffing	éraillure légère/ grippage naissant
scum	scorie/ crasse
scumming	efflorescence
sea	mer
(-) bed	fonds des (-)
mean (-) level/MSL	niveau moyen des (-)

seal | joint/rondelle d'étanchéité/obturation
(-) groove | rainure/gorge d'étanchéité
annulus (-) | presse-étoupe
hydraulic (-) | (-) hydraulique
lip (-) | (-) à lèvre
rubber (-) | (-) en caoutchouc
water (-) | (-) d'eau

sealant | agent d'étanchéité

sealed | étanche

sealers | pince à sceller

sealing | plombage/scellement

seals | plombage/scellés

seam | couche/veine/filon; fissure/ligne d'assemblage
(-) less drawn tube/(-) drawn tube | tube étiré sans soudure
(-) welding | soudage continu

seamless | sans soudure

search | recherche/prospection

season | saison

seasonal | saisonnier

seat | siège/lieu
valve (-) | (-) de soupape

secondary | auxiliaire/secondaire

section | coupe/profil; châpitre
(-) iron | fer profilé
columnar (-) | profil stratigraphique
cross (-) | (-) transversale
geological (-) | (-) géologique
locked-in/ slant (-) | forage dévié
longitudinal (-) | (-) longitudinale
record (-) | (-) sismique

sectional | sectonnel
(-) iron | fer profilé
(-) paper | papier quadrillé

security | sécurité/sûreté; caution/garantie

sediment | sédiment/dépot

sedimentary | sédimentaire
(-) deposit | dépôt (-)
(-) overlap | recouvrement (-)
(-) rocks | roches (-)

sedimentation | sédimentation
(-) tank | bassin de (-)
paralic (-) | (-) paralique

seepage | suintement

segment | segment

segregation | séparation

seism | séisme/secousse tellurique/tremblement de terre

seismic | sismique
(-) origin | épicentre
(-) prospecting | prospection (-)
(-) reflection method | méthode de sismique réflexion
(-) surge | tsunami
(-) waves | ondes (-)

seismographe | sismographe

seismology | sismologie

seismometer | sismomètre

seized | grippé

seizure | grippage

selective | sélectif

self | automatique/auto
(-) adjustable | auto-réglable
(-) cleaning cones | cônes auto nettoyant
(-) closing | à fermeture automatique
(-) contained | autonome
(-) excitation | auto-excitation
(·) lubrication | auto-graissage
(-) priming pump | pompe à amorçage automatique
(-) propelled | auto-moteur
(-) regulating | autorégulation
(-) starter | autodémarreur

semi-arid | semi-aride

semi-automatic | semi-automatique
(-) arc welding | soudage (-) à l'arc

semi-longitudinal/ semi-transverse fault | faille diagonale

semiskilled worker | ouvrier spécialisé

semisteel | fonte aciérée

semitrailer | semi-remorque

sender | émetteur

seniority | ancienneté

sensibility/ sensitivity | sensibilité/ susceptibilité

sensible | sensible; sensé
(-) heat | chaleur (-)

sensitive | sensible

sensitizer | sensibilisateur

sensor | capteur

separating	séparation/ triage
separation	séparation/ triage
(-) plane	plan de (-)
bubble-type (-)	(-) par barbotage
centrifugal (-)	(-) centrifuge
separator	épurateur/ séparateur/ purgeur
sequence	série/ succession
series	série
(-) connection	montage/ accouplement en (-)
(-) of strata	complexe de couches
(-) winding	enroulement (-)
geological (-)	(-) géologique
serrated	cannelé/ cranté/ dentelé/ strié
serration	cannelure/ dentelure/ rainure
service	fonctionnement/ service, entretien
(-) life	durée de vie/ durée de (-) utile
(-) pipe	tuyauterie/ conduite de branchement
serviceability	facilité d'entretien
servicing	entretien/ maintenance
servo control	commande asservie/ servo régulateur
set	série/ ensemble/ groupe/ cadre/ déformation
(-) back counter	compteur avec remise à zéro
(-) of joints	(-) de cassures
(-) screw	vis de blocage
(-) up	composition des garnitures de forage/ montage
electric generating (-)	groupe électrogène
permanent (-)	déformation permanente
residual (-)	déformation résiduelle
setting	installation/ mise en place/ montage; orientation
(-) over	décentrement/ désaxage
(-) time	temps de prise
(-) up	montage
(-) to zero	mise au zéro
to settle	déposer/ précipiter; installer/ régler
settled	fixe/ invariable/ établi

settlement	dépôt/ précipitation; établissement/ peuplement
(-) area	périmètre d'etablissement zone de peuplement
(-) rate	vitesse de précipitation/ vitesse de sédimentation
settler	décanteur/ séparateur; colon/ immigrant
settling	décantation/ dépôt/ séparation/ sédimentation; affaissement/ tassement
(-) basin/(-) pond	bassin de (-)
(-) crack	lézarde de tassement
(-) pit	fosse de (-)
(-) velocity	vitesse de (-)
severance	disjonction/ disruption/ rupture
(-) pay	indemnité de licenciement
severity	sévérité/ intensité
vibratory (-)	intensité vibratoire
sewage	eaux résiduaires/ eaux usées/ eaux d'égouts
(-) disposal	évacuation des (-)
(-) system	réseau d'égouts
sewer	égout
(-) opening	bouche/ regard d' (-)
shackle	manille d'attelage/ boucle de la chaîne d'ancrage
(-) line/(-) rod	tige de commande
tension (-)	tendeur
shadow	ombre; écran
shadowing	effet d'écran
shaft	arbre/ axe; puits (de mine)
(-) drive	transmission par arbre
(-) key	clavette
(-) sinking	creusement/ fonçage de puits
connecting (-)	(-) de transmission
drilling (-)	train de sonde
drive (-)	arbre moteur
driven (-)	arbre conduit
power take-off (-)	arbre de prise de force
splined (-)	arbre cannelé
shaker	crible à secousses
(-) screen	tamis oscillant
shale (-)	tamis vibrant des boues
shale	schiste argileux
sandy (-)	argile sableuse
sloughing (-)	schiste boulant
shallow	peu profond
(-) well	puits (-)
shallows	banc de sable/ bas-fond

shaly	schisteux
shank	embout fileté/ tige; flanc d'un pli
bit (-)	filetage de l'outil de forage
shape	forme/ profil
sharing	partage; participation
time (-)	temps partagé
sharp	aigu; précis
sharpening	affûtage/ aiguisage
(-) stone	pierre à aiguiser
sharpness	finesse; netteté; acuité
shatter	fragment/ morceau
(-) belt/(-) zone	zone de broyage
(-) breccia	brèche de friction
(-) proof	incassable
shattered	brisé/ broyé
shaving	copeau
shear	cisaillement
(-) folding	plissement cisaillant
(-) joint	diaclase de (-)
(-) pin	goupille de (-)
shearing	cisaillement
shears	cisaille/ ciseaux
sheath	fourreau/ gaine
sheathed	revêtu/ gainé
sheave	poulie
(-) block	moufle
shed	appentis/ hangar
sheen	éclat
sheet	feuille/ intercalation/ tôle
(-) erosion	érosion en nappes
(-) flood	écoulement/ inondation en nappe
(-) iron	tôle de fer
(-) jointing	disjonction en bancs
(-) joints	diaclases horizontales
(-) lead	plomb en feuilles
(-) metal	plaque/ tôle
(-) pile	palplanche
data (-)	fiche technique
thrust (-)	nappe de charriage
sheeted	stratifié
sheeting	blindage/ coffrage; stratification; tubage
(-) plane	plan de stratification

shelf	étagère/ rayonnage; plateau continental
(-) corrosion	corrosion en magasinage
(-) life	vie d'emmagasinage/ durée de conservation
insular (-)	socle
island (-)	plateau insulaire
shell	coquille/ chemise/ enveloppe/ calandre
(-)-and-coil condenser	condenseur à calandre et serpentins
(-)-and-tube condenser	condenseur à calandre multitubulaire
(-) auger	tarière à cuiller
(-) breccia/(-)cock	lumachelle
(-) like	conchoïdal
(-) pump	pompe à sable
cone (-) bit	coquille
pump (-)	corps de pompe
shellac	gomme laque
shelly	coquiller
(-) limestone	calcaire (-)
shelter	abri
shelving	incliné; déclivité
sherardizing	shérardisation (protection antirouille)
shield	plaque de garde/ blindage/ bouclier/ écran protecteur
(-) arc welding	soudage à l'arc avec électrode enrobée
(-) tubes	tubes de protection
thermal (-)	bouclier thermique
shift	poste de travail/ équipe; changement de vitesse/ changement; faille de dislocation/ rejet/ rejet horizontal
(-) fault	faille de dislocation
(-) fork	fourchette du changement de vitesse
gear (-)	boîte de vitesse/ changement de vitesse
shifting	déplacement/ migration
(-) dune	dune mobile
(-) of a divide	migration de la ligne de partage des eaux
(-) sand	sable mouvant
shim	cale d'épaisseur
shimmy	flottement des roues (d'une automobile)
shingle	galets de plage; bardeau
(-) bar	cordon de (-)
(-) lining	revêtement en bardeaux
shipping	embarquement/ expédition
(-) ton	unité de volume (1.132574 m³)

shirtail/bit (-)	talon de l'outil
shock	choc/à-coup/secousse
(-) absorber	amortisseur
(-) load	charge de (-)
(-) proof	anti (-)
(-) wave	onde de (-)
shoe	patin/sabot/semelle
(-) carrier	support des (-)
brake (-)	sabot/mâchoire de frein
casing (-)	sabot de tubage
float (-)	sabot à soupape
jet (-id-)	sabot à jets tourbillonnaires
shooting	tir
(-) system	système de (-)
correlation (-)	(-) de corrélation
reflection (-)	sismique réfraction
subsurface (-)	(-) enterré
well (-)	carottage sismique
shop	atelier
shore	côte/rivage/littoral; contrefiche/étrésillon/entretoise
(-) cliff	falaise littorale
shore line	côte/ligne de rivage/littoral
shoring	boisage/étayage
short	aigu/cassant/court
(-) circuit	court-circuit
(-) cut	raccourci/recoupement
shortage	manque/pénurie
shot	explosion/coup/tir; grenaille
(-) bit	couronne à grenailles
(-) break	rupture
(-) concrete	béton projeté
(-) drilling	forage à la grenaille
(-) hole drilling	forage sismique
shoulder	collerette/épaulement/saillie
(-) of a bit	portée d'un outil de forage
(-) bushing	douille bridée
box (-)	épaulement femelle (de tige de forage)
shank (-)	portée de blocage
shove	rejet horizontal
shovel	pelle/pelle mécanique/excavateur
(-) type loader	chargeuse à pelle
back action (-)/ mechanical (-)/crowd (-)/ (-)dredge	(-) à godet/excavateur à godet
power (-)	(-) mécanique

show	indice/indication/venue
drilled (-)	venue en cours de forage
showings	traces
shrink	retrécissement/retrait
(-) fit	emmanchement par retrait
shrinkable	rétractable
heat (-)	thermo (-)
shrinkage	contraction/retrait
(-) cavity/(-) hole	retassure/cavité de retrait
(-) crack	fente de dessication/fente de retrait
(-) of steel	gauchissement de l'acier
shroud	enveloppe/emboîtement/blindage/bouclier
shunt	shunt/dérivation/collecteur
(-) excitation	excitation en dérivation
(-) meter	débitmètre en dérivation
(-) motor/	moteur-shunt
(-) wound motor	
(-) resistance	résistance en dérivation
shut-in	fermé
(-) drilling	pression statique
pressure	dans un puits
(-) valve	vanne de fermeture
shut-off	fermeture/obturation; vanne/robinet d'arrêt
(-) cock	robinet d'arrêt
(-) plug	bouchon de refoulement
shut-down	arrêt/hors service/interruption
shutter	obturateur/vanne
side	côté/paroi/versant; flanc d'un pli; lèvre d'une faille
(-) boom	flèche latérale/grue à flèche latérale
(-) elevation	profil/vue latérale
(-) hole	regard
(-) lights	feux de position
(-) play	jeu latéral
(-) slip	dérapage
(-) slope	talus
(-) thrust	poussée latérale
(-) tracked hole	sondage/trou dévié
(-) tracking tools	outils de déviation
(-) view	vue de côté
(-) wall	paroi latérale
(-id-) coring	carottage latéral
(-id-) sampler	carottier latéral
lifted (-)	lèvre soulevée d'une faille
lowered (-)	lèvre inférieure d'une faille

siding	*voie de garage*	single	*unique/ simple; élément*
			unitaire de tige
sierra	*sierra*	(-) acting pump	*pompe à simple effet*
		(-) cylinder	*monocylindrique*
sieve	*tamis/ crible*	(-) deck screen	*crible à plateau unique*
(-) acceptance	*contrôle*	(-) drum hoist	*treuil à simple tambour*
	granulométrique	(-) inlet fan	*ventilateur à une*
(-) analysis	*analyse*		*seule ouïe*
	granulométrique/	(-) pass welding	*soudage en une passe*
	analyse par tamisage	(-) phase	*monophasé*
(-) filter	*filtre à tamis*	(-) stage compressor	*compresseur mono-*
(-) tray/(-) plate	*plateau perforé*		*étagé/à un étage*
mesh (-)	*(-) à maille*	(-) thread	*filetage à pas simple*
swing (-)	*(-) oscillant*		
		sink	*doline; évier*
sieving	*tamisage/ criblage*	(-) hole	*effondrement/ doline*
		collapse (-)	*doline d'effondrement*
sifting	*tamisage*	valley (-)	*couloir karstique*
sight	*vue/ regard/ viseur*	sinker	*fonceur de puits;*
(-) distance	*distance de visibilité*		*marteau de fonçage*
(-) flow indicator	*regard d'écoulement*	(-) bar	*barre de surcharge;*
(-) gauge/gage	*viseur*		*maîtresse-tige de*
			repêchage
sighting	*visée*		
(-) board	*alidade*	sinking	*affaissement/ creusage/*
(-) line	*ligne de (-)*		*enfoncement*
sign	*signe/écriteau/panneau*	sinter	*tuf/ tuffeau*
		(-) deposit	*concrétion*
signal lamp	*lampe de signalisation*		
		sintered	*aggloméré/ fritté*
silencer	*silencieux*		
	(d'échappement d'un	siphoclinometer	*inclinomètre à siphon*
	moteur)		
		siphon	*siphon*
siliceous	*siliceux*		
(-) earth	*diatomite/ terre*	site	*emplacement/ situation*
	à diatomées	(-) development	*aménagement du terrain*
(-) slag	*laitier (-)*	job (-)/work (-)	*chantier*
silicon	*silicium*	size	*grandeur/ taille/*
(-) carbide	*carbure de (-)/*		*dimensions/ format*
	carborundum	natural (-)	*(-) nature*
		nominal (-)	*taille nominale*
silicone	*silicone*		
(-) grease	*graisse à base de (-)*	sizing	*calibrage/ criblage/*
			classement volumétrique
sill	*seuil*	(-) screen	*crible classeur*
(-) depth	*profondeur de (-)*		
		skelp	*tôle pour tubes*
silt	*limon/ vase*		
		sketch	*croquis/ schéma/ plan*
silting up	*envasement/ limonage/*	(-) map	*(-) de reconnaissance*
	colmatage		
		skew	*de biais/ oblique*
silty	*vaseux/ boueux*		
		skewing	*glissade/ déplacement*
silver	*argent*		*oblique*
(-) solder	*soudure à l' (-)*		
		skewness	*asymétrie*
sine	*sinus*	offset (-)	*glissement/ dérapage*
(-) wave	*onde sinusoïdale*		*d'un outil de forage*
		skid	*traineau/ patin/ madrier/*
			cale/ support/ glissières
		(-) frame	*chassis skid*
		(-) mounted	*monté sur patins/ sur*
			cales/ sur glissières
		(-) proof	*antidérapant*
		live (-)	*traineau à roulettes*

skidding	dérapage/ripage; glissement de l'outil à molettes	slide	coulisseau/glissière; éboulement
		(-) furrow	couloir d'avalanche
		(-) rail	barre/rail de glissement
skimmer	écumoire; pelle de retenue/ godet niveleur	(-) rock	cône de déjection
(-)shovel/(-)scoop	pelle niveleuse	(-) rule	règle à calcul
		sliding	ripage/coulissant
skin	peau/croûte/film	(-) caliper	pied à coulisse
(-) hardening	trempe superficielle	(-) collar	bague coulissante
(-) of casting	croûte de la fonte	(-) gear	engrenage baladeur
(-) patching	réparation en surface	(-) surface	surface de glissement
skirt	bêche; jupe	slime	boue/limon/vase/schlamm
foundation (-)	jupe de fondation		
		slim hole drilling	filiforage/forage en diamètre réduit
skirting	bordure/socle/plinthe		
		slimy	boueux/limoneux/ visqueux
slab	dalle/panneau/plaque		
(-) ingot	brame		
(-) iron	fer en brames	sling	élingue/boucle/cravatte
(-) structure	division en plaques	(-) line	élingue/haussière
		(-id-) socket	manille d' (-)
slabbing	rupture en plaques		
		slip	glissement/éboulement; coin de retenue;fiche
slack	mou/lâche/sans tension		
(-) cable/(-) rope	câble détendu	(-) cleavage	faux clivage
(-) loop	boucle de dilatation d'une canalisation	(-) fault	fente d'affaissement
		(-) fold	pli de cisaillement
slacking	décollement/desserrage (d'un écrou)	(-) grip	bride de fixation à coins/ griffe à coins
		(-) joint	articulation coulissante/ coulisse du tube conducteur
slag	scorie/laitier/mâchefer		
		(-) knot	noeud coulant
slaked lime	chaux éteinte/chaux hydratée	(-) ring	collecteur (d'un moteur à induction)
		(-) socket	souricière
slant	inclinaison/pendage; incliné/oblique	(-) stick	tige polie
		(-) type elevator	élévateur à coins (tubes)
(-) drilling	forage oblique	(-) type hanger	dispositif de suspension à coins
(-) rig	sondeuse à pile inclinée		
slanted	dévié/oblique	slipper	sabot de freinage
(-) hole	trou incliné		
		slipping	filage (report des points d'usure du câble de forage)
sledge	masse/marteau de forgeron; traineau		
(-) hammer	marteau à devant	slips	surface de glisssement; coins grippeurs/cales
sleeper	traverse/semelle	power (-)	coins automatiques
sleeve	douille/fourreau/ manchette/manchon	slit	entaille/fente
(-) bearing	palier lisse	slope	inclinaison/pente/ pendage/talus
(-) joint	assemblage à manchon		
blanking (-)	bouchon obturateur de tubage	(-) failure	rupture de talus
		(-) line	ligne de plus grande pente
connecting (-)	manchon de raccordement	back (-)	contre-pente/revers
sliding (-)	manchon coulissant	steep (-)	pente escarpée
split (-)	manchon en deux parties		
threaded (-)	manchon fileté	slot	fente/rainure/encoche/ saignée
slice	tranche/lame	(-) welding	soudure sur entaille
thrust (-)	copeau de charriage		
slick joint	joint de tube à garnissage		

slotted	encoché/à fente
(-) pipe	tube crépiné/tube rainuré
slotting	entaillage/mortaisage
slough	bourbier/fondrière
sloughing	séparation/éboulement
(-) formation	formation boulante
hole (-)	éboulement des parois du puits
slow	lent
(-) running jet	gicleur de ralenti (carburateur)
sludge	boues/cambouis
(-) cake	sédiments de filtration
activated (-)	(-) activées
sludger	pompe à sable
slug	bouchon
sluggish	lent/paresseux
sluice	écluse/rigole/canal
slump/slumping	éboulement/glissement
slurry	boue/coulis/mortier peu épais
slush	boue/gadoue/neige fondante
(-) pit	bac/bassin à boue
(-) pump	pompe à boue
small	petit
(-) end bearing	palier de pied de bielle
smear	tache
smearing	usure des roulements
smelting	fusion
(-) plant/(-) works	fonderie
smog	fumée (smoke) et brouillard (fog)
smoke	fumée
smoothing	lissage/polissage/ajustement
smudge	fumée épaisse
snap	cassure/rupture; fermoir
(-) action control	réglage par tout ou rien
(-) head	bouterolle
(-) hook	mousqueton
(-) ring	bague à ressort
snapping up line	cordage/câble de commande de la clé de manoeuvre
snatch block	poulie à chape ouvrante; outil de repêchage à coins
snifting valve	reniflard
snips	cisailles
snitcher	balai électrique/détecteur de défaut de revêtement de canalisation
snout	bec de déversement
snubber	amortisseur
adjusting (-)	rallonge ajustable
snubbing	curage sous pression; arrêt abrupt d'un câble/d'une haussière
(-) line	câble/élingue de retenue
(-) post	pieu de retenue/d'amarrage
soak/soaking	trempage/imbibition
soap	savon
(-) stone	stéatite
(-) suds	mousse de (-)
socket	douille/manchon; raccord d'accrochage; cloche de repêchage; prise de courant
(-) joint	emboitement à tubage
(-) wrench	clé à tube
bell (-)	cloche de repêchage à emboitement
Babcock stiff(-)	cloche (rigide) de repêchage
soda	soude
(-) ash	carbonate de sodium anhydre
(-) lime	chaux sodée
(-) lye	lessive de (-)
(-) wash	lavage à la (-)
sodium	sodium
(-) alum	alun de (-)
(-) chloride	chlorure de (-)
(-) hydrate	soude caustique
soft	mou/ductile/malléable/fragile
(-) clay	argile plastique
(-) rock	roche tendre
(-) rope	merlin/cordage
(-) solder/(-) soldering	soudure tendre/soudure à l'étain
(-) water	eau douce
softening	adoucissement/amollissement
(-) agent	plastifiant/agent d'adoucissage/amollissant/émollient
(-) point	point de ramollissement
water (-)	adoucissement des eaux
software	logiciel

soil	*sol/ terrain*
(-) bearing value	*indice porteur du sol*
(-) creep	*glissement de terrain/ fluage du (-)*
sub (-)	*sous (-)*
top (-)	*couche arable*
soil	*salissure/ souillure/ impureté*
solar	*solaire*
(-) energy	*énergie (-)*
solderability	*soldabilité*
soldered	*soudé*
soldering	*soudage; brasage*
(-) bit/(-)iron	*fer à souder*
(-) flux	*fondant de soudure*
(-) lamp/(-) torch	*lampe à souder*
(-) powder	*poudre à braser*
(-) tongs	*pince à souder*
sole	*socle/ base/ substratum semelle*
(-) piece	
(-) plate	*plaque de fondation/ selle*
solenoid	*solénoïde*
(-) valve	*électrovanne*
solid	*solide; uni; continu*
(-) bearing	*palier plein*
(-) beds	*couches dures*
(-) ground/(-) soil	*terrain ferme*
(-) line	*ligne continue*
(-) wood	*bois massif*
total dissolved solids (TDS)	*quantité totale de matières dissoutes*
solubility	*solubilité*
soluble	*soluble*
solute	*soluté*
solution	*dissolution/ solution*
(-) subsidence	*tassement/ affaissement de (-)*
aqueous (-)	*solution aqueuse*
standard (-)	*solution titrée*
solvent	*solvant/ dissolvant*
sonde	*sonde*
compensated density (-)	*(-) de densité compensée*
introduction (-)	*(-) à induction*
reciprocal (-)	*(-) inverse*
sonometer	*sonomètre*
soot	*suie*
sorter	*classeur*
sorting	*classement/ triage*

sound	*son; sain/ solide; détroit/ goulet*
(-) insulation	*insonorisation*
(-) proofing	*isolation acoustique*
(-) wave	*onde sonore*
sounding	*sondage*
(-) borer	*tarière*
(-) pin	*pointe de pénétromètre*
(-) tool	*pénétromètre*
soundness	*validité/ exactitude*
sour	*acide/ corrosif*
(-) water	*eau acide/ eau sulfurée*
source	*source*
alternative energy (-)	*(-) énergétique de remplacement*
spacer	*cale/ entretoise d'écartement/ rondelle*
spacing	*écartement/ espacement/ intervalle*
spall	*éclat de pierre*
spalling	*usure par refoulement de métal (écaillage des dents d'engrenages)/ effritement*
span	*enjambement/ intervalle/ portée*
life (-)	*vie/ durée de vie*
spanner	*clef de serrage/*
adjustable (-)	*clef anglaise/ clef à molette*
box (-)/socket (-)	*clef à douille*
spare	*de rechange/ de réserve*
(-) part	*pièce (-)*
(-) wheel	*roue de secours*
spark	*étincelle*
(-) advance	*avance à l'allumage*
(-) arrester	*pare-étincelle*
(-) coil	*bobine d'allumage*
(-) gap	*écartement des électrodes de bougie*
(-) plug	*bougie d'allumage*
(-id-) points	*électrodes de bougie*
(-id-) wrench	*clé à bougies*
sparkless	*sans étincelles*
spatter	*éclaboussure*
spear	*harpon de repêchage/ arrache tube*
(-) joint head	*guide-butoir*
casing (-)	*poire de repêchage*
drill collar (-)	*arrache tube*
releasing (-)	*poire de repêchage à coins*

specific | spécifique/ déterminé
(-) energy | énergie massique
(-) gravity | densité
(-) weight | poids volumique/ poids spécifique

specifications | spécifications/ cahier de charges

specified | imposé/ exigé

spectrograph | spectrographe

spectrometer | spectromètre

spectrophotometer | spectrophotomètre

spectrum | spectre

speed | vitesse
(-) box | boîte de (-)
(-) governor | régulateur de (-)
(-) indicator | tachymètre/ indicateur de (-)
(-) range | gamme de (-)
cutting (-) | (-) de coupe
drilling (-) | (-) du forage
free (-) | (-) à vide
idling (-) | régime de ralenti
rotating (-) | régime de rotation
variable (-) | (-) variable

speedometer | tachymètre/ compteur de vitesse

spent | dépensé/ épuisé/ usé

spheroidal | sphéroïdal
(-) jointing | séparation (-)
(-) structure | division en boules

spider | collier à coins/ dispositif de retenue à coins; araignée; croisillon/ étoile
(-) gear | pignon satellite
casing (-) | support de tubage à coins
tubing (-) | support de tiges à coins

spigot | saillie/ bout mâle; robinet/ siphon
(-) end of pipe | extrémité mâle d'un tube
(-) joint | joint à emboîtement
(-) and socket pipe | tuyau à emboîtement

spike | clou/ crampon

spill | coulage/ déversement/ fuite
(-) pipe | tuyau de décharge

spillage | débordement

spillway | canal de trop plein

spin | rotation rapide/ vrille
(-) off | retombée

spindle | broche/ arbre/ axe/ fusée/ pivot
(-) capacity | puissance à l'arbre
axle (-) | fusée d'essieu
injector (-) | aiguille d'injecteur

spinner | spinner
drillpipe (-) | appareil de vissage des tiges
kelly (-) | entraîneur de la tige d'entraînement

spinning | tournoiement/ mouvement de rotation
(-) chain | chaîne de vissage
(-) line/(-) rope | câble de vissage

spiral | spirale/ serpentin
(-) bevel gear | engrenage conique à denture helicoïdale
(-) bit | trépan hélicoïdal
(-) guide | crochet redresseur
(-) spring | ressort à boudin

spire | spire/ spirale; tour

spirit | alcool

spit | digue en épi/ flèche littorale

splash | éclaboussement/ éclaboussure/ projection
(-) board/(-) guard | garde-boue
(-) lubrication | graissage par barbotage

splice | épissure/ éclisse

spline | ergot/ tenon/ clavette/ cannelure
(-) shaft | arbre cannelé

splinter | écharde/ fragment

split | fendu; fente/ fissure/ division/ scission
(-) case pump | pompe double aspiration
(-) collar/(-) sleeve | manchon en deux pièces
(-) coupling | accouplement à coquilles
(-) flow | écoulement divisé
(-) joint | tube fendu longitudinalement
(-) pin | goupille fendue
(-) tee | té fendu

splitter | inciseur de tube
casing (-) | fendeur de tubage

splitting | fendage/ refente/ fission; dédoublement de couche

spoilage | déchets/ rebuts

spoke | rais/ rayon/ échelon

sponge | éponge

sponging agent | agent gonflant

spongy | spongieux/ poreux

sponsor	*maître de l'oeuvre*	spring	*ressort; source*
spontaneous	*spontané*	(-) balance	*balance à ressort/ peson*
(-) generation	*génération (-)*	(-) bumper/(-) coil	*(-) à boudin*
(-) ignition	*auto-allumage/*	(-) clip	*pince à (-)*
	auto-ignition	(-) driven	*mû par un ressort*
		(-) grapple	*spirale agrippante*
spool	*manchette à brides/ bride*	(-) leaf	*lame de (-)*
	d'ancrage/ tambour/	(-) loaded	*chargé par (-)*
	moulinet	(-) mount	*(-) de suspension*
(-) piece	*manchette de*	(-) suspension	*suspension à (-)*
	raccordement/ bride de	(-) swivel	*émerillon à (-)*
	raccordement	(-) valve	*soupape à (-)*
casing (-)	*raccord (à double bride)*	(-) washer	*rondelle élastique*
	pour suspension de tubage	coiled (-)/helical (-)	*(-) à boudin*
drilling (-)	*raccord de forage à*	leaf (-)	*(-) à lame*
	brides	return (-)	*(-) de rappel*
tubing (-)	*raccord double bride*	torsion (-)	*(-) de torsion*
	pour tige	valve (-)	*(-) de soupape*
		(-) of salt water	*source d'eau salée*
spooling	*bobinage*	(-) water	*eau de source*
(-) flanges	*flasques d'un tambour*	mud (-)	*volcan de boue*
		outcrop (-)	*source d'affleurement*
spoon	*cuiller; affleurement*	tubular (-)	*source karstique*
spot	*tache/ point/ endroit*	sprinkler	*arroseuse/ pulvérisateur/*
(-) check	*contrôle ponctuel*		*tourniquet*
(-) height	*point coté*		
(-) welding	*soudure par point*	sprinkling	*arrosage/ aspersion*
hard (-)	*zone dure*	fire (-) system	*dispositif d'arrosage*
hot (-)	*point chaud*		*contre l'incendie*
spotting	*positionnement*	sprocket	*roue dentée/ dent de pignon*
		(-) chain	*chaîne à barbotin/*
spout	*bec/ ajutage/ goulotte/*		*chaîne-galle*
	tuyau de décharge/	(-) drum	*tambour denté*
	dégorgeoir	(-) wheel	*pignon de chaîne*
pouring (-)	*(-) verseur*		
		sprung mass	*masse suspendue*
spouting	*jaillissement*		
		spud	*spatule de dégagement*
spray	*atomisation/ embruns/*	(-) bit	*trépan-bêche*
	pulvérisation/		
	vaporisation	to spud	*forer par battage au*
(-) lubrication	*graissage par*		*câble*
	brouillard d'huile		
(-) nozzle	*gicleur/ buse de*	spudder	*machine/ atelier de*
	pulvérisation		*forage par battage*
(-) painting	*peinture au pistolet*		
		spudding	*battage au câble*
sprayer	*atomiseur/ pulvérisateur/*	(-) bit	*trépan de (-)/ trépan*
	vaporisateur		*d'attaque/ trépan-bêche*
		(-) in	*début de forage*
spread	*dispersion; dispositif*	(-) pulley	*poulie de forage par (-)*
	d'essai sismique	(-) shoe	*sabot de battage/ sabot*
(-) correction	*correction d'obliquité*		*d'attaque*
spreader	*agent mouillant; épandeuse*	spur	*contrefiche/ contre-fort/*
grit/gritter (-)	*gravillonneuse*		*éperon; ramification*
		(-) gear	*engrenage droit/*
spreading	*propagation/ épandage;*		*engrenage à denture*
	enduisage		*droite*
(-) tension	*tension d'étalement*	mountain (-)	*éperon de montagne*
		rocky (-)	*saillie de roche*
		truncated (-)	*éperon tronqué*
		spurious	*accidentel/ parasite*
		spurline	*ligne de faîte*

spurt	écoulement immédiat (recueilli en filtration avant formation du gâteau)
(-) loss	perte aux à-coups de pression
spurting out	jaillissement
squad	équipe
squall	bourrasque/grain/ coup de vent
squamate	squamé
square	carré; équerre
(-) bolt	boulon (-)
(-) head	tête (-)
(-) nut	écrou (-)
(-) pass	cannelure (-)
(-) thread	filet (-)
squeak	grincement
squeegee	raclette
squeeze	compression/esquiche
(-) cimenting	cimentation sous pression/esquichage
(-) film	effet d'éponge
squeezer	écrase-tube; pince à cingler
squirrel cage motor	moteur à cage d'écureuil
squirt	seringue
(-) can lubrication	graissage à la burette
(-) gun	pistolet-graisseur
to stab	guider une tige dans le raccord pendant le vissage
stabbing	guidage des tiges/ du tubage
stability	stabilité
stabilized	stabilisé
(-) dune	dune (-)
stabilizer	stabilisateur
bottomhole (-)	(-) de fond
link (-)	(-) des bras d'élévateur
sleeve (-)	(-) à manchon
string (-)	(-) de train de tiges
stable	stable
stack	pile/empilage/tas/gerbe; pilier/pinacle
(-) pipe	conduit de fumées
horizontal (-)	couverture multiple
stackable	gerbable
stacker	élévateur/sauterelle
stacking	empilage/piquetage
stadia	mire de précision
(-) constant	constante stadimétrique
staff	mire de précision; état major/personnel
cross (-)	équerre d'arpenteur
stage	étage/degré/phase/stade
(-) flotation	flottation étagée
(-) of early youth	stade de première jeunesse
(-) of full maturity	stade de pleine maturité
(-) of late youth	stade d'adolescence
structure process (-)	stade de développement
staggered	décalé/en quinconce
stain	tache
staining	souillure; teinture/ marquage avec indicateur
stainless	inoxydable
stake	piquet de jalonnement/ pieu/poteau
stalling	blocage/calage du moteur; perte de vitesse; arrêt
stamp	timbre/marque/tampon; pilon
stamped	embouti/estampé; broyé/ concassé; timbré/contrôlé
stamping	emboutissage/estampage
stampings	pièces embouties
stanchion	étai/béquille/montant
stand	ensemble de tiges de forage assemblées; support/socle/ piètement
(-) off	excès de longueur du filetage mâle par rapport au filetage femelle, après vissage à fond des tiges
(-) pipe	colonne montante; borne fontaine; tuyau de refoulement
standard	norme/étalon/standard/ normal/ordinaire
(-) cell	pile étalon
(-) colours	couleurs de référence
(-) conditions	conditions normalisées
(-) deviation	écart type/déviation ordinaire
(-) pipe	tuyau normalisé
(-) production	production de série
(-) solution	solution titrée
(-) tools	outils de forage au câble
standardization	normalisation
standby	en attente/en réserve/ de secours

standing	fixe/ à l'arrêt/ au repos
(-) block/(-) pulley	poulie (-)
(-) water	eau stagnante
(-) waves	ondes stationnaires
standstill	repos/ équilibre/ arrêt
staple	agrafe/ crampon/ coin
star	étoile
(-) connection	montage en (-)
(-) coupling	couplage en (-)
(-) delta	étoile-triangle
starch	amidon
start-up	démarrage
(-) time	temps de mise en route
starter	démarreur
starting	mise en route
(-) cartridge	cartouche de lancement
(-) crank/(-) handle	manivelle de (-)
(-) knock	cliquetis au démarrage
(-) lever	levier de démarrage
(-) output	puissance de démarrage
(-) torque	couple de démarrage
automatic (-)/self (-)	démarrage automatique
cold (-)	démarrage à froid
inertia (-)	lancement par inertie
state	état/ régime/ condition
solid (-)	(-) solide
steady (-)	régime stationnaire/ régime permanent
unsteady (-)	régime transitoire
statement	énoncé/ exposé; relevé de compte/ bilan
public (-)	déclaration
static	statique; parasite/ perturbation atmosphérique
(-) head/(-) lift	hauteur d'élévation du pompage
(-) pressure	pression (-)
station	poste/ emplacement
comfort (-)	toilettes publiques/ WC publics
duty (-)	lieu d'affectation/ poste
stationary	stationnaire/ fixe/ inerte
stator	stator
stave	douve
stay	support/ montant/ entretoise/ étai/ hauban
(-) block	semelle d'ancrage
(-) bolt	boulon d'ancrage
staying	haubannage/ étayage

steady	constant/ régulier
(-) fluid flow	écoulement permanent
(-) running condition	régime stable
steam	vapeur
(-) hammer	marteau pilon à (-)
(-) trap	purgeur automatique
steel	acier
(-) bloom	loupe d' (-)
(-) casting	pièce en (-) coulé
(-) pig	fonte aciéreuse
annealed (-)	(-) recuit
case hardened (-)/ cemented (-)	(-) cémenté
cold drawn (-)	(-) étiré à froid
crucible (-)	(-) au creuset
hardened (-)	(-) trempé
high speed (-)	(-) à coupe rapide
ingot (-)	lingot d' (-)
mild (-)	(-) doux
stainless (-)	(-) inoxydable
structural (-)	(-) profilé
steep	escarpé/ raide
(-) dip	pendage raide
steerable	orientable
steering	direction
(-) box	boitier de (-)
(-) lever	levier de (-)
(-) tool	indicateur de dérivation d'un forage
(-) wheel	volant de (-)
stellated structure	structure en étoile/ structure radiée
stem	tige/ queue
drilling (-)	maitresse tige/ train de (-)
valve (-)	(-) de soupape
step	marche/ gradin; phase/ stage
(-) bearing/(-) box	crapaudine/ palier de pied
(-) bit	trépan à redans
(-) fault	faille en escalier/ faille à gradins
(-) fold	pli monoclinal
stepped	étagé/ échelonné/ à gradins
(-) pulley	poulie (-)
stepping down	réduction/ démultiplication
sterile	roche stérile
stevedore	manutentionnaire
stibium	antimoine
stick	bâton/ tige
(-) friction	frottement saccadé
stickiness	collage/ gommage

sticking	coincement/grippage/ blocage	straightener	redresseur/appareil à redresser
ring (-)	collage des segments	strain	tension/fatigue/ contrainte/déformation
sticky	collant	(-) gauge	extensiomètre/jauge de déformation
stiff	raide/rigide/consistant	(-) limit	limite d'allongement
stiffener	raidissoir/contrefort/ renfort	permanent (-)	déformation permanente
		tensile (-)	effort de tension
stiffness	raideur/rigidité	strainer	tamis/filtre/crépine
still	alambic/appareil de distillation	(-) cap	bouchon-filtre
		(-) screen	tamis
stirrer	agitateur	suction (-)	crépine d'aspiration
stirring	agitation/brassage	strand	toron/brin; rivage/côte
stock	amas/réserve/provision/ stock	(-) of cable	(-) de câble
		(-) line	ancienne ligne de rivage
(-) piling	emmagasinage/stockage de réserves	central (-)	âme d'un câble
		wire (-)	toron métallique
stone	pierre/caillou	strap	courroie/ruban métallique
(-) breaker/(-) crusher	concasseur	(-) of an eccentric	collier d'excentrique
(-) lattice	structure alvéolaire	butt (-)	couvre joint
(-) river	coulée de pierres	driving (-)	courroie d'entraînement
stony	pierreux/rocailleux	strapped joint	joint à recouvrement
(-) ground	terrain rocailleux	strata	couches géologiques/ strates
stool pigeon	détecteur de conduite	disrupted (-)	(-) déchirées
stop	arrêt/interruption	overlying (-)	(-) sus-jacentes
(-) cock	robinet d' (-)	tilted (-)	(-) basculées
(-) nut	écrou de blocage	underlying (-)	(-) sous-jacentes
(-) screw	vis d' (-)	upturned (-)	(-) redressées
(-) watch	chronomètre	stratified	stratifié
stopper	bouchon/obturateur	stratigraphic	stratigraphique
stopping	arrêt	(-) break/(-) gap/	lacune (-)
(-) device	dispositif d' (-)	(-) hiatus	
stopple	bouchon temporaire d'un branchement piqué sur une conduite	(-) separation/	rejet (-)
		(-) throw	
		(-) trap	piège (-)
storage	emmagasinage	stray	égaré/errant; dispersion
(-) battery	batterie d'accumulateurs	(-) block	bloc erratique
store	magasin	(-) currents	courants vagabonds
(-) keeper	magasinier	(-) sand	lentille de sable incidentelle
stowage	arrimage	streak	bande/liséré/trainée
stowing	remblayage/remblai	stream	stream/rivière/fleuve; courant/circulation
straddle	chevauchement	(-) bed	lit de fleuve
straggling	dispersion/ dissémination	streamlet	ruisseau
straight	droit/rectiligne	streamline	courant naturel d'un fluide
(-) hole drilling/(-) well	forage vertical	(-) flow	écoulement laminaire
(-) shank drill	mèche à queue cylindrique		
(-) swivel	tête de rotation/tête d'injection		
(-) through	passage direct		

strength	force/résistance/ solidité	strut	contre-fiche/étai/ jambe de force
bending (-)	résistance à la flexion	strutting	entretoisement
breaking (-)	résistance à la rupture	stub	ergot/mentonnet; tronçon; tuyau à passage direct
dielectric (-)	rigidité diélectrique		
impact (-)	résistance au choc	(-) end	tête de bielle
shear (-)	résistance au cisaillement	stubbing	raboutage des masse-tiges
stress	effort/tension	stuck	bloqué
(-) limit	limite de fatigue	(-) bearing	palier grippé
stretch	allongement/extension	stud	tenon/tourillon/plot; montant/poteau/ entretoise; boulon/goujon
stria	rayure/strie		
strike	orientation d'une couche d'une faille; découverte d'un gisement; grève (arrêt de travail)		
		(-) bolt	boulon fileté sur sa longueur
		cylindre head (-)	boulon de culasse
string	train de tiges; veinule/ mince couche géologique; corde/ficelle	stuffing	garniture/rembourrage
		(-) box	presse-étoupe
		(-id-) gland/	garniture de presse-
(-) bead	passe étroite de soudage	(-id-) packing	étoupe
(-) of casing	colonne de tubage	sub	raccord double femelle; réduction
(-) of drill pipes/	train de tiges de forage		
(-) of rods		(-) basket	panier à sédiments
(-) of tools	chapelet d'outils	crossover (-)	réduction
fishing (-)	garniture de repêchage	kelly-saver (-)	raccord d'usure de la tige carrée
washover (-)	garniture de surforage		
stringing	alignement de tiges; bardage; mouflage	lifting (-)	tête de levage
		rotary (-)	réduction de tiges
(-) pipe	bardage des tubes	subassembly	préassemblage/sous ensemble
(-) up	mouflage		
strip	bande/ruban/feuillard	subcontracting	sous-traitance
(-) pit	carrière/exploitation à ciel ouvert	subdued	subordonné; usé/atténué
		(-) mountain	montagne à relief réduit
stripe	raie/bande/hachure		
stripping	épuisement; dépouillement/ découverture	submergence	submersion/affaissement
		subsidence	effondrement/ affaissement
(-) pipe	collecteur d'assèchement		
(-) shovel	pelle excavatrice	subsiding area	zone d'affaissement
stroke	coup; course	subsiding area	zone d'affaissement
piston (-)	course du piston	subsurface	souterrain
two (-) engine	moteur à deux temps	(-) exploration	reconnaissance du sous-sol
structural	structurel	(-) water	eau souterraine
(-) basin	cuvette synclinale	sucker rod	tige de pompage
(-) bulge	saillant anticlinal	(-) line	câble pour (-)
(-) contours	courbes de niveau	(-) sub	raccord pour (-)
(-) datum	niveau de référence	sucking	suction
(-) discordance	discordance tectonique	(-) pump	pompe aspirante
(-) iron	fer profilé	suction	aspiration
(-) relief	amplitude maximale de surélévation	(-) pit	bassin d' (-)
(-) terrace	terrasse tectonique	suds	solution savonneuse
structure	structure; constitution	sullage	limon/vase
geological (-)	(-) géologique		
imbricate (-)	(-) en écailles		
interlocked (-)	(-) entrelacée		
shut (-)	(-) en gros bancs		
slump (-)	(-) pliée		

sump	siphon/puisard/bassin à boue/fond de carter
(-) pit	puisard de vidange
(-) pump	pompe d'assèchement
wet (-)	carter à bain d'huile
supercharging	suralimentation
superincumbent/ superjacent	superposé
(-) bed	couche de toît
supply	alimentation/fourniture/ arrivée
(-) connection	raccord d'(-)
(-) line/(-) pipe	tuyau d'(-)
power (-)	source d'énergie
supporting	soutènement/support
(-) beam	solive de (-)
surface	surface/aire/ superficie
(-) casing	tube guide
(-) hardness	dureté superficielle
(-) of unconformity	(-) de discordance
(-) outcroppings	affleurements
(-) wear	usure superficielle
surfactant	agent tensio-actif
surge	surtension/saute de pression ou d'intensité
(-) chamber	chambre d'équilibre/ chambre anti-bélier
pressure (-)	à-coup de pression
survey	levé topographique; étude/examen
(-) instrument	instruments d'arpentage
(-) net	canevas topographique
(-) of heights	nivellement
geological (-)	études géologiques
surveying	prospection
(-) with chain	arpentage
geophysical (-)	(-) géophysique
surveyor	arpenteur/géomètre/ topographe
(-)'s compass	boussole topographique
(-)'s level	niveau à lunette
(-)'s stake	jalon
suspended	en suspension/flottant
suspension	suspension
(-) cable	câble de (-)/câble porteur
swab	piston râcleur/ hérisson
swaging	étampage
swallow-hole	gouffre/abîme/aven
sway	balancement/débattement transversal/oscillation
(-) brace	cornière de renforcement/ entretoise

sweep	balayage
sweet water	eau douce
sweetening	adoucissement
swell	bombement/renflement; foisonnement; houle
swelling	renflement/gonflement
(-) agent	agent gonflant
(-) clay	argile gonflante
swept volume	cylindrée/volume balayé
swing	balancement/oscillation; rotation
(-) axle	essieu oscillant
(-) crane	grue à rotation totale
(-) joint	genouillère
(-) line	câble de manoeuvre
(-) sieve	tamis oscillant
swirl	turbulence/tourbillon
switch	interrupteur/contacteur-disjoncteur
(-) board	panneau de commande/ tableau de distribution
(-) box	coffret d'(-)
(-) gear	poste de coupure
cut-out (-)	disjoncteur
float (-)	(-) à flotteur
micro (-)	microrupteur
pressure (-)	pressostat
push button (-)	(-) à boutons poussoirs
swivel	tête d'injection; pivot; émerillon
(-) bail	anse de la (-)
(-) body	corps de la (-)
(-) hook	raccord au câble/ crochet tournant
(-) joint	joint articulé
(-) rod	attache à tournant
(-) socket	tourillon
power (-)	(-) d'entraînement
synchro mesh transmission	boîte de vitesses synchronisées
synclase	fissure de retrait/ synclase
synclinal	synclinal
(-) bend	charnière (-)
(-) closure	cuvette (-)/bassin structural
(-) fold	pli synclinal
(-) limb	flanc synclinal
syncline	synclinal/pli synclinal
closed (-)	(-) fermé
pseudo (-)	faux (-)
synlube	lubrifiant synthétique

system	*système*
(-) of faults	*(-) de failles*
control (-)	*circuit de réglage*
distribution (-)	*réseau de distribution*
feeder (-)	*réseau d'alimentation*
grid (-)	*réseau de transport (électr.)*
ring main (-)	*réseau maillé*

T

table	*table/ tableau (de nombres); table de rotation; plateau/ tablier; massif; nappe*
(-) mountain	*montagne tabulaire*
rotary (-)	*table de rotation*
turn (-)	*plaque tournante*
water (-)	*nappe d'eau*
perched (-id-)	*(-id-) suspendue*
tablet	*tablette*
tabular	*plat/ aplati/ tabulaire*
tachometer	*compte-tours/ tachymètre*
tack	*semence/ petit clou; point de soudure*
(-) welding	*soudure de pointage*
tackle	*palan/ treuil/ moufle/ poulie*
(-) assembly	*appareil de levage*
(-) block	*poulie de palan*
hoisting/lifting (-)	*palan de levage*
oil (-)	*patte d'arraignée*
tacky	*adhésif/ collant/ gluant*
tag	*étiquette/ marqueur*
tail	*queue*
(-) chain	*chaine de manutention à crochet*
(-) pipe	*tuyau d'échappement*
(-) post	*support d'arbre de treuil de puisage*
(-) pulley	*poulie de retour*
(-) stock	*poupée mobile d'un tour*
to take	*prendre/ prélever/ soulever*
(-) a strain	*rattraper le jeu*
(-) down	*démonter*
(-) off	*enlever/ décoller*
take-off	*branchement/ prise latérale*
(-) post	*bras de balancier*
power (-)	*prise de force*
take-up	*tendeur*

tallow	*suif*
tally count	*comptage/ pointage*
talus	*pente d'éboulis/ talus*
tamper	*dame/ fouloir/ appareil à bourrer/ à compacter*
backfill (-)	*appareil à damer les remblais*
power (-)	*(-) mécanique*
tamping	*bourrage/ compactage/ pilonnage*
tangential	*tangentiel*
(-) thrust	*charriage (-)*
tank	*réservoir/ cuve/ citerne*
(-) bottom	*fond de (-)*
(-) capacity	*contenance/ volume d'un (-)*
feed (-)	*bâche*
sump (-)	*réservoir collecteur*
tanker	*camion ou wagon-citerne*
tap	*robinet; taraud*
box (-)	*cloche taraudée*
(-) drill	*mèche*
(-) draining (-)	*(-) de vidange*
draw-off (-)	*de puisage*
(-) thread	*taraud*
bottoming (-)	*(-) finisseur*
pin (-)	*(-) agrippeur du joint femelle (box) d'une tige*
taper	*cône/ conicité/ rétrécissement*
(-) pipe	*raccord conique*
(-) roller bearing	*palier/ roulement à rouleaux coniques*
(-) tap	*taraud fileté conique*
tappet	*taquet/ poussoir/ came*
valve (-)	*poussoir de soupape*
(-) clearance	*jeu des poussoirs*
(-) cover	*cache soupape*
tapping	*soutirage*
(-) bar	*ringard*
(-) nipple	*bague de piquage*
tar	*goudron/ brai*
(-) board	*carton goudronné*
(-) paper	*papier goudronné*
(-) pitch	*brai*
target	*cible/ mire*
(-) rod	*mire à voyant*
taring	*tarage*
tarpaulin	*bâche/ prélart/ toile cirée*
taut	*bandé/ raide/ tendu*
(-) cable	*câble tendu*
team	*équipe*

tear   *déchirement*
  (-) proof   *undéchirable*

tearing down   *démontage*

teflon   *téflon*
  (polytetrafluorethylene)

telltale   *indicateur/jauge*
  (-) lamp   *lampe témoin*

telluric   *tellurique*

temper   *trempe*
  (-) brittleness   *fragilité de revenu*
  (-) screw   *vis de rallonge*

temperature   *température*
  (-) drop   *chute de (-)*
  (-) range   *intervalle de (-)*
  (-) rise   *échauffement*
  flowline (-)   *(-) à la goulotte*
  room (-)   *(-) ambiante*

tempering   *revenu*

template   *gabarit/calibre; plaque de base/chassis de guidage*

temporary   *temporaire*
  (-) water   *eau (-)*

tensile   *(effet de) traction/ tension*
  (-) force   *force de (-)*
  (-) strength   *résistance à la traction*

tension   *tension/traction; voltage*
  (-) fault   *faille d'extension*
  (-) pulley   *poulie de (-)*
  (-) regulator   *regulator/stabilisateur de (-)*
  high (-)   *haute (-)/voltage élevé*

terminal   *borne (élect.); terminal*
  negative (-)   *(-) négative*
  positive (-)   *(-) positive*
  continental (-)   *en Afrique, couches sédimentaires de recouvrement du socle*

terrace   *terrasse*
  alluvial (-)   *(-) d'accumulation/ (-) alluviale*
  erosion   *(-) d'érosion*
  matched (-)   *(-) couplées*
  structural (-)   *replat structural*

terrain   *terrain*

test/testing   *essai/épreuve/test*
  (-) bench   *banc d' (-)*
  breaking (-)   *(-) de rupture*
  fatigue (-)   *(-) d'endurance*
  fineness (-)   *(-) granulométrique*
  field (-)   *(-) sur chantier*
  no-load (-)   *(-) de marche à vide*
  (-) piece/sample   *éprouvette/ échantillon*

texture   *texture*
  banded (-)   *(-) rubannée*
  cell (-)   *(-) cellulaire*
  lattice (-)   *(-) fenestrée*
  serrate (-)   *(-) engrenée*

thalweg   *talweg/fond de vallée*

thaw   *dégel*
  (-) depression   *dépression thermokarstique*

thermal   *thermique/ thermal*
  (-) expansion   *dilatation thermique*
  (-) value   *pouvoir calorifique*

thermocouple   *couple thermoélectrique*

thermometre   *thermomètre*
  bimetallic (-)   *(-) à bilame*

thermoplastic   *thermoplastique*

thermosetting   *thermodurcissable*

thick   *épais*
  (-) bed   *couche puissante*

thickener/thickening   *épaississeur/ épaississant*

thicket   *taillis/fourré*

thickness   *épaisseur*
  wall (-)   *(-) de parois*

thief   *échantillonneur*
  (-) formation   *formation fissurée*
  (-) sand   *sable de capture*
  (-) zone (in a well)   *zone de perte de circulation*

thimble   *cosse/oeillet de câble*

thin   *mince/clair*
  (-) film lubrication   *graissage par film (-)*
  (-) seam   *couche (-)*

thinner   *amincissant/diluant (peint.)/fludifiant (boues)*

thread   *filet/filetage*
  (-) chaser   *peigne à fileter*
  (-) depth   *profondeur de (-)*
  (-) galling   *éraillure de filetage*
  left hand (-)   *pas à gauche*
  pitch of (-)   *pas du filetage*
  (-) protector   *embout protecteur de filetage*

three
(-) phase current
(-) way cock/valve

trois
  courant triphasé
  robinet/vanne à trois
  voies

threshold

seuil/limite inférieure

throttle

(-) blade

régulateur/obturateur;
  accélérateur
papillon

throughout

capacité/consommation

throw
(-) of fault

rejet; déviation/écart
(-) de faille

throwing

lancement

thrust

ball (-)
(-) bearing

(-) ball bearing
(-) block
(-) collar

(-) fault/over (-)
(-) load/axial (-)

(-) plate

(-) ring
(-) washer

butée; poussée; faille
  anormale/faille inversée
(-) à billes
palier de (-)/
  (-) tournante
(-id-) à billes
bâti de (-)
anneau de (-)/ de
  poussée/collet de (-)
chevauchement
effort axial/poussée
  axiale
plaque de (-)/plaque
  d'ancrage
anneau de (-)
rondelle de (-)

thumbscrew

vis papillon

thump/thumping

battement/cognement/
  pilonnement

tide

marée

tideland area/
tidelands

région/terres inondables

tie

(-) bar
(-) bolt
(-) down
(-)-in weld
(-) rod
cross (-)

attache/lien/
  tirant/traverse
tirant
boulon de fondation
point d'ancrage
soudure de racordement
barre d'accouplement
tirant

tight

(-) fit
(-) formation
hand (-)
(-) hole

(-) seat
(-) side (of a
belt)

(-) spot

ajusté/assuré/bloqué/
  étanche/fixe/hermétique/
  imperméable/solide/
  tendu
emmanchement à force
formation peu poreuse
serré à la main
trou rétréci/foré avec
  un trépan usé, sous-
  dimensionné
ajustement serré
brin tendu/brin
  conducteur (d'une
  courroie)
étranglement

belt tightener

tendeur de courroie

tightening

blocage/serrage à fond

tightness

étanchéité

tilt
(-) dozer
(-) meter

basculement/inclinaison
boutoir à dévers
indicateur de pente/
  clinomètre

timber

(-) prop
(-) support
(-) trestle
(-) work

bois de charpente/
  de construction
étai en bois
soutènement en bois
échafaudage en bois
charpente en bois

time
dead (-)/down (-)
(-) setting
rig (-)/set-up (-)

temps
(-) mort
réglage
(-) de montage

timer

compteur de temps/
  dateur/minuterie

timing
(-) gear

advanced (-)
retarded (-)
valve (-)

réglage/calage
dispositif de réglage
  du temps
avance à l'allumage
retard à l'allumage
calage de la
  distribution

tin
(-) foil

(-) hat
(-) plate

étain
feuille d'étain/
  papier d'aluminium
casque de foreur
fer blanc

tintometer

colorimètre

tip

(-) bucket
(-) cart
carbide (-)
(-) up seat

extrémité/bout rapporté;
  pastille d'outil; décharge
auger/benne basculante
camion à (-id-)
pastille de carbure
siège basculant

tipping
(-) truck

basculant
camion (-)

tire/tyre

(-) casing
(-) lever
(-) patch
(-) pump
(-) tread

radial-ply (-)
spiked (-)
tubeless (-)

pneu/pneumatique/
  bandage
toile/carcasse de (-)
démonte-pneu
"rustine"/pièce
gonfleur
bande de roulement
  d'un (-)
(-) radial
(-) clouté
(-) sans chambre à air

titration

titrage/dosage

to-and-fro
movement

mouvement de
  va-et-vient

toe	bout/ pointe/ bord	torsion	torsion
(-) of weld	bord d'une soudure	(-) bar	barre de (-)
(-) wall	mur de talus	(-) fault	faille de décrochement
toggle	rotule/ articulation	total	total, totale
toll	péage/ droit de passage	(-) depth	profondeur finale (d'un puits)
tonging	opération de serrage	(-) head	perte de charge (-)
tongs	clés/ tenailles/ pinces	touchdown	contact sur le fond
back-up (-)/break-out (-)	(-) de dévissage	tough	dur/ résistant/ tenace
chain (-)	(-) à chaine/ serre-tube	tow line/towing	câble de remorquage
(-) torque indicator	(-) à indicateur de couple de serrage/ (-) dynamométrique	tow	étoupe/ filasse
insulated (-)	pinces isolantes	tower	tour/ colonne
working (-)	(-) de vissage	towing	remorquage
tongue	langue/ languette/ coulisseau	tracer	traceur/ indicateur
(-) and groove joint	emboîtement mâle et femelle	tracing	traçage/ calquage; calque/ tracé
(-) washer	rondelle de sûreté	track	chemin de roulement/ piste/ voie; chenille
tool	outil	(-) bolt	boulon d'éclisse
(-) grab	grappin de repêchage	(-) cable	câble porteur
(-) holder	porte-outil	(-) rod	barre d'accouplement
(-) jack	verin de serrage d' (-)	(-) roller	galet de chenille
(-) kit	trousse à (-)	(-) vehicle	véhicule à chenille
drilling (-)	(-) de forage		
fishing (-)	(-) de repêchage	tractor	tracteur
machine (-)	machine (-)	(-) loader	chargeuse/ pelleteuse
pneumatic (-)	(-) pneumatique	(-) shovel	pelleteuse chargeuse
tool-joint	raccord de tige	trailer	remorque/ roulotte
(-) box	boîte/ raccord femelle de tiges creuses	transformer	transformateur
		welding (-)	(-) de sondage
tool pusher	chef de chantier de forage	transient	transitoire
tools	outils/ outillage	transmission	transmission
tooth	dent d'un outil de forage	(-) constant	coefficient de perméabilité
(-) crest	crête de la (-)	(-) gear	boîte de vitesses
(-) root	racine de la (-)	transverse	transversal
top	haut/ cime/ sommet; appoint	(-) fault	faille (-)
(-) dead center	point mort haut	trap	collecteur/ récepteur/ siphon
to top-up	compléter/ rétablir le niveau/ faire un appoint	air (-)	purgeur d'air
		bucket (-)	purgeur à cloche
topsoil	terre végétale	drip (-)	siphon
torch	chalumeau/ lampe à souder/ torche	float (-)	purgeur à flotteur
		trash	déchet/ ordures/ rebut
(-) cutting	découpage au (-)	travel	avance/ course/ parcours
soldering (-)/	lampe à souder	(-) path	trajectoire
welding (-)		piston (-)	course du piston
torque	couple/ moment de torsion	traveller	curseur
(-) converter	convertisseur de (-)		
(-) motor	moteur à (-) constant		
(-) wrench	clé dynamométrique		
make-up (-)	(-) de serrage/ de vissage		

travelling	translation/ mobile
(-) block	moufle/ palan mobile; baladeur
(-) crane/bridge	pont roulant
(-) rope	câble d'entraînement du tambour
tray downspout	déversoir
tread	bande de roulement d'un pneu
treading	rechapage
treating/treatment	traitement/ épuration
(-) agents	produits de (-)
(-) plant	installation/ unité de (-)
water (-)	épuration de l'eau
trench	tranchée/ fossé/ fouille
(-) compactor	dame/ fouloir
(-) digger	excavateur de (-)
(-) excavator	excavatrice
(-) hoe	pelle rétrocaveuse
(-) shore	étrésillon
trend	axes préférentiels; tendance
(-) of a fault	direction d'une faille
trestle	chevalet/ support/ portique/ tréteau
trial	essai/ épreuve/ concours
by trial-and-error	par approximations successives
(-) run	marche d'essai
triangulation	triangulation
(-) point	point géodésique/ point de (-)
tributary	affluent/ tributaire
trickle/trickling	filet de liquide/ ruissellement/ goutte à goutte
(-) flow	écoulement ruisselant
(-) filter	filtre bactérien
(-) water	eau suintante
tricone/tricone rock bit	trépan à molettes
trigger	détente/ crochet
(-) bit	carottier à cliquet
(-) switch	interrupteur à bascule
trim	compensation/ équilibrage
trimming	arrangement/ ébarbage
(-) machine	ébarbeuse
trims/trimmings	accessoires/ garnitures/ robinetterie

trip	manoeuvre; dispositif de déclenchement
(-) casing spear	arrache-tube
(-) coil	bobine de déclenchement
tripod	trépied/ tripode
tripping	déclenchement
round (-)	manoeuvre du train de tiges/ aller retour du train de tiges
trolley	chariot/ diable/ fardier
trommel/trommel screen	crible rotatif/ trommel
trouble	panne; faille/ dislocation
(-) free	bon fonctionnement/ sans incident
(-) proof	indéréglable
(-) shooter	dépanneur
trough	auge/ bac/ cuve/ gouttière; pli synclinal/ dépression
(-) bend	charnière synclinale
(-) conveyor	transporteur à auges
fault (-)	fossé d'effondrement
trowel	taloche/ truelle
truck	camion/ chariot
(-) capacity	charge utile d'un camion
crane (-)	(-) grue
flat bed (-)	(-) à berceau surbaissé
fork (-)	chariot à fourche/ transpalette
fork lift (-)	chariot élévateur à fourche
hand (-)	diable
off highway (-)	(-) tous terrains
true	véritable/ réel
(-) bore	calibré
(-) dip	pendage réel
truncated	tronqué/ arasé/ émoussé
troncation	troncature
trunk	coffre; tronc
(-) line	conduite principale
trunnion	tourillon
truss	bâti/ support/ traverse
try	essai
tsunami (seismic surge)	vague de fond d'origine sismique
tub	baquet/ cuffat/ cuve

tube	tube/ tuyau
(-) bundle	faisceau de (-)
(-) clamp	serre (-)
(-) cutter	coupe (-)
(-) expander	dudgeon/ mandrin d'expansion
(-) extractor	extracteur de (-)
(-) fittings	raccords de tuyauterie
(-) hanger	support de (-)
(-) joint	raccord de tuyau
(-) packing	bague d'étanchéité
(-) wrench	clé à (-)
tubing	tube/ tiges/ colonne de production/ colonne montante
(-) anchor	fixation de la colonne de production/ de la colonne montante
(-) catcher	mâchoires de suspension/ appareil de repêchage
(-) packer	garniture d'étanchéité
(-) spear	arrache-tube
(-) spider	table ouvrante
(-) tong	clé de serrage
tubular	tubulaire
(-) drill	cloche/ cuiller/ soupape
(-) shaft	arbre creux
tug rim	poulie d'entraînement à gorge
tumbler	culbuteur
(-) switch	interrupteur à bascule
turbid	trouble/ épais/ opaque
turbidimeter	opacimètre/ turbidimètre
turbidity	opacité/ turbidité
turbine	turbine
(-) pump	turbopompe
flush (-)	(-) de forage
turbocharger/ turboblower	turbo soufflante
turbo compressor	turbo compresseur
turbo drill	turbo foreuse
turbo drilling	turboforage
turn	tour/ révolution; spire
(-) plate/(-) table	table de rotation; plaque tournante
left hand (-)	rotation à gauche
right hand (-)	rotation à droite
rough (-) (on a lathe)	chariotage d'ébauchage (sur un tour)
smooth (-)	chariotage de finition (-id-)
turnbuckle	ridoir/ tendeur à vis

turpentine/turps/ turpentine oil	térébenthine/ essence de térébenthine
turret	tourelle
(-) lathe	tour revolver
twin	jumelé/ conjugué; maclé
(-) engine	moteur à deux cylindres
(-) lead cable	câble à deux brins
twine	ficelle
twist	tors/ torsion
(-) drill	foret hélicoïdal/ foret américain
twistoff	cassure/ rupture
twisted	tordu/ torsadé
twisting moment	couple de torsion

U

U-bend	coude en U/ raccord en U
U-bolt	étrier fileté
upper dead center (udc)	point mort haut
UHF (ultra high frequency)	très haute fréquence
U-iron/U-shaped iron	poutrelle/ profilé en U
ullage	espace d'un réservoir non occupé par le contenu
ultimate	ultime/ final/ limite
(-) load	charge limite
(-) resistance	résistance (-)
(-) stress	tension de rupture
ultrafiltration	ultrafiltration
unbalance	balourd/ déséquilibre/ équilibre instable
dynamic (-)	balourd dynamique
unbedded deposit	dépôt non stratifié
unbreakable	incassable
uncased	non tubé
uncoiling	déroulement/ dévidement
unconfined	sans limite/ libre
(-) aquifer/	nappe phréatique/
(-) groundwater	nappe libre
unconformable	discordant
unconformity	lacune/ discordance stratigraphique

unconsolidated	*boulant/ meuble/ non-consolidé*	unused	*inutilisé*
(-) formation	*formation non consolidée*	unweathered	*non altéré/ inaltéré*
(-) sand	*sable boulant*	unwieldy	*lourd/ peu maniable*
uncovered	*découvert/ dénudé*	unworkable	*inexploitable/ non rentable*
unctuous	*onctueux*	updating	*mise à jour*
(-) clay	*argile grasse*	upfault	*faille inverse*
undercut	*affouillement/ sape/ sous-cavage*	uplift	*exhaussement/ soulèvement*
underground	*souterrain (e)/ enterré*	upper	*supérieur*
(-) cable	*câble (-)/ câble enterré*	(-) bed	*couche (-)/ couche du toit*
(-) corrosion	*corrosion (-)*	(-) layer	*couche de couverture*
(-) drainage	*drainage (-)*	(-) leaf	*partie supérieure de la couche*
undergrowth	*broussailles*	upright	*vertical/ debout; montant*
underlay	*inclinaison*	upset	*refoulement; bouleversement*
underlying	*sous-jacent*	(-) end	*bout refoulé*
(-) rock	*soubassement/ bedrock*	(-) pipe	*tube à extrêmités refoulées*
undermining	*affouillement/ entaillement/ sapement/ sous-cavage*	(-) welding	*soudage par refoulement*
under reamer	*élargisseur*	upstream	*en amont*
undersize	*refus du crible/ déclassé*	upstroke	*course montante*
under thrust	*sous-chariage*	upswelling	*bombement/ gonflement/ renflement*
undisturbed	*non disloqué/ non pertubé*	uptake	*montée; colonne montante*
uneven	*irrégulier/ inégal*	upthrow	*rejet/ côté relevé/ masse chevauchée*
unfavorable	*contraire/ défavorable*	upthrust	*soulèvement*
(-) wind	*vent (-)*	upturning	*rebroussement/ déferlement d'une nappe*
unglazed	*non vernissé*	upward	*ascendant/ montant*
(-) porcelain	*porcelaine poreuse*	(-) stroke	*course montante d'un piston*
unindurated	*non consolidé*	upwelling	*remontée d'eau*
union/union coupling	*raccord-union/ raccord 3 pièces*	urinal	*urinoir*
unit	*unité; installation/ appareil*	useful	*utile*
(-) of measurement	*(-) de mesure*	(-) elastic limit	*limite élastique*
compressor (-)	*compresseur/ installation de compression*	useless	*inutile*
universal	*universel*	utilities	*services publics (eau/ gaz/ électricité/ air comprimé/ chauffage urbain)*
(-) joint	*joint de cardan/ joint (-)*	utilization	*utilisation/ exploitation/ usage*
unloading	*déchargement*	UV	*ultra violet*
(-) rack	*porte de (-)*		
unmatched	*désassorti/ inégalé*		
unracking	*dégerbage*		
unreactive	*inerte*		
unserviceable	*inutilisable*		
unslaked lime	*chaux vive*		
unstable	*instable*		

V

V-belt	*courroie trapézoïdale*
(-) drive	*entraînement/commande par (-)*
(-) sheave	*poulie à (-)*
vacancy	*lacune*
vacuum	*vide*
vadose water	*eau d'infiltration*
valley	*vallée*
anticlinal (-)	*(-) anticlinale*
(-) floor	*fond (plat) de vallée/ plaine alluviale*
(-) outcrop	*affleurement de (-)*
(-) spring	*source de thalweg*
(-) wall	*versant d'une (-)*
collapse (-)/rift (-)	*(-) d'effondrement*
destructional (-)	*(-) d'érosion*
structural (-)/	*(-) tectonique/*
constructional (-)	*(-) structurale*
valve	*soupape/vanne/ clapet/robinet*
(-) adjustment	*réglage de (-)*
(-) body	*corps de (-)/robinet/ clapet*
(-) box	*boîte à clapet/ boitier de clapet/ chapelle*
(-) cage	*corbeille/cage de clapet/boîte de soupape*
(-) cap	*bouchon de valve*
(-) chamber	*boîte/chapelle*
(-) clearance	*jeu des (-)*
(-) cock	*robinet vanne*
(-) cut off	*clapet de vanne*
(-) face	*portée de (-)*
(-) flapper	*clapet de vanne*
(-) grinding	*rôdage de (-)*
(-) head/(-) disc	*tête de (-)*
(-) insert	*corbeille de (-)*
(-) lever	*culbuteur/linguet de (-)*
(-) lifter	*poussoir de (-)*
(-) needle	*aiguille de pointeau*
(-) plug	*pointeau/opercule de vanne/boisseau*
(-) rocker/(-) rocker arm	*culbuteur/linguet de (-)*
(-) rod	*queue de (-)*
(-) seat	*siège de (-)*
(-id-) insert/ring	*siège rapporté de (-)*
(-) spindle/spear/ stem	*queue de (-)*
(-) taffet	*poussoir de (-)*
automatic (-)	*(-) automatique*
back circulating (-)	*(-) de circulation inverse*
bailer (-)	*clapet de soupape*
ball (-)	*vanne à boulet/à bille*
blow off (-)	*vanne/robinet de purge*

breather (-)	*reniflard*
butterfly (-)	*robinet à papillon*
check (-)	*clapet de retenue/ clapet anti retour*
cock (-)	*robinet à boisseau*
diaphragm (-)	*robinet à membrane/ à diaphragme*
drain (-)/drain off (-)	*vanne de purge/vanne de vidange*
exhaust (-)	*(-) d'échappement*
float (-)	*(-) à flotteur*
foot (-)	*crépine d'aspiration*
globe (-)	*robinet à (-)/(-) à boulet*
inlet/intake (-)	*(-) d'admission*
master (-)	*vanne maîtresse*
plug (-)/ball plug (-)	*vanne/robinet à boissau*
pressure reducing (-)	*détendeur*
pressure relief (-)	*(-) de décharge.*
relief (-)/safety (-)	*(-) de sûreté*
shut off (-)/stop (-)	*vanne d'arrêt*
van	*camionnette/fourgon*
vane	*ailette (de turbine)/ palette/aube*
vapor	*vapeur*
(-) barrier	*écran pare-vapeur*
(-) lock	*bouchon de (-)*
(-) permeability	*perméabilité à la (-)*
(-) pressure	*tension de (-)*
(-id-) lamp	*lampe à pétrole à pression*
variable	*variable*
(-) displacement pump	*pompe à débit variable*
variation	*variation/variante; déclinaison magnétique*
abnormal (-)	*anomalie magnétique*
variegated	*bariolé/bigarré*
(-) sandstone	*grès bigarré*
varnish	*vernis/laque*
vehicle	*véhicule/voiture*
tracked (-)	*(-) à chenille*
wheeled (-)	*(-) sur roues*
velocity	*vitesse*
mud-return (-)	*(-) de circulation de la boue*
veneer	*plaquage/feuille de plaquage*
vent	*évent/prise d'air*
(-) pipe	*tuyau d'aération*
ventilating duct	*gaine d'aération*
vertex	*sommet d'une courbe*

vesicular	*vacuolaire*
vessel	*récipient/ vase/ réservoir*
vibrator	*vibreur/ vibrateur*
vibro driving	*vibrofonçage*
view	*vue*
cutaway (-)	*(-) écorchée*
front (-)	*élévation/(-) de face*
sectional (-)	*(-) en coupe*
top (-)	*(-) en plan*
(-) tube	*tube de visée*
VIP latrine (ventilated improved pit latrine)	*latrine améliorée auto ventilée*
viscosity	*viscosité*
viscous	*visqueux*
vise	*étau*
(-) jaws	*mâchoires d'étau/ mordaches*
parallel (-)	*(-) à mors parallèle*
pipe (-)	*(-) à tube*
vision panel	*panneau de visite*
visor	*visière/ regards*
visual examination	*examen à l'oeil nu*
void	*vide/ pore/ interstice/ bulle*
(-) space	*espace interstitiel*
volcanic	*volcanique*
(-) flow	*coulée de lave*
(-) pile	*cône (-)*
(-) plug	*bouchon (-)*
voltage	*tension*
(-) drop	*chute de (-)*
(-) regulator	*stabilisateur de (-)*
primary (-)	*(-) d'amorçage*
voltaic	*voltaïque*
voltmetre	*voltmètre*
volume	*volume*
specific (-)	*volume massique*
swept (-)	*cylindrée*
volumetric	*volumétrique*
(-) efficiency	*rendement (-)*
volute	*diffuseur/ volute*
vortex	*tourbillon*

W

W (watt)	*watt*
wad/wadding	*tampon/ bourre/ étoupe*
wainscoting	*boisage/ cloisonnage/ lambris*
walking beam	*balancier/ levier de battage*
(-) pump	*pompe à (-)*
(-) saddle	*selle du (-)*
walkway	*passerelle*
wall	*mur/ paroi; lèvre d'une faille*
(-) face	*front de taille*
(-) hook	*caracole/ sifflet de repêchage*
(-) sample	*carotte latérale*
(-) scraper	*élargisseur rotatif*
(-) thickness	*épaisseur de paroi*
walled-up	*maçonné/ colmaté*
wandering	*migration*
warehouse	*entrepôt/ magasin*
warming up	*réchauffement/ mise en température*
warning	*avertissement*
(-) light	*voyant lumineux/ lampe-témoin*
warping	*gauchissement/ gondolement*
wash	*lavage; badigeonnage*
rain (-)	*ruissellement diffus*
rill (-)	*ruissellement en filets*
sheet (-)/surface (-)	*ruissellement en nappes*
washer	*rondelle; laveur/ décanteur*
lock (-)	*(-) frein*
sealing (-)	*(-) d'étanchéité*
shakeproof (-)	*(-) non desserrable*
spring (-)	*(-) élastique*
washing	*lavage; affouillement*
(-) soda	*carbonate de sodium/ de soude*
washlands	*terres inondables*
washout	*ravinement*
washover	*surforage*
(-) pipe/(-) tube	*tube de (-)*
(-) shoe	*couronne de (-)*

waste	déchet/résidu; perte/ rebut	wax	paraffine/cire
(-) disposal	évacuation/élimination des déchets	earth (-)	cire minérale
(-) dump/(-) tip	terril/décharge publique	wear/wear & tear	usure
(-) recovery	récupération des déchets	(-) bushing	fourrure de protection
(-) rocks	stériles	gauge (-)	perte de diamètre de l'outil (par usure)
(-) water	eaux résiduelles		
household (-)	ordures ménagères	(-) plate	plaque de protection
industrial (-)	déchet industriel	normal (-)	usure normale
wasting	gaspillage	weather	temps
water	eau	weathered	altéré/désagrégé
(-) bearing/	aquifère/formation	weathering	altération due aux agents atmosphériques
(-id-) formation	aquifère		
(-) cement	ciment hydraulique	mechanical (-)	désagrégation mécanique
(-) hammer	coup de bélier	web	âme d'une poutre/nervure
(-) hardening	trempe à l'(-)		
(-) hardness	dûreté de l'(-)	wedge	coin/cale/biseau
(-) harvesting	collecte d'(-) de pluie	(-) key	clé de serrage
(-) piping	conduite d'(-)	(-) ring	collier à coins
(-) proof	imperméable à l'(-)		
(-) repellent	hydrofuge	weight	poids/charge
(-) seal	joint hydraulique	(-) on bit (wob)	poids sur l'outil
(-) softening	adoucissement de l'(-)	breaking (-)	charge de rupture
(-) supply	approvisionnement en (-)	clump (-)	gueuse
(-) swivel	tête d'injection	dead (-)	(-) mort
(-) tight	étanche à l'(-)	empty (-)	(-) à vide
(-) tower	château d'(-)		
(-) treatment plant	station d'épuration	gross vehicle weight (GVW)	poids total roulant
(-) well	puits d'(-)		
(-) wheel	roue à (-)	weighted	pondéré/lesté/taré
artesian (-)	(-) artésienne	(-) average	moyenne pondéré
attached (-)	(-) connexe		
bound (-)	(-) liée	weir	déversoir/barrage
brackish (-)	(-) saumâtre		
confined ground (-)	(-) captive	weld	soudure
connate (-)	(-) connée	back (-)	(-) sur l'envers
filtered (-)	(-) filtrée	(-) bead/(-) seam	cordon de (-)
flush (-)	eau de rinçage	butt (-)	(-) bout à bout
grey(-)	(-) grasses/(-) (eaux usées domestiques provenant du lavage de la vaisselle et ustensiles de cuisine)	(-) crack	soufflure de (-)
		fillet (-)	(-) d'angle
		flash (-)	(-) par étincelage
		lap (-)	(-) à clin/(-) par recouvrement
ground (-)	(-) souterraine	(-) metal	métal d'apport
(-id-) run off	écoulement souterrain	seal (-)	(-) d'étanchéité
(-id-) table	nappe phréatique	spot (-)	(-) par point
hard (-)	(-) dure		
native (-)	(-) connée/(-) incluse/ (-) d'origine	welder	soudeur
rain (-)	(-) de pluie	welding	soudage
raw (-)	(-) brute/(-) non traitée	arc (-)	(-) à l'arc
		autogenous (-)	(-) autogène
waste (-)	(-) usée	(-) burner	chalumeau à souder
		(-) clamp	bride de (-)
waterfall	chute d'eau	(-) électrodes	électrodes de (-)
		(-) goggles	lunettes de (-)
watering	arrosage	(-) leads	câbles d'alimentation
		(-) machine/(-) set	machine à souder
watershed	ligne de partage des eaux	(-) rod	baguette d'apport
		(-) shield	bouclier de (-)
wave	onde/vague	(-) tongs	pinces à souder
wavy	ondulé		

well	*puits/forage*	winch	*treuil de levage*
(-) casing	*tubage/revêtement*	(-) barrel	*tambour de (-)*
(-) cleaning tools	*outils de curage*	crane (-)	*(-) de grue*
(-) location	*emplacement du forage*	crank (-)/hand (-)	*(-) à main/à manivelle*
(-) logging	*diagraphie*		
(-) site	*chantier de forage*	wind	*vent*
(-) workover	*reconditionnement*	(-) deposit/	
	des puits	(-) sediment	*dépot éolien*
abandonned (-)	*(-) abandonné*	(-) dial/(-) gage	*anémomètre*
bare footed (-)	*(-) non tubé*	(-) mill	*moulin à (-)*
depleted (-)	*(-) épuisé*	(-) shield/(-) screen	*pare-brise*

well head	*tête de puits*	winding	*enroulement/bobinage*

wet	*humide*	wind lass	*cabestan/guindeau/treuil*
(-) bulb temperature	*température de bulbe humide*		
		wing	*aile*
		(-) nut	*écrou à papillon*
		(-) pump	*pompe à ailette*

wetstone	*pierre à aiguiser*	wire	*fil/fil métallique*
		barbed (-)	*fil de fer barbelé*
wettability	*mouillabilité*	(-) clamp	*collier de fil de fer*
		(-) cloth/(-) gauze	*toîle métallique*
wetting	*humidification/mouillage*	fuse (-)	*fusible*
(-) agent	*agent mouillant*	live (-)	*fil sous tension*

wheel	*roue*	wireline	*câble de forage*
(-) barrow	*brouette*	(-) clamp/wire	
(-) ditcher	*trancheuse à (-)*	rope clamp	*serre-câble*
(-) flutter	*flottement des (-)*	(-) cutter/wire	
(-) hop	*débattement de la (-)*	rope knife	*coupe-câble*
(-) hub	*moyeu de (-)*	(-) wiper	*essuie-câble*
(-) rim	*jante de (-)*		
(-) wobble	*flottement des (-)*	wire rope	*câble métallique*
abrasive (-)	*meule abrasive*		
band/belt (-)	*poulie pour courroie*	wiring	*câblage*
chain (-)	*poulie à chaîne*	(-) diagram	*schéma de (-)*
driving (-)	*(-) motrice*	withdrawal of casing	*extraction des tubes*
fly (-)	*volant d'inertie*		
hand (-)	*volant (de manoeuvre)*	wobble	*flottement*
idle (-)	*(-) libre/folle/*		
	poulie folle	woodwork	*charpente*
paddle (-)	*(-) à aubes*		
ratchet (-)	*(-) à rochet*	wool	*laine*
sprocket (-)	*pignon de chaîne*	cotton (-)	*ouate*
spur (-)	*(-) dentée*	glass (-)	*(-) de verre*
steering (-)	*volant de direction*		
worm (-)	*roue à vis sans fin*	working	*marche/fonctionnement/*
			exploitation/travail
whitewash	*badigeon/lait de chaux*	(-) depth capacity	*profondeur limite de*
			travail du trépan
whiting	*blanc d'Espagne*	(-) load	*charge de service*
		(-) order	*état/ordre de marche*
Whitworth thread	*filetage/pas de*	(-) pressure	*pression de régime/*
	Whitworth		*pression de marche*
		(-) speed	*vitesse de régime*

wick	*mèche*	workover	*reconditionnement*
(-) feed lubricator	*graisseur par (-)*	(-) rig	*chèvre/derrick/*
			trépied de (-)

wide	*large*	worm	*vis sans fin*
(-) meshed	*à grosse mailles*	(-) gear	*engrenage à (-)*
		(-) wheel	*roue tangente/*
wiggle	*agitation*		*roue à (-)*
(-) stick	*balancier; baguette de sourcier*		
		worn	*usé*
wildcat	*forage de reconnaissance*	(-) out	*complètement (-)*

wrapping — revêtement/ enrobage
  (-) tape — bande de (-)/ couvre joint

wrecking — sauvetage
  (-) truck — camion de dépannage

wrench — clé
  adjustable (-) — (-) à molette
  box (-)/socket (-) — (-) à douille
  chain (-) — (-) à chaîne
  monkey (-) — (-) anglaise/ (-) à molette
  pipe (-) — (-) à tube
  ratchet (-) — (-) à rochet/ à cliquet
  tap (-) — tourne à gauche

wrinkling — plissement/ gauchissement

wrist — tourillon
  (-) pin — axe de piston
  (-id-) bushing — douille d' (-id-)

wrought — forgé

wye connection — montage en étoile

X

X bit — taillant/ trépan en croix

X rays — rayons X

X lab — abréviation pour laboratoire expérimental

Y

Y branch — té oblique/ tubulure oblique
Y-connection/ Y-grouping — montage en étoile (électr.)

yank — secousse donnée à une corde coincée

yard — unité de longueur anglo saxonne; cour/ chantier/ dépôt/ parc
  (-) stick — instrument de mesure/ référence
  water (-) — ensemble moto-pompe/ réservoir alimentant une bourgade rurale

yarn — fil textile
  cabled (-) — fil câblé

yield — rendement/ production/ débit

yielding — élasticité/ déformation/ rendement

yoke — collier de raccordement

Z

zenith — zenith

zeolite — zéolite
  (-) process — adoucissement de l'eau (par zéolites)

zero — zéro
  (-) adjustment/ (-) setting — réglage à (-)/ mise à (-)

zinc — zinc

zincification/ zincing/ zincking — zingage/ galvanisation

zone — zone/ plage/ région
  (-) of brecciation — (-) de brèche
  (-) of faulting — (-) de faille
  (-) of lost returns — (-) de pertes de circulation
  (-) of weathering — (-) d'altérations
  fault (-) — (-) de failles
  vadose (-) — (-) de l'eau d'infiltration

Terminologie de l'approvisionnement en eau et de l'assainissement du milieu

Français—anglais

A

abaisseur — depressant

abandonné — derelict

abaque — calculation chart

abattant — flap
siège (-) — tilting seat/toilet seat

abattage — blasting

abime — chasm

about/aboutement — butt/scarfing

abrasion — abrasion
(-) éolienne — wind (-)

abri — cab/shelter

abrupt — scarped

accessoires de tuyauterie — fittings

accident — accident/mishaps
(-) de terrain — ground irregularity

accouplement — clutch; coupling
(-) élastique — flexible coupling

accrochage — grappling; scaffold
(repêchage)

accrocheur de repêchage — latch jack/grab/grab iron

accumulateur (électr.) — battery

activité respiratoire (d'une boue résiduaire) — respiratory activity (of sludge)

additif — additive/agent
(-) anti-mousse — defoamer/defoaming agent

adduction — adduction/conveying/piping of water

adoucissement — softening
(-) par échange de cations — (-) by cation exchange
(-) à la chaux (essai) — (-) lime softening (test)
(-) des eaux — water (-)

adsorption — adsorption
(-) sur charbon actif — (-) by activated carbon

aérateur de surface (eaux résiduaires) — surface aerator (waste water)

aération des eaux de consommation — aeration of water supplies
(-) des eaux résiduaires — (-) of waste water

affaissement — depression/downthrow/sag/settling/submergence/subsidence

affilé — sharp
tranchant (-) — fine edge

affleurement — outcrop/blow/surface outcroppings
(-) masqué — concealed/buried (-)
(-) de faille — fault (-)
(-) du fond — fanning the bottom of the well, drilling lightly to avoid a deviation

affluent — tributary river

affouillement — undermining/undercut/scour/scouring

affût — frame/stand/mounting

affûtage (d'un outil) — dressing (of a tool)/sharpening

affûteuse — grinder

agent — agent/factor; assistant
(-) mouillant — wetting (-)
(-) technique — technical assistant
(-) désémulsionnant — demulsifier
(-) d'étanchéité — sealant
(-) tension-actif — surfactant

agglomérat — conglomerate
(-) non consolidés — unindurated aggregates

agglomérant — binder

aggloméré — sintered

agrafe de courroie — belt clamp

agrandissement — magnification

agrégat — aggregate
(-) grossier poreux — open-graded (-)

aggressivité carbonique — agressivity of carbonic acid

aigu — sharp

aiguisage — sharpening

aile (de cornière) — leg (of angle)

ailette — fin/paddle
tube à (-) — (-) tube

ailerons — fins

aimant — magnet
(-) de repêchage — fishing (-)
(-id-) à carottier — core (-id-)

air	air	*analyses de contrôle*	analysis of water
(-) aspiré	intake (-)	*(-) bactériologiques*	bacteriological (-)
(-) de balayage	scavenging (-)		
(-) comprimé	compressed (-)	*ancienneté*	seniority
(-) de refoulement	discharge (-)		
		ancrage	fastening/anchorage
aire	area/surface	*(-) du haubannage*	guy anchor
(-) continentale	continental (-)		
(-) d'érosion	(-) of truncation	*angle*	angle
		(-) de déviation	deviation (-)
ajustage	fit	*(-) d'inclinaison*	(-) of dip
		ou de pendage	
ajustement	smoothing/setting	*(-) d'inclinaison*	hade of fault
		d'une faille	
ajusteur	fitter	*(-) d'incidence d'un*	bottom rake
		outil	
alcalin	alkaline		
		angulaire	angular/angle
alésage	bore (of a cylinder);	*retard (-)*	delay angle
	reaming		
		annuaire	directory
aléseur	reamer		
(-) pour tubage	casing scraper	*anticlinal*	anticline
		(-) affleurant	exposed (-)
alimentation	feed	*(-) allongé*	elongated (-)
(-) par gravité	gravity (-)	*(-) asymétrique*	asymmetric (-)
		(-) complexe	composite (-)
allure	rating; speed	*(-) déversé*	overturned (-)
(-) tectonique	tectonic features	*(-) droit*	erect (-)
		(-) renversé	recumbent (-)
alliage	alloy	*(-) tronqué*	arrested (-)
(-) coulé sous	die cast (-)		
pression		*antimoine*	stibium
allumage	firing/ignition	*appareil respiratoire*	SCUBA (self-contained
retour d'(-)	back (-)	*autonome de plongée*	underwater breathing
		sous-marine	apparatus)
alluvion	alluvium/deposit		
(-) côtières	coastal deposits	*appareillage*	device/equipment
(-) glaciaires	glacial till	*(-) de contrôle*	control (-)
		(-) enregistreur	recording (-)
altération	deterioration/	*(-) de serrage*	clamping (-)
	weathering		
		appentis	shed/lean-to
couverture d'(-)	overburden/		
	weathered layer	*apport*	drift/deposit; influx
		(-) d'oxygène	oxygen input
altérites	(-id-)		
		par approximations	by trial-and-error
amas	cluster	*successives*	
âme d'un câble/	filling	*aquifère*	aquifer/water bearing
d'un cordage			formation/ground water
			reservoir
amont	upstream	*couche (-)*	(-id-)
(-) pendage	updip	*(-) perchée*	perched (-)
amolissant	softening agent	*arable (terre)*	top soil
amortisseur	shock absorber/buffer/	*araignée*	oil tackle
	bumper/snubber; damper/	*patte d'(-)*	oil groove
	dashpot		
		arbre	shaft/axle/spindle;
(-) de moufle fixe	crown block bumper		tree
(-id-) mobile	traveling bloc bumper	*(-) moteur ou*	drive (-)
(-) de sautes de	surge damper	*d'entraînement*	
pression		*(-) entraîné ou*	driven (-)
		conduit	
amovible	detachable/removable	*(-) cannelé*	splined (-)
		(-) creux	tubular shaft
analyse des	sample examination	*(-) principal*	line/main (-)
carottes			

arènes	grit
arénage	sandy
arête	crest/ridge; edge
(-) anticlinale	anticlinal (-)
(-) synclinale	trough line
argile	clay
(-) à blocaux	boulder (-)
(-) à silex	flint (-)
(-) colloïdale	colloidal/burned (-)
(-) de faille	fault gouge
(-) gonflante	swelling (-)
(-) gypsifère	anhydritic shale
(-) limoneuse	(-) loam
(-) litée	bedded (-)
(-) plastique	bearing clay
(-) sableuse	sandy shale
(-) schisteuse	shale
(-) stratifiée	laminated shale
aride	arid
arm	bras
rocker (-)	brinquebale
aronde	dove
(assemblage) en queue d' (-)	dovetail/dove-tailed (mounting)
arrache-câble	rope spear/rope grab
arrache-cuvelage	casing spear/casing ring and slips/pulling jar
arrache-tube	tubing spear/bell socket/bull spear
(-) à mâchoires	spider bushing and slips
arrêt	stop off
marche (-)	on-off
arrière-plan	background
arrimage	stowage
assainissement	sanitation
assèchement	drainage/dewatering/ pumping-out
pompe d' (-)	dewatering pump
assemblage	assembly
(-) à mi-bois	scarf
(-) en sifflet	scarfing joint
assise	base
assurance	dependability; insurance
atelier	workshop
(-) de mécanique	machine shop
(-) de forage	drilling rig
attache	tie/clip/fastener
(-) câble	rope/wire line socket

aubage (d'un compresseur)	blading (of a compressor)
(-) d'entrée	inducer
(-) de sortie	exducer
auge	trough/basin
auget	bucket
(-) de noria	elevator bucket
auto	self
(-) démarreur	(-) starter
(-) excitation	(-) excitation
(-) graissage	(-) lubrication
(-) moteur	(-) propelled
(-) nettoyant	(-) cleaning
(-) réglable	(-) adjustable
(-) régulation	(-) regulating
auto élévatrice à nacelle	cherry-picker/ monopod jack up
auto-épuration/ auto-purification	self-purification
automatique	automatique
à amorçage (-)	self-priming
à fermeture (-)	self-closing
semi (-)	semi (-)
autonome	self contained
auxiliaire	secondary
aval	downstream
(-) pendage	down dip
avalanche	avalanche/labor
avancement	feeding/feed/footage
vitesse d' (-)	rate of penetration/ drilling
avant-projet	draft/draft study
avant-trou	pilot hole
avarie	breakdown/damage
axe	axle/spindle/gudgeon pin/pin; axis
(-) anticlinal	anticlinal axis/saddle axis
(-) d'un crystal	(-) of crystal
(-) de piston	wrist pin
(-) de plissement	fold (-)
(-) plongeant	plunging/pitching (-)
(-) synclinal	trough (-)

B

bac	tank/vat
(-) à boue	mud pit
(-) de décantation	settling vat/ decantation tank
(-) de récupération des boues	sample trough

bâche tarpaulin; tank
  (-) d'alimentation   feed tank

bactériophage bacteriophage

badigeon white wash

bague collar/ring/bushing
  (-) coulissante   sliding (-)
  (-) d'écartement   spacing bush
  (-) de piquage   tapping nipple
  (-) de presse-étoupe   packing gland
  (-) de suspension   cable ring

baguette d'apport welding rod
  de soudure

baguette de divining rod/wiggle
  sourcier   stick

baignoire bathtub

bain bath

baisse decline

baladeur traveling block
  pignon (-)   sliding gear

balai brush
  (-) électrique   snitcher

balance scale/balance
  (-) à boue   mud balance

balancement swinging/rocking

balancier pendulum/beam
  (-) de battage   spudder/rocker beam/
    walking beam
  (-) à contrepoids   balance bob
  (-) de pompe   pumping beam

balayage scanning; scavenging/
  sweep

balourd unbalance

banc bed/bank

bande tape; strip; band;
  streak
  (-) d'enregistrement   recording tape
  (-) de terrain   strip of ground
  (-) d'absorption   absorption band

baquet tub/vat

barbotage bath
  graissage par (-)   (-) lubrication

bardage de pipe stringing
  canalisation

bardeau shingle board/lath;
  shingle
  revêtement en (-)   shingle lining

baril barrel

barillet barrel/drum
  (-) de stockage des   drill pipe carrousel
  tiges

barre bar/rod; rail
  (-) d'attelage/ de   draw bar
  traction
  (-) de glissière   rail
  (-) de surcharge   sinker bar

barrière de permeability barrier
  perméabilité

basculement tilt/tilting
  (-) des couches   (-) of strata

base (topographique) base line
  (-) de données   data base

bas-fond shallows

bassin basin; bowl/pan;
  reservoir; pit/pond
  (-) d'aspiration de   mud suction pit
  boue de forage
  (-) combiné pour   combined tank for
  eaux résiduaires   activated sludge
  (-) de décantation   settling pond
  (-) d'effondrement   fault basin
  (-) fluvial/   river basin
  (-) versant
  (-) hydrographique   drainage (-)
  (-) hydrogéologique   groundwater (-)
  (-) structural   synclinal closure

bâti frame/bedplate/skids

bâton stick

battage hammering/jarring/
  percussion
  (-) au câble   percussion drilling/
    spudding

batterie storage battery
  d'accumulateurs

batteur beater; jar

baume salve

battage beating

bec spout/nozzle/mouthpiece
  (-) de déversement   snout
  (-) verseur   pouring spout

bêche skirt

bédane chisel

bélier hydraulique hydraulic ram/hydram

benne bucket/tub/hopper
  (-) automatique   clamshell bucket
  (-) de creusement   sinking (-)
  (-) foreuse   hammer grab
  (-) preneuse   clamshell/grab/
    bucket grab
  (-) à traction   dragline bucket

béquille prop/stanchion/leg

berceau de bearer plates (of an
  moteur   engine)

béton	concrete
(-) armé	reinforced (-)
(-) précontraint	prestressed (-)
(-) projeté	shot (-)
bétonnière	concrete mixer
bichromate	dichromate
bielle	connecting rod/push rod
(-) de balancier d'une sondeuse au battage	pitman
tête de (-)	big end
pied de (-)	small end
bifurcation	fork/forking/branch
(-) des eaux	water-partition
bigorne (d'une enclume)	bickern (of an anvil)
bilan	balance; balance sheet; statement of affairs
(-) de l'eau souterraine	ground water balance
bille	ball
biseau	wedge/edge/bevel
blindage	sheeting/shield/shroud
bloc	block/stone/clump
(-) basculé	tipped block
(-) charrié	overthrust (-)
(-) continental	continental (-)
coulée de (-)	boulder stream
(-) couronne à poulies multiples	scatter sheave crown
(-) de dévissage	breakout (-)
(-) de pierre roulée/ (-) émoussée	boulder
(-) erratique	drift boulder/ perched block
(-) faillé	fault block
(-) soulevé	up thrown (-)
bobine	spool/reel/coil
(-) d'allumage	ignition coil/spark coil
boisage	shoring
bois massif	solid wood
boîte	box/case
(-) à bornes	junction (-)/ connecting (-)
(-) à boue	mud box
(-) de dérivation	branching (-)
(-) d'engrenages	gear case/gear shift
(-) à garniture	packing gland
(-) de jonction	cable box
(-) de vitesses	gearbox
bombement	belly; swell
(-) anticlinal	anticlinal bulge
bombonne	carboy
bonde	bung/plug
bord	brim
bordure	border/fringe/rim/ skirting
borne	landmark/boundary stone
(-) électrique	terminal/binding post
(-) à vis	binding screw
bossellement	dent
bouchage	stoppage/clogging
(-) au sable	sand packing
bouche	mouth/opening; estuary (river)
(-) d'égout	sewer opening
(-) d'incendie	fire hydrant
bouché	clogged
bouchon	plug/stopper/cap/blank
(-) de cimentation	cementing plug
(-) filtre	strainer cap
(-) fusible	safety cap
(-) obturateur	plug/blanking sleeve
(-) de remplissage	filler cap/plug
(-) temporaire d'un piquage sur une conduite	stopple
boucle	loop/buckle/sling
(-) de harnais	elevator link
(-) de la chaine d'ancrage	shackle
(-) de dilatation d'une canalisation	slack loop
(-) de suspension	lifting eye
bouclier	shield
(-) thermique	thermal (-)
boue	mud/sludge/slime
(-) de forage	drilling (-)
(-) de démarrage	spud (-)
boues	sludge
résiduaires	
(-) activées	activated (-)
centrifugation des (-)	(-) centrifugal separation
conditionnement des (-)	(-) conditioning
digestion des (-)	(-) digestion/anaerobic treatment
évacuation des (-)	(-) disposal/(-) tipping
filtration des (-)	dewatering of (-)
boueux	slimy
bougie	candle
(-) d'allumage	spark plug
(-) filtrante	filtering (-)
(-) de réchauffage	glow plug
boule	ball
boulettes	pellets

boulon	bolt/stay bolt/stud bolt
(-) d'ancrage	anchor bolt
(-) étrier fileté	U-bolt
(-) à oreilles	wing (-)
bourbier	slough
bourdalou (vase de nuit)	chamber pot (old, although used in sleeping cars)
bourrage	balling/balling up/ packing/pack
bourre	wadding
bourrelet	upset; flange
(-) alluvial	levée
bouse (de vache)	cow dung
boussole	compass
(-) d'inclinaison	inclinometer
(-) topographique	surveyor's (-)
bouteur	bulldozer
brai	tar pitch
brame	slab ingot
branche/ branchement	branch/branch connection
branchement particulier	household connection
bras	arm/crank/jib
(-) de balancier	take-off post
(-) d'élévateur	elevator links
(-) d'une rivière	distributary
(-) mort (-id-)	cutoff of a river/ dead arm
(-) de manivelle	crank arm
(-) de pompe	pump handle
brasage	brazing
(-) au bain	dip (-)
brasure	braze/brass soldering
brèche	breccia; gap
(-) de dislocation/	dislocation/fault
(-) de faille	breccia
(-) détritique	scree (-)
(-) de friction	shatter (-)
(-) intrusive	intrusive (-)
(-) de remplissage	solution (-)
(-) salifère	saliferous (-)
bride	flange/clamp/bridle
(-) filetée d'obturation de canalisation	saddle (-)
(-) de fixation	mounting pad
(-) pleine	blank (-)
(-) de sécurité	safety clamp
brin	strand
(-) actif	active line
(-) mort	dead line/dead end

brinquebale	rocker arm
brisé	broken/split/shattered
broche	driving pin/spindle
(-) creuse	hollow (-)
brochure	pamphlet
brouette	wheel barrow
brouillon	draft
broussaille	undergrowth/brushwood
brousse	bush/brush
bruit de fond	background noise
burette	oil can
burin	chisel
buse	nozzle
buselure de lavage (de filtres rapides)	nozzle for washing (rapid filters)
butée	stop ring/dog/thrust bearing
(-) à billes	ball thrust bearing
butoir	bumper

C

cabestan	capstan/cathead
(-) de dévissage	spinning cathead
cabine	cab
cabinet	closet
(-) d'aisance	latrine/toilet
(-id-) à fosse	pit latrine
(voir latrine)	(see latrine/closet)
câble	cable/line/rope
(-) d'alimentation	feeder
(-) armé (électr.)	armored (-)
(-) de battage	cable-tool line
(-) de cabestan	catline/cathead(-)
(-) de curage	bailing/sand(-)
(-) de forage	drilling cable/rope/ line
(-) de la clé de blocage des tiges de forage	back-up line
(-) de manoeuvre	swing/calf (-)
(-) de sondage	bull rope
(-) pour soudure	welding leads
(-) à torons	round-strand(-)
(-) antitorsion	nonspinning rope
(-) de treuil de manoeuvre	casing line
porte (-)	cable bearer/(-) hanger
serre (-)	bulldog grip/(-) clamp/ (-) clip

cadran	dial
cage (-) de roulement à billes	cage/housing ball bearing cage
cahier de charges	specifications
caillou (-) façonné	pebble sand blasted (-)
caillouteux	bouldary/flinty
caisse (-) à claire-voie (-) de criblage	case/box crate screening box
cake (-) de boue (-) de filtration (ou gâteau de sédiments)	cake mud (-) filter (-)
calamine	scale
calandre	shell
calcaire (-) argileux (-) à débris (-) concrétionné (-) crayeux (-) granulaire/ (-) granuleux/(-)grenu (-) gréseux (-) marneux	limestone/chalk stone clayey limestone skelletal (-) ball stone chalky (-) granular (-) cornstone marly limestone
cale (-) d'épaisseur	slip/dog/dowel/ spacer slim
calendrier	calendar; schedule
calfatage	caulking
calibre (-) pour fils (-) pour filetage (-) à mâchoires (-) pour tôles (-) à vis	template/gauge/caliper wire gauge thread gauge shaft caliper plate gauge caliper rule
calorifuge	insulation
calotte	cap/dome
cambouis	goo/gunk/sludge
came (-) d'admission (-) d'échappement arbre à (-) galet de la (-)	cam/tappet inlet (-) exhaust/outlet (-) camshaft (-) follower/(-) roller
camion (-) sur chenilles (-) grue (-) porteur (d'une sondeuse) (-) à plate-forme (-id-) surbaissée	truck/lorry crawler gin pole (-) rig carrier platform (-) flatbed (-)

camionnette	light truck/van/ pick-up
canal (-) d'amenée (-) d'écoulement (-) d'irrigation (-) de trop plein	channel/canal pentstock/flume/ feeder outflow channel; drain irrigation channel spillway
canalisation (-) d'eau (-) enterrée (-) d'huile (-) en matière plastique	main/pipe/pipeline/ piping/duct/cable or mains (elect.) water main/line/ pipe buried pipe oil duct plastic pipe/pipeline
canevas (d'un levé) (-) des puits (-) topographique	framework drilling pattern survey net
caniveau	gutter/ditch/drain
cannelure	groove/flute/serration
capteur	collector/sensor
caracole (-) à trépan	crowsfoot/bit hook bit hook
carborundum	silicon carbide
carburant	fuel
carbure (-) fritté	carbide sintered (-)
cardan (-) à croisillon	universal joint cross pin
carottage (-) au câble (-) au diamant (-) latéral (-) sismique	core drilling/coring cable tool coring diamond core drill sidewall (-) well shooting
carotte	core sample
carottier (-) à cliquet (-) remontable (-) latéral	core drill/sampler trigger bit removable core bit side wall sampler
carré (-) d'entraînement/ (-id-) de la tige carrée (-id-) à broches (-id-) à disques	square kelly bushing/rotary drill bushing pin drive kelly bushing rotating disk kelly drive bushing
carreau (de verre)	(glass) pane
carrière (-) à ciel ouvert	quarry/pit strip pit
carroyage	grid/checker

carte	map	chaos	block field
(-) en courbes de niveau/hypsométrique	contour (-)	chapelet d'outils	string of tools
(-) d'état major	ordnance survey (-)	chapelle	valve box
(-) de pendage	dip (-)	charge d'un bassin d'aération, massique	sludge loading factor
(-) en relief	dimensional (-)	(-id-), volumique	volume load/BOD loading
(-) schématique/ structurale	dip arrow (-)		
carter	case/casing/housing/ sump	charge	load
		(-) admissible	safe (-)
(-) à bain d'huile	wet sump	(-) de choc	shock (-)
cartographie	mapping	(-) explosive	blasting (-)
cartouche filtrante	canister	(-) de pointe	peak (-)
		(-) saturante	saturation/ concentration
casque	helmet/hard hat	(-) de service	work (-)
cassure	fracture/break/snap	chargeuse	loader
caution	guarantee/security/ deposit	(-) pelleteuse	back hoe (-)/shovel type
CCDV (latrine à compost alternante à double voûte)	DVC (double vault batch composting latrine)	rétro (-)	back (-)
		chariot	carriage/trolley/dolly
ceinture	belt	(-) élévateur à fourche	forklift truck
(-) de chevauchement	overthrust (-)		
(-) désertique	desert (-)	charnière	hinge; bend
cémentation	case hardening	(-) anticlinale	saddle bend
		(-) synclinale	trough bend/(-) turn
cendre	ash/cinders	charpente	woodwork
cercle de contrôle du calibre du trépan	bit gauge	charpie	lint
		charriage	driftage/thrust
chaîne	chain; range	sous (-)	underthrust
(-) anticlinale	anticlinal range	chasse d'eau	water flush/flushing
(-) à barbotin/ galle	sprocket (-)	chassis	frame/base frame
(-) d'entraînement de la table	rotary drive (-)	(-) de guidage	template
(-) à godets	pan conveyor	chaussée	pavement
(-) de montagne	mountain range	chaussures de sécurité	safety shoes
(-) à rouleaux	roller (-)		
(-) à roulement	block (-)	chaux	lime
(-) de suspension	sling (-)	(-) éteinte/ hydratée	slaked (-)
(-) de vissage	spinning (-)	(-) sodée	soda (-)
chaise d'attache	elevator	(-) vive	quick (-)
chaleur	heat	chef sondeur/ foreur	master driller
(-) sensible	sensible (-)		
chalumeau	blowtorch/torch/ welding burner	chemin	path
		cheminement	ground water flow
chambre d'équilibre	surge chamber	chemise	jacket/liner/lining/ shell sleeve
champ d'application	scope		
chanfrein	chamfer/bevel	chenal	channel
changement	shift	chevalement	derrick/headgear/ head-stock
chantier	work site/job site		
chanvre	hemp	chevalet	trestle

chevauchement	overlap/over-thrust/straddle
(-) en retour	back thrusting
plan de (-)	break thrust
cheville	pin/peg/dowel
chèvre	gantry crane; gin
(-) de forage	breast derrick
chicane	baffle/deflector
chiffre	digit
chignole	breast drill
chloration/ chloruration	chlorination
chloromètre	chlorinator
chlorure de chaux	bleaching powder
chromatographie	chromatography
(-) sur papier	paper (-)
chute	fall/drop
(-) de pression	pressure drop
cible	target
cicatrice	scar
cime	peak
cimentation	cementing
(-) sous pression	squeeze (-)
cintreuse	bending machine
(-) à tubes	pipe bender
circuit	circuit
(-) dérivé	branch (-)
coupe (-)	(-) breaker
circulation	circulation
(-) inverse de boue	reverse mud (-)
cire	wax
(-) minérale	earth (-)
(-) de paraffine	paraffin (-)
cisailles	shears/snips
cisaillement	shear/shearing
résistance au (-)	(-) strength
seuil de (-)	yield point
surface de (-)	(-) plane
ciseau	chisel
ciseaux	scissors
clapet	check valve/dart
(-) à battant	flap (-)
(-) à bille	ball (-)
(-) à boisseau	sleeve valve
(-) à crépine	foot valve
(-) de filtre	filter inlet (-)/clack (-)
(-) de pied	check valve/foot valve
(-) anti retour/ (-) de retenue	non-return (-)

clarificateur	secondary settling tank
classement	sizing; sorting
clavette	key/pin/spline
clé/ clef	spanner/wrench/key/tongs
(-) à chaine	chain tongs
(-) à cliquet	ratchet wrench
(-) à douille	socket (-)/box spanner
(-) à fourche	fork (-)
(-) à molette/ (-) anglaise	monkey wrench/ adjustable spanner
(-) à tiges	pipe tongs/wrench, hand dog
(-) de blocage	breakout tongs
(-id-) des tiges	backup (-)/back ups
(-) de déblocage/ dévissage	make up tongs/lay tongs
(-) dynamométrique	torque wrench
(-) de retenue	catch (-)/lie key
(-) de robinet	cock key
clenche	latch
clinomètre	clinometer/tilt meter
clinoscope	inclinometer
clinquant	foil
cliquet	ratchet/pawl
(-) d'arrêt	dog stop
clivage	cleavage
(-) principal	basal (-)
faux (-)	slip cleavage
cloche	bell/hood/cap
(-) à circulation	circulating overshot
(-) de guidage	bell guide/bowl
(-) de repêchage/ (-) de sauvetage	fishing bell/socket
(-id-) à coins	casing bowl
(-id-) à emboitement	(-) socket
cloison	partition/division
(-) taraudée (pour repêchage)	die collar
clou	nail/spike
cluse	cross valley
(-) active/(-)vive	water gap
(-) morte/(-) sèche	dry gap/wind gap
coagulation	clotting
coefficient	factor/degree
(-) de sécurité	safety (-)
coffrage	coffering (trenches); framing (concrete)/ sheeting
coffret	case
cognement (diesel)	knock (diesel)

cohésion d'une boue	sludge cohesion
coin	wedge; corner; angle
(-) agrippeur	basket grapple
(-) dentelés	serrated slips
(-) d'entrainement	rotary bushing/kelly drive bushing
(-) de retenue	slip of casing rig (spider)
(-) de tige de forage	drill pipe slips
coincement	sticking
col (de montagne)	(mountain) pass
collage	stickiness
(-) des segments	ring sticking
collant	sticky
collecteur	header/manifold/collector
(-) d'admission/ (-) d'aspiration	intake manifold
(-) d'assèchement	stripping
(-) d'échappement	exhaust manifold
(-) de moteur à induction	slip ring
(-) de refoulement	pump discharge leader
collerette	collar/shoulder/flange
collet	collar/neck
(-) de butée	thrust collar
(-) tournant	swivel neck
(-) rabattu	flare
collier	collar/ring/clamp
(-) d'arrêt	stop collar
(-) à coins	spider
(-) de frein	brake band
(-) d'obturation	band clamp
(-) de prise latéral	saddle
(-) de retenue	casing clamp
colmatage	clogging/plugging/silting up/patching
colon	settler
colonne	column; string
(-) d'aspiration	drop pipe
(-) de basalte	basaltic column
(-) de manoeuvre	floor stand
(-) montante	riser pipe/standpipe
(-) de refoulement	rising main
(-) de tubage	casing string
colorant	dye
combustible	fuel
combustion (humide) des boues	wet combustion of sludge

commande	control; drive
(-) asservie	servo control
(-) directe	direct drive
(-) à distance	remote control
(-) par câble	cable drive
(-) par courroie	belt (-)
(-) hydraulique	hydraulic (-)
communication	paper/conference paper
commutateur à balai	collector ring/slip ring/brush ring
commutatrice	rotary converter
compact	dense
compas	compass
(-) d'épaisseur	outside caliper
(-) à coulisse/ (-) à verge	beam (-)
compensation	balancing
complexe de couches	series of strata
comportement	performance
composition des garnitures de forage	set up
compresseur	compressor
(-) à deux étages	two-stage (-)
(-) mono étagé	single stage (-)
(-) à plusieurs étages	multistage (-)
(-) à vis	screw (-)
(-) volumétrique	positive displacement (-)
compression	compression/squeeze
comptage	tally count
compteur	flow meter
(-) à moulinet	screw (-)
(-) avec remise à zéro	set back counter
compte-tours	tachometer/tachymeter
conception	design
concrétion	concretion/sinter deposit
condensateur	capacitor
condenseur	condensor
(-) à calandre et serpentin	shell and coil (-)
(-) à calandre multi-tubulaire	shell and tube (-)
conditionnement	conditioning
(-) de l'eau	water (-)
(-) des boues	sludge (-)
(-id-) par charges	(-id-) with inert additives

conduite	line/pipe/pipeline/ main	*contrôle*	control/examination
(-) *d'alimentation*	supply line/feed line	(-) *destructif*	destructive examination
(-) *d'aspiration*	suction (-)	(-) *granulo-métrique*	sieve acceptance
(-) *de branchement*	service (-)		
(-) *principale*	trunk (-)	*convoyeur à bande*	band conveyor
(-) *de refoulement*	delivery/discharge outlet (-)	*coordonnées*	coordinates
		(-) *apparentes*	apparent place
cone	cone/taper	(-) *géographiques*	geographic data
(-) *à axes divergents*	offset cones	(-) *polaires*	polar coordinates
(-) *d'alluvions*	alluvial (-)/fan structure	*copeau*	shaving
(-) *déflecteur*	deflecting cone	(-) *de charriage*	thrust slice
(-) *d'éboulis*	fan	*coquille*	shell
(-) *de lave*	lava dome		
(-) *morse*	morse taper	*coquillier*	shelly
(-) *volcanique*	volcanic pile	*calcaire* (-)	(-) limestone
configuration	configuration/outline	*corbeille*	basket
(-) *d'écoulement*	flow pattern	(-) *de soupape*	valve cage
confluent	junction with a tributary	*cordage de la clé de manoeuvre*	snapping up line
(-) *en crochet*	barbed (-)	*corde*	string/rope
(-) *discordant*	hanging junction	(-) *à piano*	piano (-)
conglomérat	conglomerate	*cordon de galets*	shingle bar
(-) *de base*	basal (-)		
(-) *de piedmont*	fanglomerate	*cordon de soudure*	well bead
connecteur	connector/coupling	*cornière*	angle
console	bracket	*corps de pompe*	pump barrel/pump shell
constant	steady		
contact	contact; touch	*corps de sonde*	drilling shaft
(-) *mécanique*	tectonic contact	*corps de tête d'injection*	swivel body
(-) *sur le fond*	touchdown		
continu	solid	*corrélation*	correlation
		(-) *des diagraphies*	(-) of well logs
contraction	shrinkage/strain	*corridor*	passage/passageway
contrainte	stress	*corrosion*	corrosion
contraire	unfavorable	*inhibiteur de* (-)	(-) inhibitor
		(-) *en magasinage*	shelf (-)
contre-bride	counter flange/ companion flange	*cosse de câble électrique*	cable shoe/thimble
contre-coup	back lash	*côte*	shore/shore line/strand
contre-courant	back-flow/counter flow	*coté*	side/dimension (measured)
contre-fiche	truss/brace/strut/ spur	*couche*	layer/bed/blanket seam/stratum
contrefort	buttress/stiffener	(-) *alluvionnaire*	alluvium/over-burden
contre pente	back slope	(-) *arable*	topsoil
		(-) *basale*	bottomset bed
contre poids	balance weight	(-) *boulante*	unconsolidated formation
contre pression	back pressure	(-) *déchirées*	disrupted strata
contre-torsion	back twist (of a cable)	(-) *filtrante*	filter bed
		(-) *dure*	hard rock/solid bed

couche (suite)	layer/bed/blanket seam/stratum (cont'd)
(-) à involution	involution layer
(-) à fort pendage	highly inclined seam
(-) à faible pendage	low-dipping stratum
(-) redressées	upturned strata
(-) de toit	superjacent bed
coude	elbow/bend
(-) de tête d'injection	gooseneck
coulage	spill
coulée	coulee/flow; casting
(-) de boue/ (-) boueuse	mud flow
(-) de lave	volcanic flow
(-) de pierres	block stream
(-) de terrain	creep
(-) en coquille	die cast/casting
couleurs de référence	standard colors
coulis	slurry/grout
coulisse	slide
(-) de battage	bumper sub/backoff tool
(-) de forage	drilling jar/rotary jar
(-) de repêchage	fishing jar
coulisseau	slide
coup	stroke/shot
(-) de bélier	water hammer/ pressure surge
(-) de vent	squall
coupe	cut; section
(-) câble	wire-line knife
(-) carotte	biscuit cutter
(-) tige	pipe cutter
(-) tube	tube cutter/casing cutter/casing knife
(-) verticale	vertical section
couple	torque/moment
(-) de blocage/ (-) de vissage	make-up torque
(-) de démarrage	starting (-)
(-) de serrage	tightening (-)
coupole	dome/cupola
coupure	cut/gash
courant	current/flow/stream
(-) alternatif	alternative (-)
(-) d'arrachement	rip current
(-) continu	direct (-)
contre (-)	counter flow/back flow
(-) de flot	flood (-)
(-) naturel d'un fluide	streamline

(-) de retour	backflow
(-) vagabonds	stray (-)
courbe	curve
(-) bathymétrique	depth (-)
(-) de tarissement	depletion (-)
courbure	flexure
couronne	crown/ring/blank bit
(-) à molettes/ (-) de carottage	coring bit
(-) de carottier	core cutter bit
(-) dentée	saw tooth bit
(-) à grenaille	shot bit
courroie	belt/band/strap
cours d'eau	river/stream
(-) pirate	captor
course	stroke
court	short
(-) circuit	(-) circuit
coussinet	bearing/bushing
(-) d'axe de piston	wrist pin (-)
(-) de l'arbre à cames	camshaft (-)
(-) de tête de bielle	big end (-)
(-) en laiton	brass (-)
(-) pour tige d'entraînement	drive bushing
coûteau	knife/cutter
(-) à câble	rope knife
couverture	overburden
(-) détritique superficielle	waste mantle/ residual soil
roche (-)	cap
couvre-joint	butt strap
crampon	clamp/spike/dog
(-) pour tubes	pipe hook
cran de sûreté	safety catch
crapaudine	bottom bearing/thrust bearing
crasse	scum
cravache	jockey stick (to hold back drilling clamps)
cravatte	sling
crémaillère	rack/cog rail
crépine	liner/screen/strainer
(-) à fentes, à trous	slotted, perforated screen
(-) à enrobage en graviers	prepacked gravel pack
crête	crest/ridge
(-) anticlinale	anticlinal ridge

(-) isoclinale/	hogback
(-) monoclinale	
tension de (-)	peak voltage
valeur de (-)	peak value
creusement	hollowing/digging; scouring
(-) de puits	sinking a well/shaft sinking
(-) de tranchée	trench digging
creux	dip/dell/hollow
crevasse	cleft/crack/fissure
criblage	screening/sieving
crible	screen/sieve/jigger
(-) classeur	grading (-)/ classifying (-)/sizing (-)
(-) à grille filtrante	filter (-)
(-) laveur	rocker
(-) à plateau unique	single deck (-)
(-) rotatif	trommel
(-) à secousses	jigging screen
cric	jack
(-) hydraulique	hydraulic (-)
croc de cable	cable hook
crochet	hook
(-) à tubage	casing (-)
(-) de levage	lifting (-)
(-) de repêchage	fishing (-)
(-) redresseur	wall (-)/spiral guide
croisillon	cross brace/diagonal bracing
croix	cross; four-way tee
croquis	sketch
(-) coté	dimensional (-)
crottin(de cheval)	horse dung
croûte	crust/skin
(-) concrétionnée	concrete bed/hard pan
(-) désertique	desert varnish
(-) de la fonte	skin of casting
crue	flood
cuffat	tub/vat/bucket
cuiller	spoon/bailer
(-) à boue	mud barrel
(-) à clapet	mud socket
(-) à piston/	sand pump/sand
(-) à sable	bucket
(-) de curage	bailer/clean out bailer/dark bailer
vanne de (-)	(-) valve

culée	abutment
curage	bailing
(-) sous pression	snubbing
câble de (-)	bailing line/rope
tambour de (-)	(-) drum
curer	to bail out
curette	scraper
cuve	bath/bain/tank
cuvelage	casing/casing string; dug well lining
cuvette	basin/bowl/pan
(-) de failles	fault/pit
(-) de roulement à billes	ball bearing cup
(-) synclinale	basin fold/synclinal closure
(-) à la turque	squat plate
(-) de w.c.	toilet bowl/toilet pan
cylindrée	volume of an engine/ piston displacement/ swept volume

D

dalle	slab/apron
roche en (-)	flagstones
dame	tamper
(-) mécanique	power (-)
datation	dating
DBO (demande biochimique d'oxygène)	BOD (biochemical oxygen demand)
débattement	deflection
(-) de roue	wheel hop
(-) transversal	sway
débit	flow rate/yield/ throughput/output
(-) annuel	annual discharge
débitmètre	flowmeter/flow indicator
(-) à dérivation	shunt meter
déblai	cutting
(-) de forage	well cuttings/drill cuttings

déblocage — breaking out

débloqueur de trépan — bit breaker

débordement — spillage

débourbage — de-silting/desludging

début — beginning
  (-) de forage — spudding in

décalage — drift

décalé — staggered

décantation — settling/clarification
  (-) diffuse — flocculant settling
  (-) en piston/ — zone settling (of
  (-) freinée (des — flocculated particles)
  particules floculées)
  bassin de (-) — decanting basin/
    pond

décanteur — settling tank/clarifier
  (-) lamellaire — plate type (-)
  (-) statique — static settling tank
  (-id-) sans râclage — (-id-) without scraping
    system
  (-id-) cylindroconique — (-id-) cylindrical with
  ordinaire — conical bottom
  (-id-) à flux — (-id-) with horizontal
  horizontal — flow
  (-) statique à râclage — (-) with mechanical
  mécanique des boues — sludge scraper
  (-id-) circulaire — circular (-id-)
  (-id-) longitudinal — longitudinal rectangular
  rectangulaire — (-id-)

décanteur accéléré — accelerated clarifier
  (-) à circulation de boues — sludge circulation (-)
  (-) à lit de boue — sludge blanket (-)

décanteuse continue — continuous centrifuge

décapage — blasting/etching/
    pickling
  (-) à la grenaille — shot (-)
  (-) au sable — sand/grit (-)

décarbonatation — carbonate removal
  (-) à la chaux — (-) by lime
  (-) à froid — cold process (-)
  (-) à chaud — hot process (-)
  (-) sur échangeur — (-) by ion exchange
  d'ions/ sur résine

décentrement — setting over

décharge — unloading/lightening;
    discharge (elect.);
    eduction/waste outlet
  (-) publique — dumping site/land fill/
    waste dump

déchet — waste/waste material/
    cull/scrap/spoilage
  (-) de criblage — screenings

déclaration — public statement

déclencheur — cable release; trigger

décollement — slacking

décomposition — degradation/decay/
    weathering/digestion ·
  (-) anaérobique — anaerobic digestion

défaut — defect/flaw/fault

défavorable — unfavorable

défectueux — defective

déferrisation — iron removal
  (-) chimique — (-) by means of
    chemicals
  (-) par aération — (-) by aeration and
  et filtration — filtration
  (-) par filtration — (-) by catalytic
  catalytique — filtration

déflagration — blast

déflecteur — baffle/diverter

défluoruration — fluoride removal

déformation — distortion/strain/
    warping
  (-) permanente — permanent set/
    permanent strain
  (-) résiduelle — residual (-)

dégagement — effluence/release

dégât — damage

dégazage — degassing/deaeration
  (-) chimique — chemical (-)
  (-) physique — physical deaeration
  (-) sous pression — pressure (-)
  (-) sous vide — vacuum (-)

dégerbage — unracking

dégivrage — defrosting

dégorgeoir — spout

dégradation — decay/degradation

dégraissage — oil & grease removal

dégrillage — coarse & fine screening

dégrippant — antiseize compound

delta — delta

démagnétisation — demagnetizing/
    demagnetization/
    degaussing

démanganisation — removal of manganese

démarrage — start-up

démarreur — starter

déminéralisation — deionization

démontable — detachable

démontage	dismantling/knocking down/tearing down
dénitrification	denitrification
dénivellement	drop/difference in altitude
dénudation (d'un fil)	denudation (of a wire)
densité apparente	apparent density/bulk density
(-) d'un matériau filtrant	bulk (-) of filtering material
dentelure	serration
dépanneur	trouble shooter
déphosphatation	phosphate removal
déplacement	shifting
dépoli	frosted/ground
(-) au jet de sable	sand blasted
déport	offset
dépot	deposit/sediment; store/warehouse; garage
(-) alluvial	alluvial (-)
(-) d'un cordon de soudure	beading
(-) galvanoplastique	electro (-)
(-) salin	saline (-)
(-) sédimentaire	sedimentary (-)
(-) au trempé	dip plating
dépression	depression/structural saddle
dérivation	diversion
dérive	drift
dérouleuse	reel
derrick	derrick
(-) haubanné	guyed (-)
(-) repliable	jack knife (-)
(-) télescopique	telescopic (-)
désagrégation	crumbling/weathering/desintegration
désaxage	setting over
descente	lowering/descent/fall
(-) des outils	running-in of drilling tools
(-) du tubage tuyau de (-)	lowering of the casing downpipe
désembuage	demisting
désémulsifiant	demulsifier
désenclencher	to disengage
(-) le tambour de forage	to throw off the rope
déshuileur	oil separator
déshydratation	drying/dessication
désincrustant	scale remover
dessablage	grit removal
dessalage	desalting
dessalement	desalination
dessin	drawing
(-) à l'échelle	scale (-)
instruments de (-)	drafting/(-) instruments
planche à (-)	(-) board
dessinateur	draftsman/draughtman
destructif	destructive
contrôle (-)	(-) examination
détartrage	removal of scale/descaling
détartrant	scalant
détecteur	detector/sensor
(-) de canalisation	electronic pipe locator/stool pigeon
(-) de fuite	leak detector
(-) de joints	tool joint locator
détermination	determination/measuring
déterminé	specific
détersif	detergent
détritique	detrital
détroit	sound/straight
détubage	pulling
dévasement	desilting
développement	development
déversement	spill
déversoir	down spout
déviation	deflection/deflecting
(-) des sondages	(-) of boreholes
amorce de (-)	kickoff point
angle de (-)	deviation angle
accroissement de (-id-)	build-up
dévidoir	cable drum/cable reel
dévié	slanted
dévissage	unscrewing/break out
(-) du train de tige	breaking down the drill pipe
plaque de (-)	bit breaker plate
dévolution	devolution
diable	hand truck

diaclase | bottom joint/sheet
horizontale | joint

diagramme | diagram/chart
(-) d'écoulement | flow pattern

diagraphie | well logging/log
(-) de perméabilité | permeability log
(-) de production | production logging

diamètre | diameter
(-) de mandrin | drift (-)

diamètreur | inside caliper

diapositive | slide/transparency
| (photo)

diatomite | diatomaceous earth/
| siliceous earth

DIEPA (décennie | IDWSSD (international
internationale de l'eau | drinking water supply
potable et de | and sanitation decade)
l'assainissement) |

diésel (moteur) | diesel (engine)

difraction/ | scattering/diffusion
diffusion |

digesteur (boues) | digester (sludge)
(-) à brassage au | (-) with gas mixing
gaz | system
(-) à brassage | (-) with sludge
hydraulique | recirculation

digestion | digestion
(-) anaérobique | sludge anaerobic (-)
des boues |
(-id-) à forte | high rate (-id-)
charge |
(-id-) à moyenne | medium rate (-id-)
charge |

digue | dyke

dilacération | comminution

diluant | diluent
(-) pour peinture | paint thinner

diluvial/diluvient | diluvial
sables diluvients | (-) sands

dimension | dimension

dimensionnel | dimensional

diminué | depressed/reduced

diminution | dwindling

direction | direction; trend/
| wearing course; steering
| course of outcrop
(-) de l'affleure- |
ment |
(-) d'une faille | trend of fault
(-) du pendage | line of dip

directive | direction/guideline/
| introduction

discordance | discordance/
| unconformity
(-) de stratification | discordant bedding
(-) tectonique | structural (-)
(-) topographique | topographic
| unconformity

disjoncteur | circuit breaker/circuit
| breaker switch

disjonction | severance
(-) en bancs | sheet jointing

dislocation | disturbance switch

dispersant | detergent

dispersion | scatter/scattering/
| spread/straggling/stray

dispositif | device/system
(-) d'arrosage | fire sprinkling
contre l'incendie |
(-) de blocage de | core catcher
la carotte (dans le |
carottier) |
(-) de suspension | spider/slip type
à coins | hanger

disruption | severance

dissémination | straggling

distance | distance/length
(-) des faces | lateral separation
(-) horizontale des | normal horizontal
affleurements | separation
(-) de visibilité | sight (-)

divergent | divergent

division | parting
(-) en boules | spheridal structure
(-) en plaques | slab structure

doline | sink hole
(-) d'effondrement | collapse sink

dôme de sel | salt dome

données de base | background

dosage de réactif | reagent dosing
(-) par pompe | dosing pump feeding
| of reagent
(-) par déplacement | displacement feed of
| reagent
(-) gravimétrique | gravity feed dosing of
| reagent
(-) volumétrique | volumetric feeding of
| reagent
(-id-) à sole tournante | revolving disk (-id-)
(-id-) à vis | auger type (-id-)

double | double/dual
(-) paroi | (-) walled

douille	bushing/socket sleeve
(-) bridée	shoulder bushing
(-) de câble	rope socket
(-) en 2 parties	split bushing
(-) de serrage	collet
drague	dredger
(-) à câble	dragline scraper
drainage	drainage/draining
dresser	to erect; to compile
(-) une carte	to map out/to compile a map
(-) un plan	to plot
droit	straight/right
(-) de passage	easement
dudgeon	tube expander
dune	dune
(-) mouvante	wandering (-)
(-) de sable	sand (-)/sand hill
durée	life/duration/length of time
(-) conservation	shelf (-)
(-) utile	service (-)
(-) de vie	(-) span
dureté	hardness
indice de (-)	(-) number
(-id-) Brinell	Brinell (-id-) or BHN
duse calibrée	choke nipple

E

eau	water
(-) d'amont	head (-)
(-) d'appoint	make-up (-)
(-) brute	raw (-)/untreated (-)
(-) captive	confined ground (-)
(-) connée	connate (-)
(-) connexe	attached (-)
(-) dégazéifiée	deaerated (-)
(-) de diaclase	crevice (-)
(-) dissimulée	concealed (-)
(-) distillée	distilled (-)
(-) dormante	back (-)
(-) douce	fresh/sweet/soft (-)
(-) dure	hard (-)
(-) d'égouts	effluent
(-) d'exsudation	trickling (-)
(-) filtrée	filtered (-)
(-) de fond	bottom (-)
(-) de formation	formation (-)
(-) fossile	connate/fossil (-)
(-) grasses/(-) grises	grey (-) (domestic effluent mostly from washing up crockery plus kitchen utensils)
(-) d'imbibition	soakage

(-) incluse	native (-)
(-) industrielle	industrial (-)
(-) d'infiltration	soakage/percolation/seep/vadose (-)
(-) interstitielle	interstitial/pore (-)
(-) libre	free/gravity (-)
(-) liée	bound (-)
(-) minérale	mineral (-)
(-) oxygénée	hydrogen peroxyde
(-) pendulaire	pendular (-)
(-) phréatique	phreatic (-)
(-) peu profonde	shallow (-)
(-) pluviale	rain (-)
(-) polluée	polluted (-)
(-) potable	potable/drinking (-)
(-) résiduaire	sewage/foul (-)/waste (-)
(-id-) industrielle	industrial (-id-)
(-id-) urbaine	town sewage
(-) résiduelle	waste water
(-) de ruissellement	run off
(-) saisonnière	temporary (-)
(-) salée/ saline	salt (-)
(-) saumâtre	brackish (-)
(-) schlammeuse	slime (-)
(-) souterraine	ground (-)
(-) stagnante	standing (-)
(-) suintante	trickling (-)
(-) supérieure	perched/upper (-)
(-) usée	sewage/sewage effluent/waste water
(-) vadeuse	vadose water
venue d' (-)	water influx
ébarbage	trimming
ébarbeuse	trimming machine
éboulement	cave-in/earth slide/down fall/slip/slump
(-) des parois d'un puits	hole sloughing
éboulis	rubble/crumbling/débris
écaille	scale/flake
écart	déviation/throw/offset/distance/gap
(-) de la verticale	hade
écartement	spacing
échafaudage	scaffold/scaffolding
(-) en bois	timber trestle
échange	exchange
(-) d'ions	ion exchange
échangeur d'ions	ion exchanger
(-) d'anions	anion exchanger
(-) de cations	cation (-)
(-) à lits mélangés	mixed bed (-)
(-) à lits mobiles	moving bed (-)
(-) en adoucissement	softening by cation exchanger
(-) en décarbonation	carbonate removal by ion exchange

échantillon	sample/specimen
(-) de carottage latéral	sidewall core
(-) de forage	boring sample
(-) de formation	formation (-)
échantillonnage	sampling
échantillonneur	sampler
échappement	exhaust
course d' (-)	scavenging stroke
écharde	splinter
échec	failure
échelle	ladder; scale
(-) à coulisse	extension ladder
(-) pliante	folding (-)
(-) de dureté	scale of hardness
(-) des profondeurs/ des hauteurs	vertical scale
(-) géologique	geologic column
échelon	echelon; step
éclat	splinter/chip; sheen
éclaboussement	splash
éclisse	splice; fish plate
écope	scoop/bailer
écoulement	flow/discharge/ outflow/run off
(-) continu	streamline flow
(-) d'averse	storm runoff
(-) divisé	split (-)
(-) en nappe	sheet flood
(-) de percolation	seepage
(-) de retour	backflow
(-) sub laminaire	plug flow
(-) transversal	cross flow/cross current
écoutille	hatch
écouvillon	tube/flue brush
écran	screen/baffle/wall/ shield; shadow
(-) d'eau	water wall
effet d' (-)	shadowing
(-) protecteur	protective shield
écrasement	collapsing/crumbling/ crush
(-) du tubage	collapse of casing
écrase-tube	squeezer
écrou	nut
(-) à ailette	wing (-)
(-) de blocage	stop (-)
(-) à oreilles	butterfly (-)
(-) à créneaux/ (-) à encoches	castle nut
(-) de goujon	stud
(-) de serrage	hold down nut

(-) de verrouillage	lock (-)
écume	foam/froth
effet	effect/result
(-) d'entaille	notch (-)
(-) pendulaire	pendulum (-)
efficacité	efficiency
efflorescence	efflorescence/scumming
(-) saline	salt (-)
effluent	effluent
effondrement	collapse/downthrow/ subsidence
(-) circulaire	cauldron/fault pit/ sink hole
effort	strain/stress/pull
(-) axial	thrust load
(-) à la traction	tensile stress
(-) de compression	compressive (-)
(-) de flambage	buckling (-)
effritement	crumbling/spalling
égalisation	equalizing
doigt d' (-)	prong
raccord d' (-)	equalizing sub
égaré	stray
égout	sewer/drain
bouche d' (-)	(-) opening
gaz d' (-)	(-) gas
réseau d' (-)	sewage system
élargissement	widening/underreaming
élargisseur	under-reamer/reamer
(-) à guide	pilot reamer bit
(-) creux	hollow reamer
(-) rotatif	wall scraper
élasticité	elasticity
module d' (-)	modulus of (-)
élastique	flexible
électrode	electrode
électroforeuse de fond	downhole electro- drill
électro magnétique	electro magnetic
champ (-)	(-) field
électrophorèse	cataphoresis/electro- phoresis
électro placage	electro plating
électro vanne	solenoid valve
élément	element/unit/part/cell
(-) support	support frame
élévateur	elevator/lift/riser/ hoist
(-) à coins pour tubes	slip-type elevator

(-) à ouverture centrale	centre latch (-)	*(-) fossile couronne à (-)*	fossil imprint sprocket wheel
(-) à porte latérale	side door (-)		
(-) à tube	casing (-)	*émulsifiant agent émulsionnant*	emulsifying (-) agent
élimination	disposal		
(-) des déchets	waste (-)	*encastrement*	scarfing
élingue	sling/sling line	*enclave*	inclusion/enclosure
		(-) de roche éruptive	xenolith enclave
élution/ élutriation	elutriation	*(-) endogène*	endogenous enclosure
		(-) exogène	exogenetic inclusion
emballage	package	*(-) homogène*	cognate (-)
embase	base/baseplate	*enclanchement*	interlocking/latching
		(-) des joints de tiges	slapping of tool joints
embouage	slushing		
		encoche	slot
emboîtement	fit		
(-) à tubage	socket joint	*encrassé*	clogged
embout	piping end/ferrule	*encrassement*	clogging/fouling
(-) cannelé	teat end		
(-) fileté	shank	*enduit*	coating/grout/dope
(-) de sûreté (forage rotary)	rotary safety joint	*endommagement*	damage
		(-) par fatigue	fatigue (-)
emboutissage	drawing	*endurance*	endurance
		essai d'(-)	(-) test
embrayage	clutch/coupling		
(-) à cônes	cone (-)	*énergie*	energy
(-) à crabots/ à mâchoires	jaw (-)	*(-) massique*	specific (-)
(-) à dents	dog (-)/dog and spline (-)	*enfoncement*	sinking; dent
(-) à disques/ à plateau	disc/plate (-)	*engorgé*	clogged
(-) à friction	friction (-)/friction gear	*engrenage*	gear
		(-) à chevron	herringbone (-)
émeri	emery/grit/sand	*(-) à dents intérieures*	annular (-)
papier d'(-)	(-) paper	*(-) à denture hélicoïdale*	spiral (-)
toîle d'(-)	(-) cloth	*(-) droit*	spur (-)
		(-) d'équerre	miter (-)
émerillon	swivel	*(-) à roues coniques*	bevel (-)
joint à (-)	(-) joint	*train d'(-)*	cluster of gear wheels
émetteur	sender/transmitter	*(-) à vis sans fin*	worm (-)
émiettement	crumbling	*engrènement*	engagement
emmagasinage	stock piling	*enjambement*	span
emmanchement	fit	*enlisé*	sucked in
(-) à force	tight (-)		
		énoncé	statement
émollient	emollient/softening agent	*enraciné*	deep seated
émoussé	blunt/dull	*enregistrement*	recording
empiègement	entrapment	*enregistreur*	recorder
		(-) d'avancement	penetration (-)
empierrement	graveling/ballasting		
		enrobage	wrapping/coating/ covering/doping
empilage	stacking/piling up		
emplacement	site/location	*enrochement*	rock fill
emplâtre	patch		
emporte-pièces	punch		
empreinte	print/imprint/mark; sprocket		

enroulement	coiling/winding
(-) d'un câble	kinking of a rope
(-id-) sur un tambour	spooling of a cable
enrouleur	spooler/winder
ensablé	sanded-up
ensablement	sanding up
ensemble	set
ensouillage (canalisation)	burial (pipeline)
entablement	blanket
entaillage	slotting
entaille	notch/slit/gash/indentation
entaillement	undermining
entartrage	scaling/scale formation/scale deposit/fur deposit
enterré	buried
entonnoir	funnel; bowl/sink hole
(-) à trémie	mixing hopper
entrainement	drive
(-) hydraulique	hydraulic (-)
(-) mécanique	mechanical (-)
(-) par courroie trapézoïdale	V-belt (-)
entrée	inlet/intake; ingress; entry
entre-fer	air gap
entrepôt	warehouse
entretien	maintenance/servicing
entretoise	crossbar/cross member/brace/girt/strut
(-) de contre-ventement	sway brace
(-) de derrick	derrick girt
(-) du support de balancier	samson post braces
entretoisement	strutting
enveloppe	covering/jacket/shell/sheath/shroud housing; mantle
(-) de carotte	core shell
(-) de cordage	rope splice
(-) sédimentaire	sedimentary mantle
envergure	span
éolien	due to wind
dépôt (-)	wind deposit
éolienne	windmill/wind turbine/air motor
épaisseur	thickness
épaississement des boues	mud thickening
épanchement	extrusion/outpouring
épandage	spreading/spills/spraying
épaulement	shoulder
(-) femelle (de tige de forage)	box (-)
épave	wreck/derelict
éperon (de montagne)	(mountain) spur
épissage	splicing
épissure	splice
éponge	sponge
épontes	adjacent beds/surrounding formations
époque	epoch/era/age
épreuve	test/trial/proof
(-) hydraulique	hydraulic test
à l' (-) des éclats	splinter proof
éprouvette	test piece/sample
épuisement	depletion/dewatering/stripping
épuration	purification/purifying/scrubbing filtering/treatment
station d' (-)	treatment plant
équerre	square
(-) d'arpenteur	cross staff
équipe	team/crew/gang; shift
équipement	equipment/outfit
(-) de protection	safeguard (-)
éraillure	galling/scoring/scratching
(-) légère	scuffing
erg	sand desert
ergot	dowel/dog/finger/spline
érosion	erosion/scour/denudation
(-) éolienne	wind (-)
(-) karstique	furrowing
(-) par éclatement	plucking
(-) en nappes	sheet (-)
(-) des roches	rock weathering
(-) régressive	backward erosion
erreur	error
(-) aléatoire	accidental/random (-)

escarpé	steep
escarpement	bluff/scarp/cliff
espace	space/gap
(-) interstitiel	void space
(-) libre	clearance
espacement	spacing
esquille de roches	chips of rock
esquisse	draft/sketch
essai	test/trial; attempt
(-) de présélection	screening (-)
essence	gasoline/gas (USA)/ petrol (UK)
essieu	axle
(-) coudé	crank (-)
(-) moteur	drive (-)
(-) oscillant	swing (-)
essuie-tige	kelly wiper
estampé	drawn/stamped
établi	work bench; settled
établissement	installation/enterprise/ firm; setting up; settlement; establishment
étage	stage; level
étagé	stepped
étai	stay/strut/prop
étampage	swaging
étanche	damp proof/water proof/water tight
étançon	prop/shore/stay
état	state
(-) major	staff
étau	vise
(-) à mors parallèle	parallel (-)
(-) à tube	pipe (-)
étayage	shoring
étendue	extent
étincelle	spark
pare (-)	(-) arrester
sans (-)	sparkless
étiré	drawn
(-) à froid	cold (-)
étoile	star
(-) triangle	(-) delta
étoupe	oakum
étranger	extraneous; foreign

étranglement	choke/throttling/ restriction
(-) d'une couche	balk
étrésillon	trench shore
étrier	hanger/strap/yoke/ saddle
(-) de levage	link
(-) de serrage	clip
(-) de suspension d'une canalisation	pipe hanger
étude	study design
évacuation	discharge/disposal/ exhaust
(-) des déchets	waste disposal
évasement	flare
excavateur	excavator/digger
(-) à benne preneuse	clamshell (-)
(-) à godets	scoop dredger/power shovel/back action shovel
excavatrice	trencher/ditcher
excédent	excess
(-) de poids	(-) weight
excitation en dérivation	shunt excitation
en excès	extraneous
excréments	excreta
exhaure	pumping/de-watering
expédition	shipping
exposé	statement
exposition	exposure; exhibition
exploration radio	electric scanning
expulsion	ejection
exsudation	exudation
extincteur	extinguisher
extractible	extractable
extracteur	extractor/finger grip
extraction	extraction; drawing/ pulling
(-) du tubage	withdrawal of casing
extrapolation	scaling up/extrapolation
extrêmité	tip/end
(-) filetée	threaded end
(-) mâle d'un joint de tige	pin
(-id-) femelle	box
(-) mâle d'un tube	spigot end of pipe

extrudeuse	extruder
extrusif	extrusive
roche extrusive	(-) rock

F

face	face/side
(-) aval	lee
(-) d'appui	thrust (-)
(-) en saillie/	raised (-)
(-) surélevée	
faciès	facies
(-) continental	continental/terrestrial (-)
facilité d'entretien	serviceability
façonné	worked/shaped/profiled
faible	weak/low/poor/dim
(-) clivage	poor cleavage
(-) pendage	dip at low angle
faille	fault
(-) active	active (-)
(-) affaissée/	downthrow (-)
(-) d'effondrement	
(-) béante	gap (-)
(-) à charnière	hinge (-)/pivotal (-)
(-) en ciseaux	scissor (-)
(-) de décrochement	strike slip (-)
(-) diagonale	semilongitudinal (-)/ semitransverse (-)
(-) de dislocation	shift (-)
(-) en échelons	echelon (-)
(-) à faible pendage	low angle (-)
(-) fermée	close (-)
(-) à fort pendage	high angle (-)
(-) à gradins/ (-)en escalier	step (-)/distributive (-)
(-) inclinée	dipping (-)
(-) à rejet horizontal	strike-slip (-)
(-) à rejets multiples	multi throw (-)
(-) limite/ (-) marginale	boundary (-)
(-) transversale	dip (-)
faisceau	bundle/bunch; beam
faîte	apex/crest/top
ligne de (-)	spurline
falaise	cliff
(-) litorale	shore (-)
fanglomérat	fanglomerate
fatigue	fatigue
(-) de torsion	twisting
(-) par vibrations	vibration (-)

fêlure	crack/split
(-) par fatigue	fatigue (-)
fendage	splitting
fenêtre	window; inlier
(-) tectonique	geologic window/ nappe inlier
fente	slit/gap/crack/ split fissure
(-) de faillage	fault fissure
(-) de glissement	slip fault
fer profilé	section iron/sectional iron
fermé	close/shut in
fermentation	fermentation
fermeture	closure/shut-off
fermoir de sûreté	safety catch
feuillard	strip steel
feuille	sheet
feuillet basal	bottomset bed
(-) frontal	foreset (-)
(-) sommital	topset (-)
feux de position	side lights
ficelle	twine
fiche	plug/peg/pin/jack
fiente (d'oiseaux)	bird droppings
fil	edge; wire
filage	slipping (of the drilling rope to change the points of wear)
filet	thread
filetage	thread/threading
(-) de l'outil	bit shank
filière	die
porte (-)	(-) stocks
filiforage	slim hole drilling
filon	lode/seam/vein
filtration	filtration/filtering; percolation/leaching
(-) des boues avec autocompactage du gâteau	(-) of sludge with self-compacting of cake
(-) de l'eau avec coagulation sur filtre	water filtration with coagulation on filtre
(-) lente sur lit de sable	slow sand (-)
(-) sur couche unique	water filtration on single layer
(-) homogène	uniform grain size (-)

(-) hétérogène	nonuniform grain size (-)	*fluidifiant*	thinning agent
(-) sur support à mailles	(-) through mesh media	*(-) pour boue de forage*	mud thinner
(-) sur support à pré couche	(-) through precoated supporting media	*fluor*	fluorine
		fluoruration	fluoridation
filtre	filter/strainer/screen	*fluorure*	fluoride
(-) à boue	mud screen		
(-) à cartouche	cartridge (-)	*flux*	flux/flow/outflow
(-) à charbon	carbon (-)	*(-) axial*	axial flow
(-) à écoulement par gravité	gravity (-)	*(-) radial*	radial flow
(-) à gravier	gravel packed (-)	*fonçage/ foncement*	sinking
(-) à sable	sand (-)	*(-) de puits*	well boring/well sinking or digging
(-) lent à sable	slow sand (-)		
		foncé	sunk; dark/deep
fiole	phial		
		fonction-noyau	kernel function
fioul	fuel	*(diagraphie de puits)*	(well logging)
fissure	fissure/crack/ cleft/crevice	*fonctionnement*	running/working
		fond	bottom/floor
fixe	settled	*(-) de carter*	sump
		(-) des mers	sea bed
flacon	bottle/phial	*(-) salant*	salt pan
		(-) sondage	borehole (-)
flambement	buckling	*(-) de vallée*	valley (-)
		(-id-) plat	valley floor
flanc	flank/side/limb		
(-) anticlinal	anticlinal flank/limb	*fondant de soudure*	soldering flux
(-) d'un pli	shank		
(-) synclinal	synclinal limb	*fonds*	fund
flasques d'un tambour	spooling flanges	*fontaine*	spring/fountain; wash-basin
fléau de balance	beam/scales beam	*borne (-)*	standpipe
flèche	arrow/jib/boom; spit	*fontainier*	spring catchment specialist
(-) de grue	crane boom		
(-) de levage	jin pole	*fonte/ fonte en gueuses/ fonte en saumons*	pig iron
fleuret	borer/jumper bar; drill	*(-) aciérée*	semi steel
fleuve	river (that flows into the sea)	*forage*	drilling/boring; well/ borehole
flexible	flexible hose/cable	*(-) à air comprimé*	compressed air drilling
(-) d'aspiration	suction hose	*(-) par battage*	cable drilling/cable tool drilling
(-) d'injection	mud (-)/rotary (-)	*(-) à bras*	hand (-)
		(-) dévié	deflected/side-tracked hole/slant section
floc	floc	*(-) d'exploitation*	production well
		(-) d'exploration	exploration drilling
flocon	flake/clot	*(-) à grande profondeur*	deep (-)
floconneux	flaky	*(-) à la grenaille*	shot (-)
		(-) improductif	dry hole
floculation	flocculation/coagulation	*(-) par percussion*	percussion/cable drilling
flottation	flotation	*(-) profond*	deep hole
		(-) rotary	rotary (-)
flottement des roues	shimmy	*(-) au marteau*	down-the-hole hammer drilling (DTH)
flou	blurred/fuzzy	*fond de trou (MFT)*	drilling journal/log/ record
fluage	creep/flow	*rapport de (-)*	
fluid	fluid		
(-) boueux	mud (-)		
(-) d'entraînement	power (-)		
(-) de refroidissement	coolant		

force	force/strength/power	*(-) intermédiaire*	adapter bushing
(-) d'arrachement	pullout load		
(-) de cisaillement	shear force	*fracture*	fracture
(-) motrice	driving power/prime	*réseau de (-)*	joint pattern
	mover	*(-) horizontale*	bed joint
(-) de pénétration	penetrating power		
(-) de traction	tensile force	*fragment*	bit/chip/fragment/
			scrap
foret	drill/bit		
(-) hélicoïdal	twist drill	*fraise*	cutter/milling tool
(ou américain)		*(-) conique*	tapered mill
(-) conique/(-) à	countersink (-)	*(-id-) mâle*	pipe reamer
fraiser			
(-) au diamant	diamond (-)	*frange*	fringe
		(-) d'érosion	belt of weathering
foreur	driller		
(-) novice	"boll weevil"	*frappe*	striking
foreuse	rig/drilling machine	*frein*	brake
formation	formation	*frettage*	banding
(-) adjacentes	surrounding beds		
(-) aquifère	aquifer/water bearing	*friabilité d'un*	friability of a
	formation	*matériau filtrant*	filtering material
(-) boulante	sloughing/		
	unconsolidated (-)	*front*	front/face
(-) consolidée	consolidated (-)	*(-) d'attaque/*	face/working face
(-) éboulante	caving (-)	*(-) de taille*	
(-) épuisée	depleted (-)	*(-id-) de trépan*	bit gauge surface
(-) fissurée/	thief/cracked (-)		
(-) poreuse		*fuite*	leak/loss/spill
(-) tectonisée	disturbed/fractured (-)		
(-) de brèche	brecciation	*fumée*	smoke
		(-) et brouillard	smog (smoke and fog)
fosse	pit	*(-) épaisse*	smudge
(-) d'aisance	cesspool		
(-) à boue	mud (-)/slush (-)	*fumier*	manure
(-) de décantation	settling (-)/lagoon		
(-) marginale	marginal deep	*furet*	rabbit/pig
(-) septique	septic tank	*(débouchage de*	(cleaning of clogged
(-) tectonique	fault trough	*canalisations)*	pipelines)
fossé	ditch/trench	*fusée*	spindle
(-) d'effondrement	rift valley/fault trough	*(-) d'essieu*	axle (-)
(-) de drainage	drainage ditch		
		fusible	fuse
fouettement (du	lashing (of strings	*bouchon (-)*	safety plug
train de tige)	in the borehole)		
		fusion	smelting; melting
fouille	excavation/opening/		
	digging	*fût*	drum/cask/barrel
remplissage	padding of ditch		
de la (-)			
fouloir	tamper/trench		
	compactor		
		# G	
fourche	fork		
(-) à cliquet	boot jack	*gabarit*	gauge/caliper/
(-) à émerillon	swivel wrench		template
(-) de retenue	rod (-)		
		gadoue	slush
fourré	thicket	*gaz de (-)*	sewage (-)
fourreau	sheath/sleeve/cover	*gain*	gain/profit/earnings
(-) démontable	removable liner	*(-) en puissance*	power gain
fourrure	lining/bushing	*gainage*	cladding/sheathing
(-) d'entraînement	kelly bushing		
(-) de table	driving (-id-)	*gaine*	(-id-); gangue; duct;
			housing/sleeve

(-) de câble	cable sheath
(-) de plomb	lead sheathing
(-) d'entraînement de la tige carrée	kelly drive bushing/ master drive bushing
galerie	passage/gallery; cornice
galet	pebble; roller
(-) roulé	rounded (-)/(-) stone
(-) façonné	faceted (-)
(-) de plage	shingle
(-) roulé	rounded (-)/(-) stone
(-) strié	striated boulder/pebble
galet de chenille	track roller
(-) de guidage	jockey pulley
(-) fou	idler roller
galop (emballement d'un moteur)	galloping (of an engine fed too rich a mixture)
gamme	range
gangue	gangue/matrix
(-) de minerai	brood
gants de sécurité	safety gloves
garde	guard/clearance
(-) corps/(-) fou	handrail/guardrail
(-) au sol	ground clearance
garnissage	lining/lagging; packing
garniture	stuffing/packing/ gasket/seal/lining
(-) d'étanchéité	gland/packer/packing ring
(-id) pour tiges	tubing packer
(-) de bride	flange gasket
(-) d'embrayage	clutch lining
(-) étanche de tubage	casing packer
(-) de frein	brake shoe lining
(-) de presse étoupe	stuffing box gland/ gland packing
(-) de repêchage	fishing string
(-) de tige	rod packing
gaspillage	wasting
gâteau	cake
(-) de filtration	filter (-)
gauche/gauchissement	warping/buckling
gaz	gas
(-) carbonique	carbon dioxide
(-) de digestion	digestion gas
(-) de gadoue	sewage (-)
(-) de pétrole liquéfié (GPL)	liquefied petroleum (-)/ (LPG)
gaze	gauze
gazole	gas oil/diesel oil
gazosiphon	airlift
gel	gel
gélifiant/agent gélifiant	gelling agent
générateur/ génératrice	generator
(-) électrique	electric (-)
(-) à vapeur	boiler/steam generator
(-) de gaz	gas (-)
génie	engineering
genouillère	swing joint/toggle joint
géofracture	geosuture
géologie	geology
(-) de surface	field (-)
(-) stratigraphique	stratigraphic (-)
géologique	geological
géomètrie	geometry
(-) des puits	well pattern
géophone	geophone
géophysique	geophysical
étude (-)	(-) survey
géosynclinal	geosyncline
géothermique	geothermal
gerbable	stackable
gerbage	racking/bundling
gerbeur	stacking truck
gicleur	nozzle/jet
(-) de ralenti	slow running jet
giflard	jet gun
gisement	deposit/field
gîte	bed/deposit/vein
(-) disloqué	dislocated deposit
(-) mineral	mineral (-)
(-) métallifère	ore (-)
(-) en selle	saddle reef/saddle vein
glacis	glacis
(-) continental	continental rise
(-) de piémont	slope/piedmont slope
glissade	skewing
glissement	sliding/slipping/creeping
(-) d'un outil de forage	offset skewness
(-) de terrain	landslide/earthcreep
plan de (-)	gliding plane
surface de (-)	sliding surface
glissière	slide/groove
(-) de forage	drilling jar
gluant	sticky/tacky/gummy

GNL (gaz naturel liquifié)	LNG (liquid natural gas)
godet	bucket/scoop
(-) de drague	dredge bucket
(-) graisseur	oil/grease cup
(-) pour graissage forcé	pressure grease cup
(-) niveleur	skimmer
(-) de pelle mécanique	dipper
gommage	gumming/sticking
(-) des segments	ring/piston ring sticking
gomme	gum
(-) dans les moteurs	engine (-)
(-) lacque	shellac
gommeux	gummy
gondolement	warping/buckling
gonflement	swelling
gonfler	to swell/to blow-up
agent gonflant	swelling agent
gonflement du mur d'un forage/puits	creep/heaving of a well wall
gorge	groove/neck/gorge/ throat; pass/flume gulch/clough
(-) de torrent	gully
(-) profonde	canyon
(-) pour garniture/ joint	gasket groove
goudron	tar
gouge	gouge
gouffre	gulf/pit/abyss/ cauldron/shallowhole
goujon	stud bolt/gudgeon bolt/dowel pin
goulet	narrows/strait
goulot	spout/mouth/neck
(-) d'étranglement	bottle neck
goulotte	chute/gutter/downspout
(-) d'alimentation	feed chute
(-) à boue	mud ditch
goupille	cotter pin/pin
(-) de cisaillement	shear pin
(-) fendue	split (-)
(-) de retenue	retainer (-)
(-) pour support de tube d'usure	wash plug
chasse (-)	pin punch
gousset	gusset/gusset or corner plate
goutte	drop
(-) à goutte	drip feed

goutelette	droplet
gouttière	gutter/channel/ groove trough
GPL (gaz de pétrole liquifié)	LPG (liquefied petroleum gas)
graben	fault trough
gradient	gradient
(-) alterné	alternating gradient
(-) d'accroissement de déviation	angle built-up
(-) de décroissance de déviation	angle drop-off
(-) hydraulique	hydraulic gradient
(-) d'inclinaison	rate of build up
(-) de température/ (-) thermique	temperature/thermal (-)
gradin	step/scarp/tier/bench
(-) de confluence	confluence step
(-) de faille	scarp fault/scarp bench
(-) de plage	berm
(-) structural	rock step
graduation	scale
gradué	calibrated/graded
grain	grain/granule/bead/ texture
(-) fin	fine grain
(-) grossier	coarse (-)
(-) moyen	medium (-)
(-) régulier	smooth (-)
(-) serré	close (-)
graissage	lubrication/ lubrification
(-) à bague	ring (-)
(-) par barbotage	bath lubrication
(-) à carter sec	dry sump (-)
(-) à la burette	squirt can (-)
(-) par bain d'huile	oil bath (-)
(-) centralisé	central (-)
(-) forcé	forced (-)
(-) goutte à goutte	drop-feed (-)
(-) par film	film (-)
(-) par mèche	wick feed (-)
(-) par projection	splash (-)
graisse	grease/fat
(-) à bas point de congélation	cold setting (-)
(-) à haut point de fusion	high melting point (-)
(-) au savon de calcium	lime base (-)
(-) pour câbles métalliques	wire-rope compound
(-) sodique	soda (-)
graisseur	lubricator/oiler; greaser/ grease cup
(-) goutte à goutte	drop-feed (-)

grandeur	magnitude/size
granit	granite
(-) à deux micas	binary (-)
(-) recristallisé	recomposed (-)
granule	granule/pellet
granulométrie	grain size distribution/ granulometry
(-) d'une couche filtrante	(-) of filtering bed
(-) d'un matériau filtrant	(-) of filtering material
granulosité	coarseness of grain
graphique	graphic; diagram/chart/ graph
grappe	cluster
grappin	grapple/grab/hook
(-) à câble	rope grab
(-) de repêchage	tool extractor/grab
gratteur/ grâtoir	scraper
(-) de terrain	scratcher
(pour préparer la cimentation des parois)	(to scrub the cake off well walls)
graveleux	gritty/gravelly
gravelage	graveling
gravier	gravel/gravel stone
(-) alluvionnaire	run (-)
(-) de carrière	pit (-)
(-) de rivière	river (-)
(-) sableux	hoggin
(-) de terrasse	bench (-)
gravillon	fine gravel/grit
gravillonneuse	grit spreader
gréement	rigging-up/rig gear
grenaillage	shot blasting
grenaille	shot
grès	sandstone
griffe	grip/claw
(-) à coins	slip (-)
(-) de serrage	dog hook
grillage	wire netting/grating
grille	grate/grid/rack
(-) mécanique	mechanical bar screen
(-) à secousses	shaking grate
(-) d'accrochage/ de stockage	racking fingers (storage of string)
grippage	seizing/sticking
(-) naissant	scuffing
grippé	seized
gros, grosse	coarse/big/rough

(-) grain	coarse grain
(-) gravier	(-) gravel
(-) maille	wide meshed
grossissement	magnification/ enlargement
groupe	group/cluster/unit
(-) électrogène	electric generator
(-) moteur	power unit
(-) de crystaux	cluster of crystals
grue	crane/boom derrick
(-) à benne	grab (-)
(-) à câble	dragline cableway
(-) à flêche	jib crane
(-) à portique	gantry (-)
(-) à potence	pillar (-)
grumeau	clot
guérite	cabine/cab
guidage	guide/track
(-) du câble	wire line guide
colonne/pilier de (-)	guide post
entonnoir de (-)	(-) funnel
ligne de (-)	guideline
(-) des tiges/ (-) du tubage	stabbing
guide	guide/slide
(-) -butoir	spearpoint head
(-) de tige de pompage	-rod (-)
guipage	covering/lapping
(-) isolant	insulating cover

H

habitat	habitat
(-) à pression de fond	pressure (-)
hachure	stripe; shading
halage	haulage/towage
ligne de (-)	towline
halogénure	halide
hamada	hammada (rock desert)
harnais	harness
(-) d'engrenage	gearing
(-) de sécurité	safety harness
harpon	grapple/crowsfoot/ spear/fishing hook
(-) à câble	rope spear
(-) de repêchage	fishing (-)

hauban	brace/guy/guy wire/stay
(-) tendeur	span wire
haut, haute	top/summit; high
(-) d'un puits	top of shaft/top of well
(-) de pente	high slope
(-) hautes eaux	high water
(-) pression	(-) pressure
(-) teneur/	(-) grade
(-) qualité	
(-) tourbière	peat moor
hauteur	height/elevation/head/lift
(-) au dessus du niveau moyen de la mer	(-) above the mean sea level (msl)
(-) d'aspiration	suction head/suction lift
(-id-) d'une pompe	pump lift
(-) d'eau	water level
(-) de chute	head of water
(-) piézométrique	piezometric/hydraulic head
(-) de refoulement	delivery (-)
(-id-) d'une pompe	lift of a pump
(-) de remblayage	depth of fill
hauteurs	fells
havage	cutting/bossing
hélice	spiral/helix; propeller
(-) à vis	screw/spiral conveyor
enroulement en (-)	winding
hélico-compresseur	screw compressor
hérisson	pipe brush/swab/scratcher
hisser	to hoist/to raise/to pull up
hiverisation	winterisation
horizon	horizon/marker
(-) aquifère	water horizon
(-) argileux	clay pan
(-) d'apport	alluvial horizon
hors service	shut down
houle	swell
huile	oil
(-) chlorée	chlorinated (-)
(-) de coupe	cutting (-)
(-) d'ébauchage	roughing-cut (-)
(-) de graissage	lubricating/lube (-)
(-id-) pour mécanique fine	castor machine (-)
(-) de meulage	grinding (-)
(-) de vaseline	paraffin (-)
(-) de vidange	drain (-)
(-id-) de carter	sump (-)

humidité	moisture/humidity/dampness
hydraulique	hydraulics
hydrocarbure	hydrocarbon
hydrofuge	damp proof/water repellent
hydrogéologie	hydrogeology
hydrologie	hydrology
hydrolube	hydrolube
hydromètre	thermometric hydrometer
hydroséparateur	hydroseparator
hydrotimétrie	titration for hardness
hygiène	hygiene
(-) du milieu	environmental (-)/sanitation
hygromètre	hygrometer
hypsomètre	hypsometer/height measurer

I

idiogène	idiogenous/syngenetic
idiogéosynclinal	idiogeosyncline/marginal deep
île	island
îlot	islet
(-) de boue	mud lump
image	picture/image
imbiber	to soak up/to imbibe
imbrication	imbrication
imbriqué	imbricated/overlapping/criss-cross
immersion	dip/dipping
impact	impact/shock
test d' (-)	(-) test
imperfection	fault/defect
(-) crystalline	crystal defect/lattice defect
imperméabilisant/ imperméabilisation	water proofing/caulking
implantation	installation/positioning
impluvium	river basin

impointable	unpickable	*indicateur de niveau*	level gauge
imposé	specified	*(-id-) à membrane*	diaphragm (-)
imprécis	imprecise/faint/ inaccurate	*(-id-) capacitif*	capacitor (-)
		(-) par ultra son	ultrasonic (-)
imprécision	vagueness/looseness/ inaccuracy	*indice*	number/index; show
		(-) porteur du sol	soil bearing value
imprégnation	impregnation/ permeation	*(-) de peroxyde*	peroxyde (-)
(-) saline	salinization	*induration*	induration/hardening of sediments
impression	print/printing; primary coating of paint	*infiltration*	infiltration/leakage/ percolation
		inflammation	ignition
impulsion	impulse/pulse; impetus	*influence*	effect/influence
impuretés	soiled marks/foulness	*(-) topographique*	topographical (-)
inalterable	unalterable/ noncorrosive	*infusoires*	diatoms
		terre d' (-)	diatomaceous earth
incassable	shatter-proof	*ingénieur*	engineer
incidence	incidence	*(-) des boues*	mud (-)
angle d' (-)	angle of incidence/ angle of relief	*ingression*	ingression
incinération	incineration	*inhibiteur*	inhibitor/deterrent
(-) des boues	(-) of sludge	*(-) de boue*	sludge (-)
(-) des ordures ménagères	(-) of garbage	*(-) d'entartrage*	scale (-)
		injecteur	nozzle/injector
incise-tube	casing ripper/ casing splitter	*injection*	injection
		(-) directe	direct (-)
inclinaison	inclination/plunge/ dip/slope/gradient; pitch/slant/tilt/ declivity/strike	*(-) inverse*	reverse circulation
		inondation	flood
		(-) en nappe	sheet (-)
(-) de faille	fault strike	*inoxydable*	stainless
(-) moyenne	average hade	*acier (-)*	(-) steel
(-) de pendage	dip slope	*installation*	setting up/hooking up; plant/unit/installation
(-) primaire	primary dip		
angle d' (-)	angle of drift	*(-) d'essai*	test plant
		(-) d'évacuation des déchets	waste disposal system
inclinomètre	inclinometer		
(-) à fil tendu	taut-wire indicator	*(-) de filtration*	filtering plant/unit
(-) à orientation	single shot inclinometer	*(-) de forage*	drill rig
		(-id-) combiné	combination (-)
(-) à siphon	siphoclinometer	*instructions*	directions/briefing/ orders
inclusion	enclosure/insertion/ spot		
		instrument	instrument
inconsistant	unconsistent/soft/ loose	*(-) d'arpentage*	surveying (-)
		instrumentation	fishing/recovering (drilling equipment)
incrustation	incrustation/scale deposit/scale/fur		
		insuffisance	deficiency
indicateur	indicator/gage/ gauge	*intensité*	intensity/current; density; severity
(-) d'orientation	steering tool		
(-) de charge/ de poids	load indicator		
(-) de couple	drill torque (-)		

intercalation	insertion/interbedding/ break
(-) d'argile	clay potting/gouge
(-) de grès	sandstone band
(-) de sable	cross bedded sand
(-) de schiste	slate break
interdigitation	interfingering/ intertonguing
interprétation	significance/ interpretation
(-) monodynamique	monodynamism
(-) polydynamique	polydynamism
interrupteur	switch/breaker/circuit breaker/cut out
(-) à bascule	trigger/tumbler switch
intervalle	clearance/gap/interval/ range/span
intervention	trouble shooting/ servicing/work
intrusion	intrusion/dyke
(-) de sel/(-) saline	salt (-)
inversion	reversal/inversion
(-) de courant	back flush
(-) de phase	phase inversion
(-) de relief	inverted relief
irregularité	unevenness/irregularity
(-) de refoulement à l'extrêmité des tiges	upset wrinkles
isolation	insulation; by-passing/ cutting-off
(-) accoustique	sound proofing

J

jaillissement	spouting/gushing/
(-) de lave	blowing cone
jalon	peg/pole/surveying rod/picket
(-) d'arpenteur	leveling pole
jambe	leg/shank
(-) de chien	dog leg
(-) de force	strut
jante	rim
jauge	gage/gauge/dipstick
(-) à coulisse	caliper gage/gauge
(-) à trépan	drilling bit (-)

javellisation	chlorination
jet	stream/throw/jet
(-) d'air	air blast
(-) de boue	spatter cone
(-) de sable	sand blast
jeu	gap/clearance/set/ play
(-) axial	end play
(-) de clés	set of wrenches
(-) de piston	clearance of piston
rattrapage de (-)	taking the strain
joint	joint gasket/seal/ rift/diaclase
(-) annulaire/ (-) à bague	ring type joint
(-) bout à bout	butt (-)
(-) brasé	brazed (-)
(-) à bride	flanged (-)
(-) calfaté	caulked (-)
(-) à cardan	universal (-)
(-) de chanvre	hemp (-)
(-) en chicane	break joint
(-) de cisaillement	shear (-)
(-) coulissant	slip (-)
(-) de culasse	cylinder head gasket
(-) de dilatation	expansion joint
(-) à étriers du balancier	walking beam
(-) à francs bords	flush joint
(-) à lèvres	lip seal
(-) à queue d'aronde	dovetail joint
(-) à rotule	ball (-)/cup and ball (-)/ ball and socket (-)/ knuckle (-)
(-) à soufflets	bellows (-)
(-) de stratification	bedding joint
(-) de tige	tool (-)
(-) entre deux couches	cross (-)
(-) entre éléments de tubage	casing collar
(-) horizontal	bed joint
(-) parallèle à l'inclinaison	(-) dip
(-) virtuel	blind (-)
(-) à vis	screw (-)
joues de vilebrequin	crankshaft flanges
journal de sonde	log book
jumelles	field glasses/ binoculars
jupe	skirt
(-) de piston	piston (-)
(-) de fondation	foundation (-)

K

karst
 (-) complet/
 (-) profond
 (-) couvert
 (-) incomplet/
 (-) superficiel
 (-) sous-jacent

karst
 deep (-)

 covered (-)
 shallow (-)

 underlying (-)

karstique
 vallée (-)

karstic
 karst valley

kieselguhr

diatomite

L

LAA/ latrine à
 aération améliorée

VIP (ventilated improved
 pit latrine)

LAADV/ latrine
 améliorée à double
 voûte/ à double
 compartiment à fosse
 autoventilée

revised earth closet
 (REC), double vaulted

labourage
 (-) glaciaire

plowing/tilling
 glacial plowing

lac
 (-) cratère/(-)de
 cratère
 (-) de cirque
 (-) d'effondrement
 (-) de cuvette
 éolienne
 (-) de doline
 (-) résiduel
 (-) salé
 (-) temporaire

lake
 crater (-)/maar

 tarn
 cave-in lake
 deflation (-)

 sinkhole pond/lake
 relict (-)
 salina
 dry (-)

laçage

lacing

lâche

loose/slack/weak

lacis

network

lacune

gap/hiatus/
 unconformity/lacuna/
 vacancy
 (-) d'érosion
 (-) de sédimentation

erosion gap
 sedimentary (-)/
 break/diastem
 (-) stratigraphique

stratigraphic gap/break
 in the succession/
 stratigraphic hiatus
 discontinuité
 par (-)

paraconformity

lacustre
 calcaire (-)
 dépôts (-)
 faciès (-)
 sables (-)

lacustrine
 (-) limestone
 (-) deposits
 (-) facies
 (-) sands/lymnetic sands

lagunage
 (-) aéré

oxydation pond
 sludge activation

lagune
 (-) à marée

lagoon
 tidal (-)

laine
 (-) de verre

wool
 glass (-)

lait
 (-) de chaux
 (-) de ciment

milk/slurry
 whitewash/whitelime
 grout/cement slurry

laitier

slag/slurry

lambeau
 (-) de charriage
 (-) de recouvrement
 (-) de témoin

scrap
 nappe outlier/klippe
 thrust outlier
 roof pendant

lambourde

sleeper

lame

strip/blade/leaf;
 wave/surge; slice
 (-) de scie
 (-) de ressort

saw blade
 spring leaf

lamelle
 (-) de macle

lamina/lamella
 twinning lamella

laminage
 (-) des brames
 (-) des tubes

rolling
 slabbing
 tube rolling

lampe
 (-) à acétylène
 (-) à arc
 (-) baladeuse

lamp/bulb
 acetylene lamp
 arc (-)/arc light
 inspection/
 portable (-)
 (-) à carbure
 (-) à pétrole

carbide (-)
 oil burning (-)/
 paraffin (-)
 (-) de signalisation
 (-) à souder

signal (-)
 soldering (-)/soldering
 torch/blow (-)
 (-) témoin

pilot (-)/indicator (-)/
 pilot/warning light
 (-) tempête

hurricane (-)

lance d'incendie

fire hose

lancement

launching/throwing/
 starting
 (-) à air comprimé
 (-) par inertie

compressed air starting
 inertia starting

lande
 (-) marécageuse

moor/heath/barren land
 muskeg

langue
 (-) de terre

tong
 spit/neck of land

latérite
 (-) gravillonnaire

laterite
 concretionary (-)

latitude	latitude	*lessivage*	washing/leaching
(-) paramétrique	isometric (-)	*(-) du sol*	soil leaching
latrine (ou cabinet/	latrine/toilet	*lessive*	lye/detergent
cabinet d'aisance)		*(-) de soude*	soda (-)
(-) améliorée	improved (-)		
(-) à double	revised earth closet,	*levage*	raising/lifting/hoisting
compartiment/	double vaulted (REC)		
(-id-) à double vôute/		*levé*	survey/plotting
(LAADV)		*(-) à la boussole*	compass survey/dialling
(-id-) à fosse	ventilated improved (-)/	*(-) cadastral*	cadastral survey
autoventilée/(-id-) à	VIP (-)	*(-) par cheminement*	meander (-)
aération améliorée (LAA)		*(-) gravimétrique*	gravity (-)
(-id-) inodore	ROEC/Reed odorless	*(-) photogrammétrique*	aerial (-)
système Reed (LIR)	earth closet	*(-) à la planchette*	plane (-)
(-id-) à chasse	pour-flush (-)	*(-) terrestre*	ground (-)
d'eau		*(-) topographique*	survey
(-id-) à col de	waterseal (-)/		
cygne/(-id-) à joint	aquaprivy)	*levée*	raising/lifting;
d'eau			embankment
(-id-) à compost/	composting (-)	*(-) de blocs*	boulder wall
à humus		*(-) de galets*	boulder ridge/gravel
(-id-)alternante	batch (-id-)		rampart
(-id-) à double	double vault(-id-)/	*(-) de terre*	mound/bank
voûte/à deux	DVC (-)		
compartiments/(-)CCDV		*levier*	lever/handle/arm
(-)permanente	continuous composting (-)	*(-) de battage*	walking beam
(-) à double compartiment	double vault (-)	*(-) à cliquet*	pawl lever
(-) à fosse	pit (-)	*(-) à déclic*	trip (-)
(-) sèche	dry (-id-)	*(-) de direction*	steering (-)
(-) améliorée	improved (-id-)		
(-) permanente	permanent improved (-)	*lèvre*	lip/side/wall
améliorée/ CFPA		*(-) de faille*	fault wall
(-) à réservoir de	pip (-)	*(-id-) supérieure*	upthrown side of
chasse	flush (-)	*de faille*	a fault
(-) à tinette	bucket (-)	*(-) soulevée d'une*	lifted side
(-) à la turque	squat plate (-)	*faille*	
(-) multrum (conception	multrum (-) (swedish	*(-) inférieure*	lowered side
suédoise d'une latrine	design of double	*d'une faille*	
anaérobique permanente à	compartment anaerobic		
deux compartiments	permanent latrine)	*lézarde*	split/crack/crevice
(-) UTAFIFI (évolution	UTAFIFI (-) Tanzanian	*(-) de tassement*	settling crack
en Tanzanie du modèle	adaptation of above design		
précédent		*liaison*	bond/connection/
			fastener/link
latte	batten/lath		
		liant	binder/jointing material
lattis	lattice		
		ligne	line
lavage	washing/scrubbing	*(-) d'affleurement*	outcrop line
(-) au crible	jigging/jigger work	*(-) de charnière*	hinge (-)
		(-) de chevauchement	overthrust (-)
lécheur	wiper ring	*(-) de circulation*	boosting (-)
		(-) continue	solid (-)
lecture	reading	*(-) de faille*	fault (-)
		(-) de faîte	crest (-)/spurline
légende	caption/legend/key	*(-) de partage des*	divide
		eaux	
lent	slow/sluggish	*(-) de pente*	(-) of dip
		(-) piézométrique	hydraulic grade (-)
lenticulaire	lens shaped/lenticular	*(-) de plus grande*	slope (-)
		pente	
lentille	lens	*(-) de sonde*	plumb (-)
(-) allongée	rod	*(-) de visée*	sighting (-)/
(-) de grès	sandstone (-)		transit (-)
(-) de roche	sill		
(-) de sable	sand (-)/stray sand	*limaille*	filings

lime	file
(-) bâtarde	bastard (-)
(-) demi ronde	half round (-)
(-) tiers-point	three square (-)
limite	boundary/limit
(-) d'allongement	strain limit
(-) de charge	maximum load
(-) de faille	fault boundary
(-) d'élasticité	yield strength/yield stress
(-) de fatigue	stress limit
limon	silt/alluvium/slime/ sullage
limonage	silting up
limoneux	slimy
lingot	ingot/bar/billet
linguet	pawl/catch/rocker
LIR (latrine améliorée inodore système Reed)	ROEC (Reed odorless earth closet)
lissage	smoothing
lit	bed/layer/stratum
(-) alternés	alternating beds
(-) aquifère	water-bearing bed
(-) bactérien	bacterial floc
(-) divaguant	shifting (-)
(-) filtrant	filter (-)
(-) de fleuve/	stream/river bed
(-) de rivière	
(-) de hautes eaux	river flat
(-) imperméable	impervious (-)
lixiviation	leaching/lixiviation
localisateur	locator
(-) de canalisation	underground line (-)
logement	housing/dwelling
(-) de clavette	key way
logiciel	software
longeron	girder/stringer
loquet	latch
loupe	lens; bloom
(-) d'acier	steel (-)
lot	lot/run/batch
lubrifiant	lubricant/lubricating
(-) synthétique	synlub
lumachelle	shell breccia/shell cock
lumière	light; port/hole
(-) polarizée	polarized light
(-) de graissage	oil hole
lunettes	goggles; fieldglasses
(-) de soudage	welding goggles

lutte	fight/control
(-) contre la corrosion	corrosion control
lyre de dilatation	expansion loop/expansion bend

M

machine	machine/machine tool/ engine
(-) à affûter	grinding (-)/sharpener
(-id-) les fleurets	drill sharpener
(-) à biseauter/	beveling/chamfering (-)
(-) à chanfreiner	
(-) à cintrer les tubes	pipe bending (-)/ pipe bender
(-) à cisailler/	shearing (-)
(-) à découper	
(-) à damer le remblayage	bacfill tamper
(-) à ébarber	fettling/trimming machine
(-) à fileter	threading (-)/thread cutting (-)
(-) à fraiser	milling (-)
(-) à limer	filing (-)
(-) à meuler	grinding (-)
(-) à planer/	
(-) à rabotter/ étau limeur	planing (-)
(-) à rectifier	grinding (-)
(-) à roder	lapping (-)
(-) à souder	welding (-)
(-) à tamiser	screening (-)
mâchoire	jaw/grip
(-) d'étau	vise (-)
(-) d'obturateur	ram/pipe ram
(-) de fermeture sur tige	pipe (-)
(-) de frein	brake shoe
(-) de sécurité	safety clamp
(-) de suspension	tubing catcher
(-) pleine/(-) à fermeture totale	blind ram
macle	twin crystal
(-) de pénétration	penetration twin
maçonnerie	masonry/brick laying/ brickwork
(-) de la cuve	shaft/well lining
(-) en moellons	rubble masonry
macro tamis	macrostrainer
madrier	skid/joist/piece of lumber

magasin	store	*manchon*	coupling/nipple/
magasinier	store keeper		collar/bushing/sleeve
		(-) d'accouplement	(-) sleeve/(-) box
magnétique	magnetic/magnet	*(-id-) élastique*	yielding (-)/elastic (-)
		(-) de battage	drive head
magnétomètre	magnetometre/	*(-) de cimentation*	baffle collar
	variometre	*(-) coulissant*	sliding sleeve
		(-) double	box both ends
maillage	pattern/grid	*(-) fileté*	threaded sleeve
		(-) à friction	friction (-)
maille	mesh/grid/loop	*(-) à incandescence*	gas mantle
(-) d'un tamis	sieve mesh	*(-) protecteur*	protection sleeve
(-) étançonnée	stud link	*(-) de raccordement*	connecting sleeve
à (-) fines	close meshed	*(-) à soupape de*	float collar
		flottation	
maillechort	German silver	*(-) de sécurité des*	hose collar
		masses-tiges	
maillon	link	*(-) de tubage*	casing (-)
main	hand; labour/labor	*mandrin*	mandrel/chuck
(-) courante	railing/handrail	*(-) de repêchage*	mandrel socket
(-) d'oeuvre	manpower/labour	*(-) relève tubes*	casing spear
(-id-) intermittente	casual labor		
(-id-) saisonnière	seasonal (-)	*manette*	handle/hand lever
(-id-) spécialisée	skilled (-)		
(-) du diable	devil's hand (fishing)	*manifestation*	occurence
(repêchage)			
		manille	shackle
maintenance	servicing/maintenance	*(-) d'assemblage*	(-) clevis
		(-) d'élingue	sling line socket
maître	master		
(-) cylindre	(-) cylinder	*manivelle*	crank/handle
(-) d'oeuvre	prime contractor/	*(-) de mise en*	starting (-)
	supervisor	*route*	
(-) sondeur	tool pusher/drilling	*manoeuvre*	trip (pulling the drill
	superintendent/driller		string, attending to it,
			running it back into a
maître de l'ouvrage	sponsor		borehole); unskilled
			labour/hand
maîtresse-tige	drill/drilling stem/	*(-) complète (du*	round trip (as above)
	drill collar	*train de tiges)*	
(-) de repêchage	sinker bar		
		manoeuvre de sonde	roughneck
malaxage	mixing/kneading/	*(ouvrier)*	(labor)
	working		
		manomètre	pressure gauge/
malaxeur	mixer/churn/		manometre
	kneader	*(-) à cadran*	dial (-)
(-) à auges	trough mixer	*(-) à flotteur*	float type (-)
(-) de béton	concrete (-)	*(-) à membrane/*	diaphragm (-)
(-) éjecteur de boue	mud mixing hopper	*(-) à plaque*	
mamelon	hillock/mamelon; nipple	*manteau*	mantle/coat
(-) allongé	pipe nipple		
(-) central	meander core	*manuel*	manual/handbook
		(-) d'entretien	maintenance (-)
manche	sleeve; hose/pipe;	*(-) d'utilisation*	operator's (-)
	handle		
(-) à balai	joystick	*manutention*	handling
(-) à incendie	fire hose	*bras de (-)*	pipe-racker arm
(-) de manoeuvre	tiller/brace head		
(-) de pelle	shovel handle	*manutentionnaire*	stevedore
(-) de remplissage	filling sleeve/pipe		
(-) en toile	canvas hose	*maquette*	model
manchette	sleeve	*marais*	swamp/marsh
(-) à brides	spool	*(-) salant*	salt (-)/salt marsh

marche	running/working/ operation/progress; step	masse tige	drill collar
(-) à pleine puissance	full load (-)	(-id-) à appui sur paroi	wall supported (-)
(-) à vide	no-load (-)	(-id-) hydraulique à ancrage	hydraulic wall anchor (-)
(-) au ralenti	idling/idle (-)		
(-) arrêt	"on-off"	masse volumique	density
		(-id-) apparente	apparent (-)
mare	pond		
		massif	massive/bulk; solid mass/ block/plug
marécage	bog/marsh	(-) affaissé	sunken block
		(-) ancien	old land
marge	margin	(-) arasé	truncated upland
(-) de sécurité	safety (-)	(-) effondré	graben/trough fault
		(-) faillé	fault block
margelle	curbstone	(-) intrusif	boss
(d'un puits)	(of a well)	(-) surélevé	horst
		(-) tabulaire	table
marmite	pothole/aven/ kettle hole		
		mastic	putty/filler
marne	marl/shale		
(-) à silex	cherty (-)	mât de charge, mât	boom
(-) gonflante	heaving (-)		
(-) sableuse	sandy (-)	mât de forage	drilling mast/pole
délitage des (-)	marl sloughing	(-id-) à éléments coulissants	tubular telescopic (-)
		(-) cantilever	cantilever (-)
marnière	marl pit	(-) haubanné	guyed mast
		(-id-) démontable	(-id-) portable
marque	mark/marque/stamp	(-) non haubanné	free standing (-)
(-) de choc	percussion (-)	tête de (-)	(-) head
(-) glaciaire	glacial scratching		
		matériau	material/stuff
marqueur	tag	(-) calibré	graded (-)
		(-) détritique	land waste
marteau	hammer	(-) échoué	drifted (-)
(-) compresseur	jack (-)	(-) d'enrobage	wrapping (-)
(-) à devant	sledge (-)	(-) d'origine	parent (-)
(-) à panne sphérique	ball peen (-)	(-) de remblai	landfill/embankment (-)
(-) de fonçage	sinker	(-) superficiel	head
(-) fond de trou/ MFT	down-the-hole (-)/ DTH	matériel	equipment/material
(-) à forger/(-) à devant	forging (-)/sledge (-)	(-) de forage	drilling equipment
(-) de géologue	geologist (-)	matière	material/matter/ substance
(-) perforateur	drill (-)/(-) drill	(-) colloïdale	colloid/colloidal (-)
(-) pilon	drop (-)/ram	(-) dangereuse	hazardous (-)
(-) piqueur/	jack (-)/ram jack (-)/	(-) dissoutes totales	total dissolved solids
(-) pneumatique	rock drill/air (-)/ paving breaker	(-) filtrante	filter material
(-) pneumatique	jack (-)/rock drill/ air (-)/paving breaker	(-) inerte	inert (-)/filling substance
(-) riveur	riveting (-)	(-) inflammable	flammable (-)
		(-) isolante	insulating (-)
masse	mass/bulk; ground/ earthing (electr.)	(-) organique	organic matter
(-) charriée	overthrust/displaced (-)	(-) plastique	plastics
(-) chevauchée	upthrow	(-id-) thermodur- cissable	thermosetting plastics
(-) continentale	kratogen	(-) première	raw material
(-) rocheuse	rock mass	(-) thermoplastique	thermoplastic (-)
(-) de sel	salt plug		
(-) suspendue	sprung mass	mâtoir	matting tool
circuit de (-)	ground loop (electr.)	(-) à tubes	beading hand tool
masse moléculaire/	molecular weight	matrice	native rock; die
(-) molaire		(-) d'estampage	stamping die

mauvais, mauvaise	bad/weak/low/poor	*(-id-) par ultra*	ultrasonic (-id-)
(-) état	poor condition	*son*	
(-) conducteur	poor/bad conductor		
mauvaise qualité	low grade	*métal*	metal
		(-) antifriction	Babbitt (-)/white (-)
méandre	meander/loop	*(-) d'apport*	filler/deposited (-)
(-) abandonné	deserted loop	*(-) commun*	base (-)
(-) encaissé	enclosed/ingrown	*(-) fritté*	sintered/fritted (-)
	entrenched meander	*(-) trempé*	hardened (-)
(-) recoupé	cut off (-)		
		métamorphisme	metamorphism
mécanique	mechanics; mechanical	*(-) d'enfouissement*	burial (-)
(-) des fluides	fluid (-)	*(-) d'injection*	injection (-)
(-) des roches	rock (-)	*(-) de profondeur*	load (-)
(-) des sols	soil (-)	*(-) libre*	free (-)
		(-) périphérique	contact (-)
mécanisme	machinery/mechanism	*(-) régressif*	retrograde (-)
(-) d'alimentation	feed (-)		
(-) d'avance	pneumatic feed	*méthane*	methane/marshgas/
pneumatique			biogas
(-) d'horlogerie	clockwork		
(-) directeur	steering gear	*méthode*	method/system/process
		(-) d'approximations	trial and error (-)
mèche	wick; borebit/drill/	*successives*	
	tap	*(-) électrique*	electrical (-)
(-) à huile	oil wick	*(-id-) focalisée*	induction laterolog
(-) à queue	straight shank drill	*(-) de sismique*	seismic reflection (-)
cylindrique		*réflexion*	
(-) hélicoïdale	twist shank drill		
		meule	grindstone/grinding
mélange	blend/mixture/mix		wheel
	compound		
(-) antigel	antifreeze mixture	*meuleuse*	grinder
(-) eutectique	eutectic (-)		
		mg par litre/ par kg	parts per million (ppm)
mélangeur	mixer/blender		
(-) à palettes	blade (-)	*microbilles*	microballoons (to reduce
(-) de boue	mud gun/mud (-)		evaporation)
(-id-) à jet tour-	rolling jet (-)		
billonnaire		*microbrèche*	microbreccia
mélasse	molasses	*micromètre*	micrometer
membrane	membrane/diaphragm	*microrupteur*	microswitch
(-) à perméation	permeation selective(-)		
sélective		*microscope*	microscope
(-) semiperméable	semipermeable (-)	*(-) à contraste*	phase contrast (-)
		de phase	
mentonnet	latch pin/lug/stub	*(-) à haute résolution*	high resolution (-)
		(-) à immersion	dipping (-)
mer	sea	*(-) à réflexion*	engyscope
fonds des (-)	(-) bed		
niveau moyen	mean sea level/MSL	*migration*	shifting; migration
des (-)			
		milieu	environment/medium
méridien	meridian	*(-) continental*	continental environment
(-) d'origine	prime (-)/	*(-) filtrant*	filter medium
	standard (-)		
		minerai	ore
mesure	measure/measurement;	*(-) pauvre*	base (-)
	metering/measuring		
(-) à ruban	measuring tape	*minuterie*	timer
(-) de longueur	length measure		
(-) de pendage	dip logging	*mire*	sight pole/level rod/
(-) indicative de	level gauge		staff
niveau		*(-) graduée*	leveling rule
(-id-) à membrane	diaphragm (-id-)	*(-) de nivellement*	leveling pole
(-id-) capacitif	capacitor (-id-)	*(-) de précision*	stadia/staff
		(-) à voyant	target rod

mise	putting/setting
(-) à jour	updating
(-) à la masse (électr.)	earthing/earth connection/grounding
(-) en route	starting
(-) en place d'un outil	setting
(-) au zéro	setting to zero
mobylette	moped
modalité/mode	procedure/clause
mode opératoire	operating procedure
modèle	model/pattern/template
module	module/modulus
moisissure	mold/must
moletage	knurling
molette	knurling wheel
clé à (-)	monkey wrench
nez de (-)	cutter nose
outil à (-)	roller bit
(-id-) dentées	milled tooth bit
moment	moment/torque
monoclinal	monocline; monoclinal/uniclinal
monocylindrique	single cylinder
monophasé	single phase
mont	mount/mountain
montage	assembly/setting mounting; set up connection
(-) en étoile (électr.)	star connection
(-) en triangle (électr.)	delta (-)
(-) en parallèle (électr.)	parallel (-)
(-) en série (électr.)	cascade (-)/series connection
(-) sur patins	skid mounting
montagne	mountain
(-) à relief réduit	subdued (-)
montant	upright/stanchion/leg/stay stud
monte charge	lift/service elevator/hoist
montée	rise/upgrade/ascent/climb
monter	to climb/to rise; to erect/to assemble/to mount
monticule	hillock
monture	mount/mounting/fitting
moraine	moraine
morceau	piece/bit/scrap/shatter
mordâche (d'un étau)	clamp/claw (of a vise)
mortaisage	slotting/mortising
mort-terrain	dead ground/overburden/muck
mortier	mortar/cement
(-) de chaux/ (-) hydraulique	hydraulic (-)/lime (-)
(-) liquide	grout
(-) peu épais	slurry
mot clé, clé	keyword
moteur	engine/motor/prime mover
(-) asynchrone (électr.)	asynchronous motor
(-) à bague (électr.)	slip-ring (-)
(-) à boue (électr.)	mud (-)
(-) à couple constant (électr.)	constant torque (-)
(-) à courant triphasé (électr.)	three-phase current (-)
(-) à deux temps	two-stroke/two cycle engine
(-) hors bord	outboard engine/motor
(-) d'induction (électr.)	induction motor
(-) série (électr.)	series-wound (-)
(-) shunt (électr.)	shunt wound (-)/shunt (-)
(-) suralimenté	supercharged engine
(-) synchrone (électr.)	synchronous motor
moto pompe	power driven pump
motte	mound/clod/clump
mou (d'un câble)	slack/slackness (of a cable)
mouchard radioactif	snooper
mouflage	reeving/reeving system/block line/stringing up
(-) à brins multiples	multiple line (-)
moufle	block/pulley/sheave/block/crown
(-) crochet	hook block
(-) double	double (-)
(-) fixe	crown (-)
(-) mobile	traveling (-)
(-) à plusieurs poulies	multi-sheave (-)
moufler un câble	to reeve a wireline
mouillabilité	wettability
mouillant	penetrant agent (-) wetting agent

mouillé	wet/moist/damp
périmètre (-)	wetted perimeter
moule	mold/mould/casting form
moulin	mill
mousqueton	snap hook
mousse	foam/froth/lather
(-) de savon	soap suds
agent moussant	foaming/frothing agent
mouton	ram/pile hammer/pile driver
mouvement	movement/motion
(-) alternatif	reciprocating (-)
(-) circulaire	circular motion
(-) coulissant	sliding (-)
(-) d'horlogerie	clock (-)
(-) de terrain	subsidence effect
(-) rétrograde	backward motion
(-) de rotation	spinning
(-) transversal	cross drift
moyenne	average/mean
(-) pondérée	weighted (-)
moyeu	hub
mur	wall/floor
(-) argileux	poundstone
(-) de soutènement	retaining (-)/bearing (-)
(-) de talus	toe (-)

N

nacelle	basket/gondola/nacelle/pod
(-) de tubage	casing stabbing basket
naissant	incipient/nascent
nappe	sheet/nappe; ground water
(-) captive	confined groundwater
(-) de charriage	thrust/overthrust (-)/displaced mass
(-) chevauchantes	overlapping nappes
(-) de chevauchement	overthrust sheet/nappe
(-) d'écoulement	downsliding (-)
(-) d'intrusion/	intrusive sheet
(-) intrusive	
(-) de lave	extrusive sheet
(-) libre	unconfined ground water/water table
(-) perchée	perched (-)
(-) phréatique	phreatic surface water/ground water table
(-) de recouvrement	fold nappe
(-) de roche	rock sheet

natif	native/virgin
navette	traveling block
neck	neck
(-) volcanique	volcanic (-)/plug
nervure	rib
net	sharp; neat; nitt
netteté	sharpness
nettoyage	cleaning/scrubbing
nettoyer	to clean/to cleanse/to scrub/to pull/to crumb out
nettoyeur	cleaner/cleanser
(-) de parois	wall (-)
névé	firn/firn snow
ligne de (-)	firn line
nez	nose/nozzle
(-) d'injecteur	injector nozzle
(-) de l'outil	bit nose
nickelage	nickel plating
nid	pocket; nest
(-) d'abeille	honeycomb
(-) de pie	crow's nest
(-) de poule	pot hole
(-) de soufflure	coarse porosity
niveau	level
(-) de base	base (-)/datum line
(-id-) d'érosion	erosion base (-)
(-) à bulle	spirit (-)/bubble (-)
(-) des basses-eaux	low water datum
(-) de crêtes	peak plain
(-) à flotteur	float gauge
(-) hydrostatique	ground water (-)/water table (-)
(-) à lunette	surveyor's (-)
(-) à main	hand (-)
(-) marqueur/	marker horizon
(-) repère	
(-) du sol	ground (-)
(-) moyen de la mer	mean sea (-) (MSL)
niveleuse	grader
nivellement	grading/leveling survey/surveying/leveling
noeud	knot; node
(-) coulissant/	slip (-)/noose
(-) coulant	
(-) de cabestan/	bowline
(-) de chaise	
(-) de canalisation	mains junction
(-) lâche	loose knot
nonne	earth pillar/sand pinnacle
noria	scoop/bucket chain/chain pump

normalisation	standardization
norme	standard/norm
(-) provisoire	tentative (-)
notice	instructions/instruction booklet
noyau	kernel/nugget; salt plug/core
(-) anticlinal	anticlinal core
(-) rocheux	rock (-)
(-) de sel	salt plug
(-) synclinal	trough (-)
noyautage	coring

O

objectif	lens; objective/target
(-) anachromatique	diffused focus (-)
(-) à immersion	immersion (-)
oblique	oblique/slant/skew
forage (-)	slant drilling
obliquité	angularity/obliquity
(-) d'arête d'un outil de forage	drill rake
obstruction	obstruction/clogging/blocking
obstrué par le sable	sanded up
obturateur	stopper/closing device/shutter
(-) annulaire	annular type preventer
(-) de cimentation	cement retainer
obturation	plugging/sealing/closing
bloc d' (-)	preventer stack
obturer	to seal/to seal off
(-) un aquifère	to seal off water
(-) un puits à la boue	to seal off the hole with mud
oculaire	eye piece
oeil	eye; loop/draw hole
oeillet	eyelet/eye
(-) de câble	thimble
olive de suspension	hanger
ombres	shade/shadow
ombrelle de cimentation	cementing basket

onde	wave/pulse
(-) amortie	damped (-)
(-) de première arrivée	head wave
(-) d'arrivée directe dans l'eau	waterbreak
(-) de choc	schock wave
(-) diffusée	scattered (-)
(-) directe	direct (-)
(-) primaire	primary (-)
(-) secondaire	secondary (-)
(-) stationnaire	standing (-)
(-) de surface	surface (-)
(-) transversale	transverse/shear (-)
ondulation	corrugation/ripple
(-) de terrain	swell
onguent	salve
opacimètre	turbidimeter
opération	operation
opercule	cap/lid/plug
(-) de soupape	valve (-)
(-) de vanne	valve gate/plug
ordonnancement	scheduling
ordre	order; sequence
(-) d'achat	purchase (-)
(-) de marche	running (-)/working (-)
ordures	garbage/trash/solid wastes
(-) ménagères	household wastes
oreille	ear/lug/tab
écrou à (-)	wing nut
orgue	basaltic column
(-) géologique	sand pipe
orientation	direction/bearing; setting
(-) d'une faille	fault strike
(-) des couches	direction of dip
(-) des plis	trend
indicateur d' (-)	steering tool
orifice	port/opening/mouth/outlet/aperture/hole
(-) d'admission	intake port/inlet
(-) d'échappement	exhaust port/outlet port
(-) de dégazage	vent hole
oscillation	sway/swing/bounce
(-) de vitesse	hunting/flutter
osmose	osmosis
(-) inverse	reverse osmosis
ouïe d'aspiration (ventilateur)	ear (of a fan)

outil	tool/drilling bit/bit	*(-) de levage*	hoist (-)
(-) à carbure	carbide (-)	*(-) mobile*	traveling block
(-) de démontage	(-) puller		
du trépan		*pale*	blade
(-) à entailler	notching tool	*(-) d'hélice*	propeller (-)
(-) à molettes	cone bit/roller bit		
(-id-) dentées	milled tooth bit	*palette*	pallet; blade/paddle
(-) à pastilles	button bit	*(-) de manutention*	pallet
(-) de forage	drill bit		
(-id-) au câble	standard (-)	*paléozoïque*	paleozoic
(-) de repêchage	fishing tool		
(-id-) à coins	snatch block	*palier*	bearing/trunnion; floor/
(-) en queue de	fishtail bit/drag bit		level/landing; plateau/
poisson/(-) à lames			degree
machine (-)	machine tool	*(-) à aiguilles*	needle bearing
		(-) à anneau	ring-oil (-)
outillage	tools/equipment/	*graisseur*	
	implements	*(-) autograisseur/*	self lubricating (-)
(-) à main	hand (-)	*(-) autolubrifiant*	
		(-) de balancier	saddle (-)
outiller	to fit out/to equip	*(-) à billes*	ball (-)
		(-) de butée	thrust (-)
ouverture	opening/hole/gate/	*(-) à cousinet en*	bronze-bushed (-)
	vent/gap	*bronze*	
		(-) à douille	sleeve (-)
ouvrage	work/structure	*(-) lisse*	sleeve (-)
(-) en terre	earthwork	*(-) à rotule*	self aligning (-)/
			swivel (-)
ouvrier	worker/laborer/hand	*(-) à rouleaux*	roller (-)
(-) à la tâche	piece worker/jobber	*(-id-) coniques*	tapered roller bearing
(-) actionnant les	back-up man	*(-) usé*	scuffed (-)
clés de blocage			
(-) qualifié	skilled worker	*palissade*	fence/palissade/boarding
(-) spécialisé	semiskilled (-)		
		palmer	micrometer caliper/gauge
oxy-coupage	oxygen gas cutting		
		palonnier	equalizing yoke
oxydation	oxydation/oxidizing	*(-) de frein*	brake compensator
ozone	ozone	*palpeur*	feeler
		palplanche	sheet pile/pile plank
		palustre	paludal
P		*pan*	face/pane
		(-) coupé	cant
packer/presse	packer	*panier*	basket
étoupe/garniture		*(-) de repêchage*	fishing (-)/junk (-)
d'étanchéité		*(-) à sédiments*	sub (-)/junk sub
(-) à ancre	anchor (-)		
(-id-) pour tubage	casing anchor (-)	*panne*	breakdown/failure; face
(-) cylindrique/	openhole (-)	*(-) de marteau*	hammer face/peen
(-) de terrain			
(-) pour tubage/	casing (-)	*panneau*	panel; slab; block
(-) pour colonne de		*(-) de commande*	switchboard/control (-)
tubage		*(-) solaire*	solar array
paille (dans une tuyauterie)	straw; flaw/cleft	*papier*	paper
(-) couchée	sliver	*(-) à calquer/*	tracing (-)/
		(-) calque	transparent (-id-)
paillette	flake	*(-) d'émeri*	emery (-)
		(-) filtre/(-) filtrant	filter/filtering (-)
palan	block and tackle/tackle	*(-) de verre*	sand (-)
	hoist	*(-) millimétré*	scale (-)/plotting (-id-)
(-) à chaîne	chain tackle/hoist	*(-) quadrillé*	sectional (-)
(-) à croc	lift tackle	*(-) tournesol*	litmus (-)
		paraclase	paraclase

paraffine	paraffin
cire de (-)	(-) wax
parafoudre/	lightning protector/
paratonnerre	arrester
parallaxe	parallax
parcelle	particle; plot/lot
pare-chocs	bumper/fender
pare-feu	fire break(er)
paresseux	sluggish
paroi	wall/partition
(-) d'un puits	side of shaft/well (-)
partage	division/distribution; sharing
ligne de (-) des eaux	divide
particule	particle/grit
(-) abrasive	grit
(-) argileuse	clay particle
(-) colloïdale	colloïdal (-)
(-) dispersées	dispersed (-)
(-) en suspension	suspended (-)
pas	step/pace; pitch
(-) de vis	pitch of a screw
(-) fin	fine pitch
(-) à gauche	left hand thread
passage	crossing/passage
(-) à contre courant	counter current flow
vanne à (-) direct	straight through valve
passe (de soudure)	pass (welding)
(-) chaude	hot pass
(-) sur l'envers	back (-)
(-) étroite	string bead
(-) de pénétration	stringer (-)
(-) de soutien	backing (-)
passer	to pass
(-) à la pierre	to hone
(-) au tour	to turn/to lathe
passerelle	walkway/gang way/ catwalk/footbridge
(-) d'accrochage	safety board/platform/ monkey board
(-id-) des tiges	rod board
(-) du moufle fixe	crow's nest
passivation	passivation
passivateur de métaux	metal deactivator
passoire	strainer
pastille	pellet
(-) de carbure (pour trépan)	carbide insert (for drilling bit)

pâte	paste/compound; matrix
(-) à joint	sealing compound
(-) à roder	lapping/grinding (-)
patin	skid/pad/shoe
(-) de butée	thrust pad
(-) de frein	brake shoe
patron	pattern/model
patte	foot/lug/paw
(-) d'araignée	oil groove/oil tackle
(-) d'attache/	mounting lug
(-) de montage	
(-) de fixation	mounting bracket
pave désertique	boulder pavement/lag gravel
PEBD (polyéthylène à basse densité)	LDP (E) low-density polyethylene
PEHD (polyéthylène à haute densité)	HDP (E) high-density polyethylene
pédale	pedal
(-) d'accélérateur	accelerator (-)
(-) d'embrayage/ débrayage	clutch (-)
(-) de frein	brake (-)
pédologie	pedology
peigne	die comb
(-) à clé	tong die
(-) à fileter	thread chaser
(-) de câble	cable form
peinture	paint
(-) anti-rouille	antirust/rust protective (-)
(-) bitumineuse	asphaltic (-)
(-) au latex	rubber (-)
(-) au pistolet	(-) spraying
pelle	shovel/scoop
(-) automatique	grab
(-) à benne	drag line
(-) à godet	mechanical shovel
(-) mécanique	mechanical digger/power shovel/backshoe
(-id-) excavatrice	backshoe
pelleteuse chargeuse	multibucket loader
pellicule	film
pendage	dip/hade/inclination
amont- (-)	up the dip
(-) apparent	apparent (-)
aval- (-)	down the (-)
(-) divergent	divergent (-)
(-) inversé/(-) renversé	reverse (-)
(-) latéral	flank (-)
(-) périclinal	centroclinal (-)
(-) rayonnant	quaquaversal (-)
(-) réel	true (-)
(-) support	high (-)
pendagemètre	dipmeter

pendulaire	pendular
effet (-)	pendulum effect
pente	slope/grade/incline
(-) ascendante	upgrade
(-) d'éboulis	talus
(-) descendante	down-grade
(-) escarpée/	steep slope
(-) raide	
perçage	boring/drilling out
percement	perforation/drilling/
	sinking
perceuse	drill/power drill/drilling
	machine
(-) à colonne	pillar drilling machine
perche	pole/rod
percolation	percolation
écoulement de (-)	seepage
percussion	percussion/hammering
perforateur	drill/punch/perforator
(-) de tubage	casing perforator/casing
	gun
perforatrice	drill/hand drill/rock drill
periclinal	centroclinal
perimètre	perimeter/periphery; area
(-) d'établissement	settlement area
(-) mouillé	wetted perimeter
(-) de recherche	exploration (-)
période	period/cycle/time
perméabilité	permeability
(-) réelle	effective (-)
perte	loss/wastage/leak/
	leakage
(-) de boue	mud loss
(-) de charge	pressure (-)/pressure
	drop/head (-)
(-) de circulation	lost circulation
(-) de distribution	distribution losses
(-) en éclaboussement	spatter (-)
(-) par filtration	filter/filtration (-)
(-) à l'à-coup de	spurt/surge (-)
pression	
(-) aux parois	wall (-)
perturbation	disturbance/trouble/
	upset
(-) de fonctionnement	operating troubles
(-) magnétique	magnetic disturbance
petit, petite	small/little
(-) hangar/ appenti	lean-to
(-) versant	scarp
(-) dépression	hog wallow
photoclinomètre	photoclinometer
photocolorimètre	photocolorimetre

photovoltaïque	photovoltaïc
pic	pick/hack; peak/pike
(-) à main	hand pick
(-) de montagne	peak
pièce	piece/part; patch
(-) brute de	rough casting
fonderie	
(-) de forge	forging
(-) emboutie	stamping
(-) de rechange	spare/replacement
	part
pied	foot
(-) à coulisse	caliper square/slide
	caliper/slide gauge
(-) de biche/(-) de	claw bar
chèvre	
pied cube par	cusec
seconde	
piège	trap
(-) convexe	convex trap reservoir
(-) de faille	fault trap
(-) à sable	sand (-)
piémont	piedmont
pierraille	small stone/crushed
	stone
pierre	stone
(-) à aiguiser	sharpening stone/
	grindstone/hone
(-) à facettes	sand blasted pebble
(-) à huile	oil stone
pieu	pile/post/stake
piézométrique	piezometric
charge (-)	pressure head
ligne (-)	hydraulic grade line
pige	measuring rod
(-) de niveau	dip stick
pignon	pinion/gear
(-) conducteur	driving gear
(-) d'angle	bevel (-)
(-) droit	spur pinion
(-) entraîné	driven gear
(-) satellite	spider gear
(-) tendeur	jockey pulley
pile	battery/cell; mole/
	pier; heap
(-) chimique	chemical battery
(-) étalon	standard cell
(-) sèche	dry (-)/dry cell
(-) d'ancrage	anchor piling
pilier	stack/post/pillar/
	column
(-) d'érosion	erosion column
(-) de cabestan	knuckle post
(-) de remblai	cog

pince	tongs/pliers/hooks/ dogs/grip
(-) d'accrochage	grip
(-) à chaine	chain tongs
(-) coupante/	scissor (-)/cutting
(-) cisailles	pliers
(-) à griffe	pipe-grip
(-) de repêchage	pick-up/pick up grabs
(-) à ressort	spring clip
(-) à souder	welding tongs
pioche	pick ax/hack/pick
pipeline	pipeline
piquage (sur conduite)	branch connection (on a pipeline); pitting
piquet	peg/picket/staff
(-) d'arpenteur	cross staff
(-) de jalonment	stake
piquetage	staking
piston	plunger/piston
(-) à deux chambre	split piston (coring bit)
(-) racleur	pig/pipe scraper
(-id-) rotatif	revolving scraper
piton	pinnacle
pivot	spindle/swivel/fulcrum/ pin
(-) central	king pin
plage	beach; range
plaine	plaine/lowland
plan	even/smooth; layout/ plan; map drawing
(-) cadastral	ordnance survey map
(-) de charriage	overthrust fault
(-) de chevauchement	break thrust
(-) de clivage	cleavage plane
(-) de discontinuité	plane of unconformity
(-) de disjonction	divisional plane
(-) d'eau	water level
(-) de fracture/	slip plane
(-) de glissement	
(-) incliné	ramp/gradient; incline
(-) de marche	twinning plane
(-) de séparation	separation plane
plancher	flooring/floor
planimétrage	plotting
plancton	plancton
plaque	plate/sheet/slab
(-) d'arrêt	baffle (-)
(-) d'assise	bed (-)
(-) de dévissage/ de vissage	bit breaker
plastique	plastic
plateau	plate/tray; plateau; table
(-) -tamis	sieve tray

(-) continental	shelf
(-) d'embrayage	clutch disc/plate
(-) d'excentrique	eccentric sheave
(-) insulaire	island shelf
pli	fold/ply; creasing/ crease
(-) anticlinal	upfold
(-) concentrique	parallel folds
(-) couché	recumbent (-)
(-) déversé faillé	faulted overfold
(-) d'entraînement	drag (-)
(-)-faille	disrupted (-)/flexure fault
(-) perforé	sieve (-)/sieve tray
(-) plongeant	dipping (-)
(-) synclinal	synclinal (-)/syncline
plissement	fold/creasing/corrugation/ wrinkling/lap
(-) anticlinal	anticlinal fold
(-) cisaillant	shear folding
(-) embryonnaire	incipient folding
(-) imbriqué	imbricated (-)
(-) transversal	crossfolding
plissotement	crumpling/puckering/ minute folding
plomb	lead
fil à (-)	plumb line
(-) de sonde	plumb bob
(-) fusible	fuse/safety fuse
plombage	seals/sealing
plombagine	plumbago/black lead/ graphite
plongée	diving; dip
plongement	plunging/dipping/ inclination
(-) de l'axe du pli	(-) of a fold
(-) inverse/ contre pendage	rollover/dip reversal
(-) réel	full dip
plongeur	plunger/plunger piston; diver
(-) par déplacement	displacement (-)
(-) pousse carotte	core pusher (-)
(-) de pompe	pump plunger/piston
plot	stud/contact piece
plume	feather; pen
(-) enregistreuse/	recorder pen/
(-) traçante	recording (-)
pluviomètre	rain gauge/udometre
pneu	tyre/tire
(-) à ceinture	belted (-)
(-) ballon	balloon (-)
(-) clouté	spiked (-)
(-) radial	radial ply (-)
(-) de secours	spare tire

pneumatique	pneumatic/inflatable	*pôle*	pole
marteau (-)	pneumatic drill	*(-) magnétique*	magnetic (-)
outil (-)	air/pneumatic tool	*(-) négatif/positif*	negative/positive (-)
		migration des (-)	polar wandering
poche	pocket/bin/bunch;		
	trap; kidney	*polisseuse*	buffing/grinding
(-) d'air	air trap		machine
(-) de gaz	gas pocket		
(-) de minerai	ore bunch	*polluant*	pollutant/contaminant
poids	weight/load	*polyéthylène*	polyethylene
(-) à cavalier	rider weight	*(-) à basse densité/*	low density (-)/LDPE
(-) brut	gross (-)	*PEBD*	
(-) lourd	heavy duty vehicle	*(-) à haute*	high density (-)/
(-) mort	dead weight	*densité/ PEHD*	HDPE
(-) spécifique		*(-) expansé*	expanded (-)/
apparent	apparent specific		(-) foam
	gravity		
(-) total roulant	gross vehicle weight/	*pommade*	salve
	GVW		
(-) utile	payload	*pompage*	pumping
(-) volumétrique	bulk density	*station de (-)*	(-) station
poignée	handle/grasp	*pompe*	pump
		(-) à action	direct acting (-)
poinçon	punch/awl; die	*directe*	
		(-) à ailette	vane (-)
point	point/dot	*(-) à amorçage*	self-priming (-)
(-) d'accrochage	pick-up points	*automatique/*	
(-) bas	sag	*(-) autoamorçante*	
(-) culminant	climax	*(-) aspirante*	suction-lift pump
(-) de détérioration	node of the fault	*refoulante*	
(-) mort	dead point	*(-) d'assèchement*	sump (-)/dewatering (-)
(-) de repère	bench mark	*(-) à balancier*	beam/walking beam (-)
(-) de rosée	dew (-)	*(-) à boue*	mud (-)
(-) de rotation	fulcrum	*(-) centrifuge*	centrifugal (-)
(-) de rupture	break point	*(-id-) multicellulaire*	multistage (-id-)
		(-) à chapelet	chain (-)
pointage/pointement	pointing/picking; training	*(-) de charge/*	jet (-)
(-) comparatifs	cross plots	*à éjecteur*	
(-) de réflections	reflection picking	*(-) doseuse*	proportioning (-)
		(-) double aspiration	split case (-)
pointe	point/tip; peak	*(-) de fond de puits*	deep well (-)
(-) de charge	load peak	*(-) de gavage*	booster (-)
(-) d'électrode	electrode tip	*(-) manuelle*	hand (-)
(-) à tracer	scriber	*(-) à membrane*	diaphragm (-)
		(-) motorisée/	power (-)
pointeau	center punch; needle	*(-) commandée*	
(-) de carburateur	carburettor needle	*(-) de refoulement*	discharge (-)
		(-) de renfort	booster (-)
pointement d'une	outcrop of a seam	*(-) rotative*	rotary (-)
couche		*(-) à sable*	sand (-)/sand sucker/
(-) de sel	upright of salt		sand bucket/sludger
		(-) à vis	screw (-)
poire	pear	*(-) volumétrique*	positive displacement (-)
(-) de repêchage	casing spear/casing dog	*(-) submergée*	submersible (-)
(-id-) à coins	releasing (-)		
		pont	bridge
poisseux	sticky/pitchy	*(-) arrière*	rear axle/differential
		(-) à vis	worm axle
poisson (tout élément	fish (any part of drilling	*(-) roulant*	overhead crane
de forage qui tombe dans	equipment which has	*(-) électrique (électr.)*	bridge circuit
un puits)	become loose in a well)		
		porosité	porosity
poix	pitch	*(-) de fracture*	fracture (-)
polarimetre	polarimeter	*porte à faux*	overhang
polarisation	polarization	*porte lame*	cutter hand

portée	span/range; shoulder (of bit)
pose	laying
position	location/position
(-) *débordée*	onlap
(-) *en retrait*	offlap
(-) *géologique*	geologic position
positionnement	spotting
positionneur	air clamp
poste de travail	shift/tour/spell
poteau	pole/post/pillar
potentiel	potential
(-) *d'abaissement de niveau*	drawdown (-)
(-) *d'oxido-réduction*	redox (-)
poudre	powder/dust
(-) *abrasive*	abrasive (-)
(-) *à roder*	grinding (-)
(-) *à souder*	brazing (-)
poulie	pulley/block/sheave
(-) *à câble*	rope sheave
(-) *de câble de cabestan*	catline (-)
(-) *de câble de tubage*	casing line pulley
(-) *à chaîne*	chain wheel
(-) *à chape ouvrante*	snatch block
(-) *de curage*	sand sheave/sand line pulley
(-) *de forage*	crown pulley/crown sheave/crown block
(-id-) *au câble*	spudding pulley
(-) *mouflée*	block (-)
(-) *de palan*	tackle (-)
(-) *de tête*	crown (-)
poupée (de tour)	headstock
poussée,	thrust/pull
(-) *latérale*	side (-)
(-) *longitudinale/*	end (-)
(-) *axiale*	
poutre	girder/beam
(-) *en treillis*	lattice (-)
(-) *transversale*	sleeper/crossbeam/ traverse
poutrelle	girder/beam
pouvoir	power/force
(-) *agglutinant*	agglutinating power/ caking capacity
(-) *dispersif*	dispersive (-)
(-) *isolant*	insulating property
(-) *mouillant*	wetting (-)

précipitation	precipitation/deposit/ settlement
(-) *atmosphérique*	rainfall
précriblage	scalping
prélèvement	sample
(-) *de carotte*	core sampling
préreconnaissance	preliminary survey
presse	press
(-) *à cintrer*	bending (-)
(-) *à redresser les tiges*	pipe straightener
presse étoupe	stuffing box/packing box/gland
pression	pressure
(-) *de confinement/* (-) *de terrain*	confining (-)
(-) *de la colonne montante*	standpipe (-)
(-) *de couverture*	overburden (-)
(-) *de cuvelage*	casing (-)
(-) *d'eau*	head of water
(-) *de fracturation*	break down pressure
(-) *de marche/* (-) *de régime*	working (-)
(-) *de refoulement*	delivery (-)
(-) *de sortie*	outlet (-)
(-) *statique*	static (-)/static head
(-) *sur tiges de forage*	drill pipe (-)
pressostat	pressurestat/pressure controller
prétraitement	pretreatment
prise	hold/grasp/grip; tap; intake/offtake/inlet/ outlet
(-) *d'air*	air intake/inlet
(-) *de courant (la fiche se traduit par plug)*	socket/outlet
(-) *directe*	direct coupling
(-) *d'eau*	hydrant
(-id-) *en rivière/ en lac*	water intake
(-) *de force/* (-) *de mouvement*	power take off
(-) *en masse*	setting/hardening
(-id-) *lente*	slow hardening
(-id-) *rapide*	quick hardening
ciment à (-id-)	(-id-) cement
(-) *de terre (électr.)*	earth connection/ ground connection earthing
proclivité	slope/inclination of the ground
production	yield/output/production

produit	product/yield
(-) d'addition	additive
(-) d'apport	filler
(-) colmatants	plugging agents
(-) imprégnant	saturant
profil	profile/configuration/
	contour
(-) de dent	tooth pattern
(-) en long/	longitudinal (-)
(-) longitudinal	
(-) d'un sondage	(-) of a borehole
(-) stratigraphique	columnar section
(-) transversal	cross profile
profondeur	depth
(-) de champ	(-) of field
(-) d'enfouissement	(-) of burial
(-) forée	total measured (-)
(-) de pénétration	(-) of penetration
programme	program
projecteur	searchlight/floodlight
projection	projection/plan
(-) cartographique	map (-)
(-id-) cylindrique	cylindrical (-id-)
(-) horizontale	dip view
proportion	ratio/percentage
propriété	property/characteristic
(-) colmatante de	wall building property
la boue	of mud
prospection	prospecting/prospection/
	surveying/search
(-) électrique	electric (-)
(-) géophysique	geophysical (-)
(-) magnétique	magnetic (-)
(-) sismique	seismic (-)
protecteur	protector/guard/hood
(-) de tige	drill pipe protector
(-) de tubage	casing (-)
protection	protection/safeguard
(-) anti vibratoire	vibration insulation
(-) contre la	rust (-)
rouille	
(-) contre les	ground (-)/earthing
pertes de courant (électr.)	
protusion	protusion
province	province
(-) distributive	distributive (-)
(-) géologique	geological (-)
(-) pétrographique	petrographic (-)
pseudo-brèche	pseudo-breccia
pseudo clivage	false cleavage
puisage	bailing; water drawing
puisard	collecting pit/soak
	pit/sump

puissance	power/rating/capacity;
	thickness
(-) à l'arbre	spindle capacity
(-) au crochet	hook horsepower
(-) de démarrage	starting output
(-) au frein	brake horsepower
(-) de levée	lifting capacity
puits	well/borehole/well bore
(-) artésien	artesian (-)
(-) creusé	dug (-)
(-) éboulé	fallen-in (-)
(-) d'essai	test (-)/wildcat
(-) d'exploration	exploration (-)
(-) filtrant	filter (-)
(-) improductif	nonproducing/dry (-)
(-) muraillé	walled shaft/well
(-) d'observation	observation (-)
(-) peu profond	shallow (-)
(-) témoin	observation (-)
pulvérisateur	sprinkler
purge	drain/bleeding/
	blowcock/blowdown
robinet de (-)	blow-off cock/drain
	cock
purgeur	bleeder/petcock/trap
(-) d'air	air trap
(-) à cloche	bucket (-)
(-) à flotteur	float (-)
purification	purifying/cleansing/
	scrubbing
(-) par lavage	elutriation
pylone	mast/pylon
(-) métallique	lattice (-)

Q

quadrant	quadrant
quadricone	four-cone bit
quadrillage	grid; pattern of squares/
	checks
(-) de la carte	map (-)
méthode du (-)	grid method
qualité	quality/grade
(-) d'huile	oil grade
(-) de filtration	
(boue)	filtration quality (mud)
(-) de roulement	riding (-)
contrôle de (-)	(-) control
quantité	amount/quantity/lot
(-) de chaleur	thermal content
(-) de fluide en	throughput
circulation	
(-) totale de	total dissolved solids
matière dissoute	

quart | quart/quarter
(-) de circle | quadrant

(moteur) quatre temps | four-stroke engine

queue | tail/end/shank/ fang
(-) d'aronde | dove tail
(-) d'un outil | fang/shank of a tool
(-) de chargement | loading boom
(-) de clapet/ | valve rod
(-) de robinet/
(-) de soupape
(-) de rat (lime) | rat tail/round file

quincaillerie | hardware

quinconce | five spot pattern/staggered

R

rabattage | retreating

rabattement | lowering/folding back/ drawdown
(-) de nappe | groundwater (-)/ drawdown

rabot | plane/planer

raboteuse | planing machine

raboutage (de masse tige) | stubbing (of drill-collar)

raccord | sub/joint/connection/ coupling/attachment/ pipe fitting/union
(-) d'accrochage du câble | wireline socket
(-) d'alimentation | supply connection
(-) à brides | flanged fitting
(-) de câble | rope coupling/cable socket
(-) en col de cygne | gooseneck coupling
(-) conique | taper pipe
(-) coudé | bent sub
(-) à épaulement | shoulder nipple
(-) d'enveloppe | casing fitting
(-) d'étanchéité | seal nipple
(-) femelle | box sub/female
(-) fileté | threaded connection
(-) de flexible | mud hose connection/ rotary hose connection
(-) de forage à brides | drilling spool
(-) de levage | hoisting sub/lifting nipple
(-) mâle | pin/male connection
(-id-) double de calibres différents | pin to pin sub/swaged nipple

(-) de montage | hook-up nipple
(-) panier | boot sub
(-) rapide pour canalisation | quick union/rapid connection
(-) de réduction | pipe reducer/reducing sub/reducing union
(-) souple | flexible coupling
(-) en té | tee/T-union
(-) de tête de puits | mud cross
(-) pour tige de forage | drill pipe coupling/ tool joint/tubing spool
(-) pour tige de pompage | sucker rod sub
(-) union | union

raccordement | joining/hook up/ tie-in/connection
(-) en surface | surface tie-in
(-) transversal | cross connection
(-) vissé | screw connection
colonne de (-) | tie back string

raccourci | short cut

raccourcissement | reducing/shortening

racine | root
(-) de filetage | thread root
(-) d'une nappe de charriage | root of a fold

râclage | scraping/scouring

raclette | scraper/squeeze/blade

racleur/racloir | scraper/pig/wiper
(-) d'huile | oil saver
(-) de parois | wall scratcher
(-id-) type hérisson | hinge lock (-id-)
(-) de tubage | casing scraper

radeau | raft

radier | apron/floor/bed/raft
(-) de fondation | foundation raft

raide | stiff/tight/taut

rail de glissement | slide rail

rainure | groove/slot/notch
(-) de clavette | key way
(-) de graissage | oil groove
(-) de repêchage | catching (-)

ralenti | idling/throttling

rallonge | extension/lengthening rod
(-) adjustable | adjusting snubber
(-) d'arbre | extension shaft

rame (de tiges de forage) | string (of drill pipes)

ramification | splitting/branching
(-) d'une faille | spur fault

ramonage | chimney sweeping
(-) des canalisations | pigging

rampe	grade/gradient/ incline/ramp; spray pipe/ rack	*recouvrement*	lap/covering/overburden/ weathering/heave; scarf
(-) *d'aspersion*	spray pipe	*rectification*	grinding/honing/ rectification
(-) *de chargement*	loading ramp		
(-) *montante*	upgrade	*rectiligne*	rectiliner
rape (lime grossière)	grater/rasp (coarse file)	*recuit (après trempe)*	annealing (after hardening)
rapiéçage	patch work	*recul*	recoil/retreat
rapport	ratio/rate; report/ log/record	*reculée*	blind valley
		récupération	recovery/retrieval/ fishing
(-) *de transformation*	transformer (-)	(-) *de carotte*	core (-)
(-) *de forage*	drilling log/boring journal log	(-) *des déchets*	waste (-)/waste disposal
		outil de (-)	retrieving tool
rapporteur (d'angle)	protractor (of angles)	*récurage*	cleaning/scouring
râtelier	rack	(-) *d'un puits*	(-) a well
(-) *à outils*	tool (-)	(-) *du fonds*	bottom hole scavenging
(-) *à tiges*	pipe fingers/pipe sway/ finger board	*recuveler*	to recase
(-) *à tubage*	casing rack	*recyclage*	recycling/recirculation
ravin	gorge/ravine/gulch/ flume	*redox*	redox/oxidation-reduction
ravinement	gully erosion	*redressé*	straightened; upturned
rayage	scoring/scratching	*redressement*	straightening/uplift/tilt
rayon	spoke; ray; beam	*réducteur*	reducer
		(-) *de vitesse*	speed (-)
rayure	streak/scratch/score/ groove	*réduction*	crossover sub; reducer; reduction
réa	sheave/tie-down sheave/deadline anchor	(-) *de frottement*	drag reduction
		(-) *de tiges*	rotary sub
réactif	reagent	*réfection*	revamping/remaking
rebord	edge/lip/ledge	*réflection*	reflexion
rebouchage	back filling	*refoulement*	discharge/delivery/lift/ output/backflow
(-) *d'un sondage*	plugging back a well	(-) *d'une pompe*	pump discharge
rebroussement	upturning	(-) *externe*	external upset
rebut	waste/refuse/trash/ scrap	(-) *interne*	internal (-)
rechange	replacement	*refus*	refusal/reject
pièces de (-)	spare parts/spares	(-) *de crible*	undersize particles/ elements
recherche	research/investigation/ prospecting	(-) *de tamisage*	screenings
récipient	vessel/receptacle/ container	*regard*	sight/inspection hole
		(-) *de visite*	inspection port/manhole
recirculation	recycling/recirculation	*régime*	state/condition; rate
recoin	nook/recess	(-) *de fonctionnement*	operating rate
		(-) *permanent*	steady (-)
reconditionnement de puits	well workover	(-) *stable*	steady running condition
		réglage	setting/adjustment
reconnaissance	recognition/exploration	*règle*	rule/ruler
forage de (-)	exploration drilling	(-) *graduée*	measuring (-)

réglementation	byelaws	*rendement*	efficiency/yield/output
régulateur	regulator/controller/ governor	*renflement*	bulge/boss/swelling
(-) d'aspiration	suction-flow (-)	*reniflard*	snifter valve/breaker valve
(-) centrifuge	centrifugal governor		
(-) de débit	flow (-)	*renversement*	inversion/reversal/ overthrow
(-) des filtres	filter (-)		
(-) de niveau	level (-)	*renvoi*	return; crossreference
(-) pas à pas	step controller	*(-) de commande*	idle gear
(-) de pression	pressure controller	*(-) de tiges*	rod swing
régule	white metal	*réparation*	repair/mending
		(-) d'entretien	maintenance (-)
rejet	rejection/downthrow or upthrow/disposal/waste; shift	*(-) urgente*	emergency (-)
		répartiteur	manifold/distributor; dispatcher
(-) domestiques	household wastes		
(-) de faille	fault throw	*répartition*	distribution/dispatching
(-) horizontal	strike slip/fault heave	*repêchage*	fish job/fishing
(-) industriels	industrial wastes	*garniture de (-)*	fishing string
(-) vertical	vertical throw		
relais	relay	*repère*	mark/bench mark/ master/datum point
(-) à maximum *d'intensité*	overload (-)	*répertoire*	index/directory/list/ table
relevage	hoisting/lifting	*reptation*	creeping
relevé	plotting; chart/record; survey	*réseau*	net/network/grid/ lattice
(-) des compteurs	meter reading	*(-) d'alimentation*	feeder system/mains
(-) du terrain	ground (-)	*(-) collecteur*	gathering
		(-) cristallin	crystal lattice
relief	relief	*(-) de distribution*	distribution system/ distribution network
(-) adouci	subdued landscape		
(-) enterré	buried structure	*(-) d'égouts*	sewage (-)
(-) escarpé	alpine relief	*(-) de failles*	fault network/group of faults
remblai	fill/land fill/back fill		
(-) de sable	sand foundation	*(-) de fractures*	joint pattern
(-) déversé	dumped fill	*(-) maillé*	ring mains/ring system
		(-) ramifié	dendritic pattern/branch line system
remblayeuse	back filler		
(-) mécanique	gob stower/stowing machine	*(-) de transport* *(électr.)*	grid system (electr.)
rembourrage	padding	*(-) de tuyauteries*	piping system
remise	shed/lean to; discount; restoration/putting back	*réservoir*	tank/container/cistern/ basin/receiver; reservoir
(-) en état	reconditioning	*(-) à air comprimé*	air receiver
(-) en marche	restarting	*(-) d'alimentation*	feed tank
(-) à véhicules	garage	*(-) amortisseur/*	surge (-)
(-) à zéro	zero point setting	*(-) intermédiaire*	
		(-) collecteur/(-) de dépôt	sump (-)
remontée	upthrown; rise/pulling	*(-) à combustible*	fuel (-)
(-) des outils	pulling tools/pull out	*(-) de décantation*	settling (-)
		(-) enterré	underground (-)
remorquage	towing/haulage	*(-) en terre*	earthen reservoir
remorque	trailer	*résidu*	residue/waste
(-) surbaissée	low bed (-)		
		résiduaire	residual
rempart	rampart	*eaux (-)*	foul water/grey water/sewage
remplissage	filling/refilling		
renard	dog/scab/cant hook	*résiliation*	cancellation
renardage	channeling		

résilience	impact resistance/ resilience	*retrait*	shrinkage/withdrawed/ recess
résine	resin	*(-) du moufle et du crochet*	block and hook retraction
(-) acrylique	acrylic (-)		
(-) anionique	anion exchange (-)	*rétrécissement*	shrink
(-) cationique	cation exchange (-)	*rétro alimentation*	feed back
(-) échangeuse d'ions	ion exchange (-)		
(-) époxide	epoxy (-)	*rétro caveuse*	back hoe/back digger
(-) thermodurcissable	thermo setting (-)	*rétro chargeuse*	back loader
(-) thermoplastique	thermoplastic (-)		
résistance	resistance/strength; drag	*rétro charriage*	back thrusting
(-) au choc	impact strength	*rétrograder*	to shift down
(-) à l'écrasement	crushing strength	*retroussement*	distorsion
(-) à l'érosion	abrasion resistance/ erosion resistance	*(-) en bas*	downward drag
(-) à la fatigue	fatigue strength/ endurance limit	*(-) en haut*	upward (-)
(-) à la rupture/	tensile strength	*revers*	back-slope
(-) à la traction		*revêtement*	coating/lining/lagging/ facing/sheath
(-) des tubages à la pression externe	collapse resistance	*(-) de puits*	well casing/walling
(-) vive	resilience	*(-) de tube*	pipe coating
résistant	resistant/tough/strong	*ride*	ripple/wrinkle/fold
(-) à la chaleur	heat proof	*rigidité*	stiffness/strength
(-) au choc	resilient	*rigole*	ditch/gully/drain/ channel
(-) au gel	frost proof	*(-) à boues*	mud (-)
(-) aux intempéries	weatherproof	*(-) de ruissellement*	rain rill
résistivité	resistivity	*ringard*	poker/tapping bar
ressort	spring	*ripage*	skidding/sliding
(-) amortisseur	buffer (-)	*rivage*	shore/coast
(-) à boudin	coil/spiral (-)	*rive*	bank/shore
(-) à lames	leaf (-)		
(-) de rappel	return (-)	*riverain*	riparian/bordering
(-) de suspension	suspension (-)/ (-) mount	*rivet*	rivet
		(-) à tête fraisée	countersunk (-)
retard	delay/lag/slippage	*(-) à tête ronde*	round head (-)
(-) à l'allumage	ignition lag	*rivière*	river/stream
(-) de phase (électr.)	phase (-)	*(-) à marée*	tidal (-)
retassure	shrinkage cavity	*(-) régularisée*	graded (-)
rétention	retention/hold up	*rivoir*	riveting hammer
retenue	witholding/holding back; deduction	*rivure*	riveted joint/riveting
(-) amont	upper round level	*robinet*	faucet/valve/tap/cock
barrage de (-)	dam/weir/barrage	*(-) à aiguille*	neddle valve
		(-) d'arrêt	shut off valve/stopcock
réticulaire	reticular/networklike	*(-) à bec courbé*	bibcock
retirer	to withdraw/to pull out	*(-) à boisseau*	cock valve/plug valve
(-) les tiges/ le tubage d'un puits	to strip out a well	*(-id-) à 3 voies*	3-way (-id-)
		(-) à boisseau sphérique	ball valve
retombée	spinoff	*(-) à flotteur*	float (-)
retour	return	*(-) en laiton*	brass (-)
(-) sur l'emplacement	relocation	*(-) à membrane*	diaphragm (-)
(-) du fluide de circulation	returns	*(-) de non retour*	check (-)
(-) de manivelle	kick back	*(-) purgeur*	pet cock/drain cock
(-) à la masse (électr.)	ground connection		

(-) vanne	gate valve
(-id-) papillon	butterfly (-)
robinetterie	cocks and fittings
roche	rock/stone
(-) arénacée	sandy (-)
(-) argileuse	clayey/argillaceous rock
(-) broyée	shattered (-)
(-) clastique	clastic (-)
(-) fissurée	seamy (-)
(-id-) litée	shale
(-) du socle	basement (-)
rocher	boulder/rock/crag
rochet	ratchet/pawl
rodage	breaking in; grinding/lapping
rodoir	grinding/lapping tool
rognures	paring
rondelle	washer/spacer
(-) d'arrêt	lock (-)
(-) de cisaillement	shearing (-)
(-) d'étanchéité	sealing (-)
rosée	dew
rotation	rotation
rotor	rotor/impeller
rotule	ball/knuckle joint
roue	wheel
(-) à aubes	paddle (-)/impeller
(-) à augets	bucket (-)
(-) à boudin	flanged (-)
(-) à cliquet	dog (-)
(-) folle	idle wheel
(-) à gorge	grooved (-)
(-) voilée	buckled (-)/crooked (-)
roulement	bearing
(-) à aiguilles	needle (-)
(-) à billes	ball (-)
(-) à rouleaux	roller (-)
(-id-) autocentreurs	self aligning (-id-)
(-) de butée à billes	ball thrust (-)
roulette	castor wheel/roller
roulotte	trailer/caravan
ruban	tape/strip/band
(-) d'arpenteur	measuring reel
(-) isolant	insulating tape
rugosité	roughness/ruggedness
ruiniforme	castellated
ruisseau	brook/rivulet/streamlet/creek
ruisseler	to trickle/to drip/to run off

rupture	fracture/break/disruption
(-) de canalisation	pipe breakage
(-) de pente	slope break
(-) en plaques	slabbing
(-) de talus	slope failure
(-) de tube de forage (torsion excessive)	twist-off

S

sable	sand
(-) aquifère	water bearing (-)
(-) boulant/ (-) coulant	loose (-)/running (-)
(-) de capture	thief (-)
(-) à grains fins	fine-grained (-)/fine (-)
(-) à gros grains	coarse grained (-)/coarse (-)
(-) mouvant	quick (-)
(-) stérile	barren (-)
(-) usé	old (-)
(-) volcanique	ash rock
sableux	sandy
sablière	sand pit
sabot	shoe/slide
(-) d'attaque/ (-) de battage	spudding (-)
(-) de cloche de repêchage	guide overshot
(-) de cuvelage	casing slide/casing shoe
(-) denté	milling (-)
(-) flottant	floating (-)
(-) fraise/ (-) de fraisage	milling (-)
(-) de frein	brake (-)
(-) de guidage/ (-) de guide	casing guide (-)/foot (-)
(-) de surforage	washover (-)
(-) de tubage	casing (-)
sac	bag/sack
saccade	jolt/jerk/yank
saignée	trench/ditch/slot/cut
saillant	spur/salient; projecting
(-) anticlinal	nose/anticlinal nose/structural bulge
saillie	spurt/ledge/shoulder

saisie des données	data acquisition	*sédimentation*	settling
salin	saline/salty/briny	*segment*	segment; piston ring
salinité	salinity/salt content	*(-) râcleur*	oil wiper/oil scraping ring
saper	to sap/to undermine	*séisme*	earthquake/seism
sas	pressure lock/lock/ trap	*sel*	salt
(-) pour piston racleur	scraper trap/pig trap	*(-) ferreux*	ferrous (-)
		(-) ferrique	ferric (-)
saumâtre	brackish	*(-) fondu*	fused (-)
		(-) gemme	rock (-)/mine (-)
saumure	brine	*(-) tampon*	buffer (-)
saut	leap/jump	*selle*	saddle/base plate; stool
saute	jump/change	*(-) anticlinale*	anticlinal (-)
(-) de pression	surge	*(-) de balancier*	walking beam (-)
sauterelle	loader/unloader; lining up tool for pipe welding	*(-) de raccordement*	pipe (-)
		(fixation rapide d'une dérivation sur tuyau)	(attaching quickly a branch line on a pipe)
sauvetage	rescue/fishing	*semelle*	base/bed plate/sill plate/foot piece/ shoe/pad
scellement	sealing		
(-) de tubage	casing landing	*(-) à boue*	mud sill
schéma	sketch/line drawing/ diagram/pattern	*(-) de renfort*	reinforcing pad
(-) de connections électriques	wiring diagram (électr.)	*semence*	tack/sprig nail
(-) d'écoulement	flow pattern	*semi-automatique*	semiautomatic
(-) de fonctionnement	flowsheet/flow diagram	*semi-circulaire*	half round
(-) de montage	construction/assembly diagram	*sens*	direction/way/sense; meaning
schiste	shale/schist	*(-) direct/(-) inverse des aiguilles d'une montre*	positive direction; anticlockwise/counter- clockwise rotation
schistosité	foliation/cleavage	*(-) rétrograde*	negative direction; clockwise rotation
schlamm	slime/tailings/sludge	*(-) de rotation*	direction of rotation
scie	saw	*sensibilité*	sensitivity; susceptibility
(-) à contourner	compass (-)	*(-) chromatique*	colour response
(-) à plusieurs lames	gang (-)	*grande (-)*	high sensitivity
(-) à main	hand (-)		
(-) passe partout/ (-) à refendre	crosscut (-)	*sentier*	foot path
(-) sauteuse	jig (-)	*séparateur*	separator/trap/ settler/elutriator
secondaire	secondary/subsidiary	*(-) d'air*	air (-)
secouage	shaking/jolting	*(-) d'huile*	oil (-)
secousse	jerk/jolt/shaking	*(-) d'impuretés*	scale trap
		(-) magnétique	magnetic separator
section	section	*séparation*	separation/separating/ settling/parting/severing
(-) de carotte	core (-)		
(-) inférieure de la garniture	minor string	*(-) en plaquettes*	platy parting
(-) supérieure de la garniture	surface string	*(-) sphéroidale*	spheroidal jointing/ spheroidal parting
(-) transversale	cross section	*séquence de soudage*	welding sequence
sédiment	deposit/sediment/ settling	*(-id-) en cascade*	cascade (-id-)
		(-id-) par dépots discontinus	block (-id-)
(-) de filtration	sludge cake		

série	series; set/lot/run
(-) carbonifère	carboniferous series
(-) de cassures	set of joints
(-) d'échantillons	line of samples
(-) géologique	geological series
grande (-)	long run/mass production
montage en (-) (électr.)	cascade connection
serpentin	coil/spiral/worm
serrage	tightening/clamping/grip/screwing up/make-up
(-) à la main	hand tightening/hand make-up
(-) des manchons	coupling make-up
serre	dog/clamp/grip
(-) câble	wire rop chip/cable clamp/bulldog grip
(-id-) de sécurité	catline grip
(-) joint	screw clamp
(-) tube	tube (-)
(-id-) à chaînes	chain tongs
serrement	squeezing/closure
serrure	lock
(-) à secret	combination (-)
(-) de sûreté	safety (-)
service	operation/attendance; duty; department/branch
(-) cadastral	cadastral survey
(-) d'entretien	maintenance department
(-) géologique	geological survey
en (-)	on/operating/working
de (-)	on duty
servo	servo/power assisted controlling or operating device
seuil	threshold; sill/shelf/ridge
(-) continental	continental shelf
(-) de cisaillement	yield point
(-) d'écoulement/	yield valve
(-) de fluage	
profondeur de (-)	sill depth
(-) rocheux	cross cliff
shell	coquille
bearing (-)	*(-) de palier*
sherardisation (galvanisation)	sherardization
siccité	dryness
siège	seat; head office
(-) de soupape	valve (-)
(-id-) rapporté	inserted (-id-)
(-) à la turque (WC)	squat plate (toilet)

sifflet	whistle
(-) de déviation/ déviateur	wipstock
(-id-) amovible	retrievable (-id-)
(-) de repêchage	wall hook
signal	signal/pulse/sign/alarm
signalisation	marking/indication/signalling
silencieux	silencer/muffler/baffle, silent
(-) d'échappement	exhaust silencer/muffler
silex	flint/flintstone
silo	bin
silice	silica
(-) impure	chirt
sillon	furrow/groove/rill/trench
simoun	sandstorm
sinistre	disaster/casualty; accident
siphon	syphon/drip trap
(-) isolateur	water seal
sismo/ sismographe	seismograph/geophone/pick up/"doodlebug"
site	site
situation	situation/location
skip	skip
(-) basculant	tilting (-)
(-) à déversement automatique	self dumping (-)
socle	basement/base/base plate/bed plate/plinth/bedrock
(-) continental	continental terrace
(-) crystallin	crystalline basement
sol	ground/soil/earth
(-) argileux	clayey soil
(-) caillouteux	bouldery (-)
(-) embryonnaire	immature (-)
(-) mamelonné	hogwallowed (-)
(-) mourant	quaking bog
solide	rugged/hardy/solid
solive	joist/beam/rafter/balk
sommet	apex/summit/crest/peak

sondage	borehole/well bore/ well; boring/drilling/ well boring
(-) au câble	rope drilling
(-) d'exploration	test boring/ exploratory hole
(-) devié	crooked hole/deflected well
(-) par percussion/	percussion/cable
(-) au battage	tool drilling
(-) profond	deep boring
(-) rotary/	rotary boring/
(-) par rotation	rotary drilling
(-) stérile	batten well
(-) tubé	cased well
sonde/ sondeuse	drilling rig/borer/ drilling machine; sonde/ probe
sondeur	driller/tool pusher
(-) acoustique	sonic depth finder
sortie	exit/outlet/delivery end; output
soubassement	base plate/subframe; underlying rock/ basement; background
souche	stub/stump
soudage	welding
(-) à l'acétylène	acethylene (-)
(-) par amorces	lap (-)
(-) à l'arc	arc (-)
(-id-) électrique	electric (-id-)
(-id-) avec electrode enrobée	shield (-id-)
(-) avec electrode nue	bare metal (-id-)
(-) autogène	autogenous (-)
(-) bout à bout	butt welding
(-) continu	seam (-)/continuous (-)
(-) discontinu	intermittent (-)
(-) en descendant	downhill (-)
(-) par étincelage	flash (-)
(-) de pointage/	tack (-)/spot (-)
(-) par points	
(-) par rapprochement	butt (-)
(-) à recouvrement	overlap (-)
(-) en remontant	uphill (-)
(-) tendre	soldering
soudure	soldered joint/weld; solder/soldering compound
(-) affleurée	flush weld
(-) à l'argent	silver solder
(-) bord à bord	butt weld
(-) à clin	lap (-)
(-) à l'étain	soft solder/tin solder
(-) étanche	caulk weld
(-) sur l'envers	back (-)
(-) à recouvrement	scarf weld/overlap weld
(-) de renforcement	backing weld
sans (-)	seamless
souflante	fan blower
(-) de suralimentation	supercharger
soufflet	bellows:
(-) de dilatation	expansion (-)
soufflure	blister/blowhole/ blasthole/gas pocket
soulèvement	upheaval/uplift
soupape	valve
(-) anti retour	non return (-)/flap (-)
(-) à boisseau	plug (-)
(-) à boulet	ball (-)/globe (-)
(-) à charnière	clack (-)
(-) à clapet	flap (-)/disc (-)
(-) de déviation	bypass (-)
(-) à membrane	diaphragm (-)
(-) de sûreté	safety (-)
(-id-) à contrepoids	weighted (-id-)
(-id-) à ressort	spring loaded (-id-)
souplisseau	conduit (flexible)
source	spring/source
(-) d'affleurement	outcrop (-)
(-) d'énergie	power supply
(-) karstique	tubular spring
sourcier	dowser/diviner
souricière (de repêchage)	combination socket/ slip socket (for fishing)
(-) à tige	overshot
soute	bunker/bin/ compartment
soutènement	support/prop
souterrain	underground
soutirage	draw off/withdrawal/ bleeding/tapping
sphérique	ball shaped
spirale	spiral/helix
(-) agrippante	spiral grapple
stabilisant	stabilizer
(-) de suspension	suspension (-)
stabilisateur	stabilizer
(-) de tension (électr.)	voltage regulator
(-) de train de tiges	string (-)
(-) des bras d'élévateur	link (-)
station	station
(-) de pompage	pump/pumping (-)
stérile	barren/dead/sterile/ unproductive
stock	stock/stockpile
stockage	storage
stratification	bedding/stratification

strie	score/scratch/ corrugation
strié	banded
structure	structure/configuration/ pattern
stylet	pen/scriber/indicator pen
sublimé	sublimate
submergé	submerged/flooded
pompe submergée	submersible pump
substance	substance/matter/ material/stuff
(-) chimique	chemical (-)
(-) colloidale	colloidal material
(-) génératrice	parent substance
(-) minérale	mineral product
substitution	replacement/substitution
énergie de (-)	alternative energy
substrat	substrate
substratum	substratum/bottom
succession	succession/sequence
(-) stratigraphique	stratigraphic sequence
(-) de couches	(-) of beds
succion	suction
suie	soot
suif	tallow
suint	wool fat/suint
suintant	oozing/dripping
suintement	seepage/seeping/ leakings
suite	following/follow-up/ continuation
(-) normale	normal superposition
suivre	to follow
(-) la direction de	to strike
(-) un banc dominant	to walk a bed/ to walk out
(-) une réflexion	to carry a reflexion
sulfate	sulfate
sulfité	sulfite
sulfone	sulfone
sulfure	sulfide
superposé	superposed/ superincumbent
superposition	superposition
(-) d'origine	original order
superstructure	superstructure
(-) d'un derrick/ d'une sondeuse	headgear

support	bearer/support/base saddle/bracket/holder/ truss/pedestral/prop/ stand/stay/rest
(-) annulaire	ring stand
(-) d'arbre de treuil de puisage	tail post
(-) de balancier (sondeuse à battage)	Samson post (percussion rig)
(-) de canalisation	pipe hanger
(-) de coins	slip holder
(-id-) à déclenchement	slip launcher
(-) d'essieu	journal bearing
(-) de tige d'entrainement	pull rod carrier
(-) de tubage à coins	casing spider
(-) de tube	tube hanger/tube support
élément (-)	support frame
(-) à chariot	slide rest
suralimentation	supercharging
(-) par tubine	turbo charging
pompe de (-)	booster pump
surbaissé	dipped/dropped/ underslung
remorque à plateforme (-)	low-bed trailer
surcharge	overloaded
surdimensionné	oversized
surexploitation	overworking/ overdrawing/excessive exploitation
surface	surface/area
(-) d'appui	bearing surface/ bearing face
(-) d'érosions étagées	downstepping surfaces
(-) de charriage	thrust/overthrust plane
(-) de continuité	surface of continuity
(-) de discontinuité	discontinuity (-)
(-) de discordance	plane of unconformity
(-) structurale	back slope
surforage	washover
surhaussement	elevation
surintensité (électr.)	overcurrent
surplomb	overhang
surpresseur	booster/supercharger/ booster pump
surrection	uplift
surtension (électr.)	voltage surge/excess pressure

surveillance	monitoring/watching/ surveillance
suspendu	hanging
nappe suspendue	perched water table
suspension	suspension
olive de (-)	hanger
synclinal	syncline; synclinal
(-) bordier	rim (-)
(-) fermé	closed (-)
synergie	synergism
système	system/method/scheme
(-) asservi	servo system
(-) de faille	fault (-)

T

table	table/board; chart
(-) à dessin	drawing board
(-) de rotation	rotary table/turntable
(-) de concentration/	concentrating table
(-) à secousses	
(-) de contrôle	observation desk
(-) de triage	picking table
tableau	panel/board
(-) d'affichage	bulletin board
(-) de bord	dash (-)/ instrument (-)
(-) de commande	control (-)/ instrument (-)
tablier	apron; floor/deck
tabulaire	platy/tabular
tache	spot/stain
tâche	task/job
tachymètre	speed indicator/ speedometer
taillant	bit; cutter/cutting edge
(-) amovible	jack (-)
(-) double	double-arc (-)
(-) en couronne	multi-point (-)
(-) en croix	rose (-)
taille	cut; cutting/dressing; size
front de (-)	breast
(-) nominale	nominal size
taillis	thicket
taloche	trowel
talon	heel/end piece/spur/ stub; counterfoil

(-) de l'outil	bit shirt tail
talus	slope/bank/side slope escarpement
(-) continental	continental (-)
(-) d'éboulis	talus (-)/scree
(-) naturel	natural (-)
tambour	drum/spool/reel
(-) à câble	hoisting (-)
(-) de câble	cable reel/cable (-)
(-) de curage	sand reel/bailing (-)
(-) débourbeur	clearing cylinder
(-) denté	sprocket drum
(-) dessableur	rumbler/tumbler
(-) d'enroulement	hose reel/root (-)
(-) d'épuisement/ (-) d'évacuation	pump-out drum
(-) de forage	bull wheel
(-) de frein	brake (-)
(-) de levage	calf wheel
(-) de manoeuvre	hoisting (-) calf wheel
(-) mélangeur	mixing (-)
(-) de tamisage	screening (-)
tamis	sieve/sifter/cribble/ strainer/screen/grate/ grid
(-) filtrant	filter sieve
(-) à mailles fines	close meshed (-)
(-) métallique	wire gauze
(-) oscillant	shaker screen
(-) de pompe	pump strainer
(-) rotatif	revolving screen/ trommel screen
(-) à sable	sand screen/sieve
(-) à secousses	shaking sieve
(-) vibrant	shale shaker/vibrating mudscreen
(-) vibreur	impact screen
tamisage	screening/sifting/ sieving
refus de (-)	screenings
tambour de (-)	(-) drum
tampon	plug/pad; buffer/ bumper
(-) graisseur	pad lubricator
(-) obturateur	sealing plug
solution (-)	buffer solution
tangage	pitch
tanin	tannin
taquet	cleat/wedge/dog/ lug/stop/catch/cam
tarage	calibration/taring
taraud	tap/threading tap
(-) conique	taper (-)
(-) fileté	(-) thread
(-) finisseur	bottoming (-)
(-) mère	master (-)
(-) de repêchage	fishing (-)/taper (-)
(-) à tubes	pipe (-)

tarière	auger/ground auger/ gouge bit/borer
(-) à argile	claying bar
(-) à cuiller	shell auger
(-) à filet/	screw (-)
(-) rubannée	
(-) à tranchant	chisel bit
tarissement	depletion
tartre	scale/scale deposit/ scale crust/fur/scab
tas	pile/heap/stack
formation sur le (-)	on-the-job training/ in-service training
tassage	ramming/packing
tassé	packed/compressed/ compact
tasseau	cleat/strip/brace
tassement	sinking/settling/ shrinkage
(-) d'une couche	warping down of strata
(-) de remblai	shrinkage of backfill
(-) du sol	land subsidence
lézarde de (-)	settling crack
tate-ferraille (repêchage)	junk feeler (fishing tool)
taux	rate/ratio/rating
té	tee
(-) double	crossover (-)
(-) oblique	Y branch
(-) de raccordement	split tee
tectonique	tectonics
(-) de failles	fault (-)
(-) de glissement	sliding (-)
(-) de plissement	folding (-)
teinte	tint/hue/colour/ shade
teinture	dye/staining
télécommande	remote control
télédétection	remote sensing
télémesure	telemetering
tellurique	telluric
témoin	witness; boundary mark; island hill/farewell rock
(-) de chevauchement	nappe outlier
tempête	storm
(-) de sable	sand (-)
temps	time; weather
(-) d'instrumentation	fishing (-)
(-) de descente et de remontée du trépan	trip (-)
(-) de montage	rig time; set up time

(-) partagé	sharing
(-) de prise	setting (-)
(-) de remontée des tiges de forage	pulling-out time for drill pipes
tenailles	tong/dog
(-) à déclic	devil's claw dogs
(-) coupe fils	wire cutter
tendeur	stretcher/tightener/ stay bolt/tension shackle turnbuckle
(-) à vis pour haubans	
(-) de chaîne	chain bolt/chain adjuster
teneur	content/grade/amount/ proportion
tenon	spline/stud/tenon
tension	voltage; stress
térébenthine	turpentine/turp/ turpentine oil
terrain	ground/land/formation/ soil
(-) accidenté	rough ground
(-) boulant/	driftage
(-) charriés	
(-) ébouleux	caving (-)/caving formation
(-) ferme	solid (-)
(-) érratique	boulder clay
(-) de recouvrement	cap/capping
terrasse	terrace/embankment
(-) d'accumulation	drift (-)/build-up (-)
(-) rocheuse	rock/strath (-)
(-) tectonique	structural (-)
terrassement	earthwork/embanking/ grading
engin de (-)	stripping machine
terre	earth/ground
(-) d'alluvion	alluvia/dirt
(-) de bruyère	peat moss
(-) à diatomées	siliceous (-)
(-) filtrante/	filter clay
(-) à filtration	
(-) glaise	loam
(-) inondable	washland
(-) de remblayage	back fill
terril	hillcock/heap/refuse or waste dump
tertre	hillcock/knoll/mound
tête	head/crown
(-) d'agrippage	casing racker (-)
(-) d'arrachage	pulling (-)
(-) de bielle	big end (of connecting rod)/crank end
(-) de boulon	bolt (-)
(-) de cabestan	capstan drum (-)
(-) de câble	pot (-)
(-) de clou	nail (-)

tête (suite)	head/crown (cont'd)
(-) coupante	cutting (-)
(-) cylindrique	cheese (-)
(-) d'écoulement	flow (-)
(-) de faille	fault ridge/hoist
(-) de fraisage	cutter head/milling tool
(-) flottante	floating (-)
(-) d'injection	swivel/flushing head/ injector nipple
(-id-) d'entraînement	power swivel
(-id-) de rotary	rotary swivel
(-) de levage	lifting sub/elevator plug
(-) de mât	mast head
(-) de piston	cross head/piston crown
(-) de pompe	pump head
(-id-) à boue	hog (-)
(-) de puits	well (-)
(-id-) encapsulé/ fermé	dry (-id-)
(-) ronde	cheese (-)
(-) de soudage	welding (-)
(-) de soupape	valve (-)/valve disc
(-) de tubage/	casing (-)/braden (-)
(-) de sonde	
(-) de tube	drive (-)
(-) tournante	swivel head
(-) de vis	screw (-)
texture	texture
(-) alvéolaire	honeycomb(-)/cell (-)
(-) bréchoïde	brecciated (-)
(-) en chevrons	herringbone (-)
(-) en cocarde	cockade (-)
(-) engrenée	serrate (-)
(-) fenestrée	lattice (-)
(-) fibreuse	linear formation
(-) granoblastique	granoblastic (-)
(-) granuloblastique	granulose (-)
(-) rubanée	banded (-)
(-) schisteuse	cleavage (-)
(-) zonée	streaked (-)
thalweg	thalweg/drainage line
thermoforage	jet piercing
tige	rod/stick/pull rod/ stem/shank
(-) d'accélération	hurry up stick
(-) d'attelage	pull rod
(-) carrée d'entraînement	kelly/kelly bar/ square kelly
(-) de clapet	valve spindle
(-) coincée	stuck pipe/frozen pipe
(-) de commande	pull line/shackle line/ shackle (-)
(-) creuse	hollow rod
(-) à extrémités refoulées	upset pipe
entraîneur de (-)/ (-) d'entraînement	kelly spinner
(-) faussée	bent rod
(-) de forage	drill pipe
(-id-) à refoulement externe	external-upset (-)
(-id-) à refoulement interne	internal-upset (-)
(-) gradué	dividing rod
(-) hexagonale d'entraînement	hexagonal kelly
(-) de jauge	gauge rod
(-) de jonction	pull rod
(-) de lin (agent colmatant de boue)	flax stalk (plugging agent for drilling mud)
(-) octogonale	octogon kelly
(-) de piston	piston rod
(-) polie	slip stick
(-) de pompage	sucker (-)
(-) de poussée	push (-)
(-) de rallonge	adjusting (-)
(-) rallongée	extension stem
(-) de soupape	valve spindle/valve stem
(-) de suspension	hanger
timbre	maximum permissible pressure; stamp
timonerie de frein	brake linkage
tir	shooting/tir
tirage	blasting/draught/draft; pulling/dragging; printing forced draught
(-) artificiel/ (-) forcé	
(-) induit	induced draught
tirant	stretcher/stay/brace/ tie
tire bouchon (de repêchage)	rope worm (for fishing)
tire fond	draw bolt/lye bolt
toile	cloth/canvas/fabric
(-) à calquer	tracing (-)
(-) ciré	oil (-)
(-) émeri	emery (-)/abrasive (-)
(-) métallique	wire gauze
toilettes	toilet/lavatory
toit	roof/ridge/overlying bed
(-) d'une couche	top of a bed
(-) d'une faille	hanging wall
(-) imperméable	confining layer
tôle	sheet/sheeting/plate
(-) d'acier	steel (-)
(-) de chicane	baffle plate
(-) emboutie	dished plate
(-) galvanisée	galvanised (-)
(-) laminée	rolled plate
(-) striée	checkered (-)
(-) pour tubes	skelp
tolérance	tolerance/allowance
topographe	land surveyor

toron	strand/ply	*trait*	dash/line/score
(-) de câble	(-) of cable	*(-) à la craie*	chalk line
		(-) de graduation	division
torrent	torrent/mountain stream	*(-) de repère*	check mark
		tranche	slice
tors	twist		
		tranchée	trench/ditch
torsion	twisting/torsion		
		trancheuse	trencher/"mucker"
tour	tower; lathe; revolution/ turn; spire	*transfert*	transfer
(-) à fileter	screw cutting lathe	*transformateur*	transformer
(-) de forage/(-) de sondage	derrick/well rig	*transmission*	transmission/drive
(-) à banc rompu	gap lathe	*(-) par arbre*	shaft drive
(-) parallèle	engine (-)	*(-) par balancier*	beam drive
(-) à revolver	capstan (-)	*(-) par courroie*	belt (-)
		(-) par vis sans fin	worm (-)
tours par minute	revolutions per minute	*(-) hydraulique*	hydraulic (-)
tourbe	peat/turf	*transporteur*	transporter/conveyor; carrier
(-) lacustre	limnic (-)	*(-) à auges/*	bucket conveyor
tourbière	bog/wet moor	*(-) à godets*	
		(-) à balancelles	pendulum (-)
touret	reel/cable drum	*(-) à bande/*	belt (-)
		(-) à courroie	
tourie	carboy	*(-) à câble*	ropeway
tourillon	journal/stud/gudgeon/ trunnion	*travaux*	work/working/ operation
tourne à gauche	tap wrench/brace head	*(-) de reprise*	workover
tournevis	screw driver	*traverse*	cross beam/cross head/ truss
tourniquet	turnstile/swivel	*(-) d'appui*	headboard
tournoiement	spinning	*treillis*	lattice/grid
TPM (tours par minute)	RPM (revolutions per minute)	*tremblement de terre*	earthquake/seism
trace	trace; trail/track/scan	*trémie*	hopper/funnel/bin
tracé	plotting/profile/contour/ route	*trempage*	soaking
(-) d'une canalisation	pipeline route	*trempe*	hardening; quenching/ soaking
(-) de faille	fault trace	*(-) superficielle*	case (-)/skin (-)
traces	showings	*trépan*	bit/drill bit
tracteur	tractor	*(-) aléseur*	reaming (-)
(-) à chenilles	crawler/tracked (-)	*(-) d'attaque*	spudding (-)
(-id-) à grue	boom cat	*(-) de battage/*	spudding (-)
		(-) bêche	
tracto chargeur	front end loader	*(-) benne*	hammer grab
train	train/string/line	*(-) à biseau*	chisel bit
(-) baladeur	sliding gear	*(-) à boue*	mud (-)
(-) de tiges de forage	string of drill pipes/ drill stem	*(-) carottier*	core (-)
		(-) à cônes	cone (-)
traineau	skid/sledge	*(-) en croix*	star (-)
(-) à roulettes	live (-)	*(-) à couronne*	crown (-)
		(-) décentré	eccentric (-)
train de tiges	string	*(-) à deux taillants*	four wing (-)
		(-) au diamant	diamond (-)
trainée	streak	*(-) à doigts*	blue demon (-)
		(-) à effacement	collapsible (-)

trépan (suite)	bit/drill bit (cont'd)
(-) *émoussé*	dull (-)
(-) *hélicoïdal*	spiral (-)
(-) *à lames*	blade (-)/drag (-)
(-) *à 2 lames*	fish tail (-)
(-) *à 3 lames*	three way (-)
(-) *à molettes*	rock (-)/roller (-)
(-) *usé*	worn (-)
trépied	tripod
tresse	braid/plait
tréteau	trestle/prop
treuil	winch/windlass/capstan
(-) *auxiliaire*	carworks
(-) *à câble*	rope (-)
(-) *de curage*	sand reel/bailing pulley/sand drum
(-) *de forage*	draw works
(-) *de levage*	geared winch/lifting winch
(-) *de manoeuvre*	working winch/bull reel
(-) *à moufle*	capstan (-)
(-) *rotary*	rotary draw works
(-) *à simple tambour*	single drum hoist
triage	sorting/grading
tricone	three cone bit
tringle	rod/connecting rod
trommel	trommel/revolving screen/screening drum
troncature	truncation
tronçon	stub
trop plein	overflow
trou	hole/gap/aperture
(-) *à l'avancement*	pilot borehole
(-) *borgne*	blind hole
(-) *de garage de la tige carrée*	rat (-)
(-) *incliné*	slanted (-)
(-) *d'injection*	grout (-)
(-) *d'inspection/*	hand hole
(-) *de poing*	
(-) *de souris*	mouse hole
(-) *de visite*	manhole
trousse	kit/set/outfit
trusquin	marking gauge
tsunami	seismic surge
tubage	casing
(-) *à l'avancement*	working (-)/continuous (-)/(-) while drilling
(-) *à emboitement/*	collar joint (-)
(-) *à retreint*	
(-) *de puits*	well casing
tête de (-)	casing head cap

tube	pipe/tube/conduit
(-) *à brides*	flanged (-)
(-) *carottier*	core/coring barrel
(-) *à clapet*	bailer/American pump
(-) *coincé*	frozen pipe
(-) *à crépine*	strainer
(-) *crépiné à fentes*	slotted liner
(-) *de cuvelage*	casing pipe
(-) *fontaine*	bell nipple
(-) *guide*	surface casing
(-) *à extrêmités refoulées*	upset (-)
(-) *de protection*	shield tube
(-) *de repêchage*	fishing (-)/horn socket
(-) *à sable/*	basket sub/basket (-)
(-) *à sédiments*	
(-) *d'usure*	wash (-)/swivel wash (-)
tubulure	pipe manifold/nozzle
(-) *d'embranchement*	branch pipe
tuf/tuffeau	sinter
turbo foreuse	turbodrill
turbo pompe	turbine pump
turbo soufflante	turbocharger
turbulence	swirl/flutter
tuyau	pipe/tuyau/hose
(-) *d'échappement*	exhaust pipe/tail pipe
(-) *à emboitement*	faucet pipe/socket pipe
(-) *d'embranchement/*	branch (-)
(-) *de dérivation*	
(-) *de décharge*	spill (-)
(-) *de refoulement*	discharge line
(-) *de vidange*	drain pipe/purge pipe
tuyauterie	piping/pipes and fittings

U

udomètre	pluviometre/rain gauge
ultime	ultimate
ultrafiltration	ultra filtration
union	union/union joint or coupling
unité	unit
urbain	urban
urinoir	urinal
usine	plant/factory/works

ustensil · utensil

usure · wear/wear and tear
(-) ondulée · rippling
(-) par refoulement/
par écrouissage
(dents d'engrenage) · (gear teeth)
(-) des roulements · smearing
(-) en sillons · ridging

utile · useful

V

va-et-vient · push and pull/hauling
line

valet · dog/clip/support

validité · soundness

vallée · valley/dale/dip head
(-) d'effondrement · rift (-)
(-) d'érosion · destructional (-)
(-) tectonique/ · constructional (-)/
(-) structurale · structural (-)
affleurement de (-) · (-) outcrop

valve · valve
(-) à clapet · flap (-)

vanne · valve/gate
(-) à arcade · yoke (-)
(-) à boisseau · plug (-)
(-) d'isolement · shut off (-)
(-) à opercule · plug (-)
(-) à papillon · butterfly (-)
(-) à passage direct · gate (-)/straight way (-)
(-) à pointeau · needle (-)
(-) de purge · bleed (-)/drain (-)
(-) à tiroir · slide (-)
(-) à 3 voies · three-way (-)
(-) de vidange · drain off (-)

vapeur · vapor; steam

vase · slime/sludge/sullage;
container/vessel
(-) de nuit · chamber pot

veine · seam/vein/lode

vent · wind/drift
(-) de sable · sand drift
rafale de (-) · wind gust

ventilateur · fan/blower

venue · inflow/irruption
(-) en cours de · drilled show
forage

vérification · verification/checking
(-) de verticalité · (-) survey

verin · jack
(-) à vis · screw (-)
(-) hydraulique · hydraulic (-)
(-) pneumatique · ruckers/pneumatic (-)

vernis · varnish

verrou · lock/latch

verrouillage · latching/locking
(-) automatique · self locking

versant · side/slope
(-) de faille · fault scarp
(-) d'une vallée · valley wall

vibrateur · vibrator/shale shaker

vibrofonçage · vibrodriving

vidange · discharge/drain/
emptying

vide · vacuum; void

vieillissement · ageing

vilebrequin · crankshaft; brace
drill

virole · ferrule/collar/sleeve/
ring

vis · screw
(-) autofileteuse · self tapping (-)
(-) papillon · thumb (-)
(-) à tête · cheese head (-)
cylindrique
(-) à tête fendue · slotted head (-)
(-) à tête fraisée · countersunk head (-)
(-) à tête ronde · round head (-)

visée · sighting/viewing

visqueux · viscous

vissage · screwing/make-up/
making-up
(-) exagéré aux clés · overtonging
appareil de (-) des · drillpipe spinner
tiges

vitesse · speed/rate/velocity
(-) annulaire · annular velocity
(-) d'avancement · rate of penetration
(-) d'emballement · runaway speed
(-) d'extraction · rope/winding speed
(-) de remontée des · pulling rate
tiges

voilé · buckled/bent

volant · fly wheel; hand wheel

volet · shutter

volcanique · volcanic
bouchon (-) · (-) plug
cone (-) · (-) pile

voltmètre · voltmetre

volume	volume
(-) *massique*	specific (-)
voûte	vault/arch/upfold; saddle
(-) *du terrain*	ground arch
voyant	signal/mark
vrille	gimlet/borer
vrombissement	hum/throbbing
vue	view
(-) *en coupe*	cross section (-)
(-) *en écartelé*	exploded (-)
(-) *en écorché*	cutaway (-)
(-) *d'en haut*	top (-)
(-) *de face*	front (-)
(-) *latérale/*	side elevation
(-) *de côté*	
(-) *transversale*	sectional (-)

W

wagon	waggon/car/carriage
W (Watt)	Watt
white spirit	naphta/petroleum spirit

Z

zéolithe/ zéolite	zeolite
zingage	zinc plating process
zone	zone/belt/area; horizon
(-) *d'altérations*	belt of weathering
(-) *altérée*	weathered layer
(-) *aqueuse*	water layer
(-) *d'affaissement*	structure depression/ subsiding area
(-) *de brèche*	(-) of brecciation
(-) *de broyage*	crushed (-)/ shatter (-)
(-) *d'écoulement*	(-) of flow
(-) *de failles*	fault (-)
(-) *de lessivage*	leached (-)
(-) *de perte de circulation (boue)*	(-) of lost returns/ thief zone (mud)
(-) *plissé*	bow area

Annex 1—Health
Annexe 1—Santé

ANNEXE 1

ANNEX 1

SANTÉ

HEALTH

MALADIES attribuables aux insuffisances de l'approvisionnement en eau potable et/ou de l'assainissement (suivies du nom de l'agent infectieux ou du vecteur) selon la classification suggérée par D. J. Bradley (1977) et modification proposée par R. Feachem (1977).

DISEASES related to deficiencies in water supply and/or sanitation (followed by name of infecting agent or vector) according to the classification suggested by D. J. Bradley (1977), and revised proposal of R. Feachem (1977).

Cat. 1

Cat. 1

Maladies d'origine fécale à transmission orale, dues à l'ingestion d'organismes pathogènes rejetés par les excrétions d'une personne ou d'un animal infecté :

Faecal-oral diseases, transmitted by pathogenic organisms passing out in the excreta of an infected person or animal and subsequently being ingested:

Amibiase/Dysenterie amibienne (protozoaire entamoeba histolytica);

Amoebic dysentery/Amebiasis (Protozoa-Entamoeba histolytica);

Ascaridiose (Helminthes-Ascarises);

Ascariasis (Helminth-Ascaris/Ascarides);

Dysenterie bacillaire/shigellose (Bactérie du genre shigella);

Bacillary dysentery/shigellosis (Bacteria-shigella);

Dysenterie balantidienne/Balantidiose (protozoaire-Balantidium Coli.);

Balantidiasis/Balantidial dysentery (Protozoa-Balantidium Coli.);

Choléra (Bactérie-Vibrion virgule/vibrion El Tor);

Cholera (bacteria-vibrio comma/El Tor vibrio);

Maladies diarrhéiques/Entérites (organismes divers);

Diarrhoeal diseases (miscellaneous);

Enterobiases/Oxyurose (Helminthes-Enterobius vermicularis);

Enterobiasis/Oxyure disease (Pinworm disease (Helminth-enterobius Vermacularis);

Virus entériques;

Enteric viruses (various viruses);

Echinococcoses/Hydatidose (Helminthe-Echinococcus granulosis);

Echinococcosis/Hydatid disease (Helminth-Echinococcus granulosis);

Gastro-entérites (organismes divers);

Gastro-enteritis (miscellaneous);

Giardiase/Lambliase (protozoaires-Giardia ou Lamblia intestinalis);

Giardiasis (protozoa-Giardia or Lamblia intestinalis);

Hépatite infectieuse/Hépatite virale/hépatite épidémique (virus);

Infectious hepatitis/virus hepatitis/Epidemic hepatitis/epidemic jaundice (virus);

Leptospirose (protozoaire spirochète Leptospira);

Leptospirosis/Weil's disease (protozoa spirochaete-Leptospira);

Paratyphoïde (bactérie-salmonella paratyphi);

Paratyphoid (bacteria-salmonella paratyphi);

Tricocéphalose (helminthe tricocéphale);

Trichuriasis (helminth-whipworm);

Tularémie (bactérie-Pasteurella tularensis);

Tularaemia (bacteria-Pasteurella tularensis);

Poliomyélite/paralysie infantile/maladie de Heine Médine (virus);

Poliomyelitis/Infantile paralysis/Heine Medine disease (virus);

*Typhoïde/ fièvre typhoïde
(bactérie-salmonella typhii).*

Cat. 2

*Maladies contrôlables par ablutions,
résultant d'une hygiène corporelle
médiocre (manque d'eau ou difficultés
d'accès) et absence de moyens
satisfaisants de contrôle des excrétions.*

*Infections oculaires et cutanées
(organismes divers):*

   Trachome/ conjonctivite granuleuse;

   Conjonctivites infectieuses;

   Gale (Scarcoptes scabiei);

   Lèpre (mycobacterium leprae);

   Pian (spirochète-treponema pertenue);

   Infections cutanées et ulcérations.

Autres affections;

   Parasitoses:

   *Typhus exanthématique (Rickettsia-
Prowaseki);*

   *Fièvre récurrente (spirochete-
Borrelia).*

Cat. 3

*Maladies contagieuses par contact ou
ingestion de pathogènes dont une
partie du cycle vital se développe
dans un hôte aquatique:*

Avec lésions cutanées:

   *Schistosomiases urinaires et
rectales (Douves Schistosome mansoni;
Sch. haematobium; Sch. Japonicum);*

   *Dermatites à schistosomes
cercaires.*

Par ingestion:

   *Clonorchiase/ distomatose hépatique
(Douves);*

   *Bothriocéphalose (Bothriocephale-
Diphyllobotrium latrium);*

   *Dracunculose/ maladie du ver de Guinée
(Helminthe-Dracunculus medinensis);*

   *Paragonimose/ Distomatose pulmonaire
(douve-paragonimus westermani);*

   Fasciolase (Douve-Fasciolopsis buski).

Cat. 4

*Maladies dont les vecteurs de
contagion sont des insectes ayant
une connection avec l'eau:*

Habitat proche de l'eau:

   *Trypanosomiase/ Maladie du sommeil
(glossine ou mouche tsétsé);*

   *Tularémie (Bactérie-Pasteurella
tularensis).*

Typhoid/typhoid fever/enteric fever
(salmonella typhi/salmonella typhosa).

Cat. 2

Water washed diseases, due to poor
personal hygiene (lack of or limited
access to water) and lack of proper
human waste disposal.

Skin and eye infections
(miscellaneous):

   Trachoma (chlamydia trachomistis);

   Infectious conjunctivitis;

   Scabies;

   Leprosy/Hansen's disease
(mycobacterium leprae);

   Yaws (treponema pertenue);

   Skin sepsis and ulcers.

Other diseases:

   Louse-borne diseases:

   Typhus fever (Rickettsia-
Prowazeki);

   Relapsing fever (spirochaeti-
Borrelia).

Cat. 3

Water-based diseases, spread by contact
with or ingestion of pathogens which
spend part of their life cycle in an
aquatic animal:

Penetrating skin:

   Urinary and rectal Schistosomiasis/
Snail fever (blood flukes -
Schistosoma mansoni; S. haematoblium;
S. Japonicum);

   Schistosome dermatis/swamp itch
(schistosome circariae).

Ingested:

   Clonorchiasis/liver fluke disease
(Helminth—clonorchis sinensis);

   Diphyllobothriasis (tapeworm);

   Dracontiosis/Guinea worm disease
(Helminth—Dracunculus medinensis);

   Paragonimiasis (fluke—paragonimus
westermani);

   Fasciolopsiasis (fluke—fasciolopsis
buski).

Cat. 4

Diseases transmitted by insect vectors
related to water:

Living near water:

   Tripanosomiasis/Sleeping sickness
(glossinidae or tsetse fly);

   Tularaemia (bacteria-Pasteurella
tularensis).

Reproduction dans l'eau
  Arboviroses;
  *Dengue (virus - moustique Aedes-
    Aegypti);*
  Encéphalites;
  Filariose;
  Paludisme (moustique anophèle)
  Onchocercose (mouche simuli);

  Fièvre jaune (moustique stégomya)

Breeding in water
  Arboviral infections;
  Dengue/breakbone fever/Dandy
    fever (mosquito Aedes Aegypti);
  Encephalites;
  Filariasis;
  Malaria (anopheles mosquito);
  Onchocerciasis (simuliidae flies/
    black flies);
  Yellow fever (mosquito stegomya).

Annex 2—Formulae
Annexe 2—Formulaire

ANNEXE 2 / ANNEX 2

FORMULAIRE / FORMULAE

I. SYSTEME INTERNATIONAL D'UNITES (S.I.) / INTERNATIONAL SYSTEM OF UNITS

1.1 Unités de base — Basic Units

Grandeur	Unité/Unit	Symbole/Symbol	Quantity
Longueur	mètre/metre	m	Length
Masse	kilogramme	kg	Mass
Temps	seconde/second	s	Time
Intensité de courant électrique	ampère/ampere	A	Intensity of electric current
Température thermodynamique	kelvin	K	Thermodynamic temperature
Quantity de matière	mole	mol	Amount of substance
Intensité lumineuse	candela	cd	Luminous intensity

1.2 Unités supplémentaires — Supplementary Units

Grandeur	Unité/Unit	Symbole/Symbol	Quantity
Angle plan	radian	rad	Plane angle
Angle solide	stéradian/steradian	sr	Solid angle

1.3 Unités dérivées — Derived Units

Grandeur	Unité/Unit	Symbole/Symbol	Quantity
Aire, superficie	mètre carré/square metre	m^2	Area, surface
Volume	mètre cube/cubic metre 1 litre = 1 dm^3	m^3 l	Volume
Angle plan	degré/degree minute seconde/second	° ' "	Plane angle
Temps	minute heure/hour jour/day	min h d	Time
Vitesse	mètre par seconde/meter per second	m/s	Speed
Vitesse angulaire	radian par seconde/radian per second	rad/s	Angular velocity
Accélération	mètre par seconde carrée/meter per second squared	m/s^2	Acceleration
Fréquence	hertz	Hz	Frequency

Grandeur	Unité/Unit	Symbole/Symbol	Quantity
Masse	*tonne*	**t**	**Mass**
Masse volumique	*kilogramme par mètre cube*/kilogram per cu. metre	**kg/m³**	**Density**
Débit-masse	*kilogramme par seconde*/kilogram per second	**kg/s**	**Mass rate of flow**
Débit-volume	*mètre cube par seconde*/meter cubed per second	**m³/s**	**Volume rate of flow**
Quantité de mouvement	*kilogramme-mètre par seconde*/kilogram meter per second	**kg.m/s**	**Momentum**
Moment cinétique	*kilogramme-mètre carré par seconde*/kilogram meter squared per second	**kg.m²/s**	**Angular momentum**
Moment d'inertie	*kilogramme-mètre carré*/kilogram meter squared	**kg.m²**	**Moment of inertia**
Force	*newton* $(1\,N = 1\,kg.m/s^2)$	**N**	**Force**
Moment d'une force	*newton mètre*/newton meter	**N.m**	**Moment of force**
Pression, contrainte	*pascal* $(1\,Pa = 1\,N/m^2)$	**Pa**	**Pressure, stress**
Viscosité dynamique	*pascal seconde*/pascal second	**Pa.s**	**Dynamic viscosity**
Viscosité cinématique	*mètre carré par seconde*/meter squared per second	**m²/s**	**Kinematic viscosity**
Tension superficielle	*newton par mètre*/newton per meter	**N/m**	**Surface tension**
Energie, travail, Quantité de chaleur	*joule* $(1\,J = 1\,N.m)$	**J**	**Energy, work, amount of heat**
Puissance	*watt* $(1\,W = 1\,J/s)$	**W**	**Power**
Coefficient de dilatation linéique	*kelvin à la puissance moins un*/kelvin to the power of minus one	**K⁻¹**	**Linear expansion coefficient**
Conductivité thermique	*watt par mètre - kelvin*/watt per meter - kelvin	**W/(m.K)**	**Thermal conductivity**
Chaleur massique	*joule par kilogramme kelvin*/joule per kilogram kelvin	**J/(kg.K)**	**Specific heat capacity**
Entropie	*joule par kelvin*/joule per kelvin	**J/K**	**Entropy**
Energie interne enthalpie	*joule* $(1\,J = 1\,N.m)$	**J**	**Internal energy enthalpy**
Flux lumineux	*lumen*	**lm**	**Luminous flux**

Grandeur	Unité/Unit	Symbole/Symbol	Quantity
Eclairement	lux $(1\ lx = 1\ lm/m^2)$	lx	Illumination
Charge électrique	coulomb $(1\ C = 1\ A.s)$	C	Electric charge
Potentiel, tension, différence de potentiel	volt $(1\ V = 1\ W/A)$	V	Voltage, potential, potential difference
Champ électrique	volt par mètre/ Volt per meter	V/m	Electric field strength
Capacité	farad $(1\ F = 1\ C/V)$	F	Capacitance
Champ magnétique	ampère par mètre/ ampere per meter	A/m	Magnetic field strength
Flux d'induction magnétique	weber $(1\ Wb = 1\ V.s)$	Wb	Magnetic flux
Induction magnétique	tesla $(1\ T = 1\ Wb/m^2)$	T	Magnetic flux density
Inductance, perméance	henry $(1\ H = 1\ Wb/A)$	H	Inductance, permeance
Résistance, impédance, réactance	ohm $(1\ \Omega = 1\ V/A)$	Ω	Resistance, impedance, reactance
Conductance	siemens $(1\ S = 1\ A/V)$	S	Conductance
Résistivité	ohm · mètre/ ohm · meter	Ω/m	Resistivity
Conductivité	siemens par mètre siemens per meter	S/m	Conductivity
Masse molaire	kilogramme per mole	kg/mol	Molar mass
Volume molaire	mètre cube par mole/cubic meter per mole	m^3/mol	Molar volume
Concentration	kilogramme par mètre cube/kilogramme per cubic meter	kg/m^3	Concentration
Concentration molaire	mole par mètre cube/mole per cubic meter	mol/m^3	Molar concentration
Molalité	mole par kilogramme/ mole per kilogram	mol/kg	Molality

1.4 Préfixes et symboles pour les multiples et sous multiples
Prefixes and symbols for multiples and submultiples

Facteur/Factor	Préfixe/Prefix	Symbole/Symbol
10^{18}	exa	E
10^{15}	peta	P
10^{12}	tera	T
10^9	giga	G
10^6	mega	M
10^3	kilo	k
10^2	hecto	h
10	deca	da

1.4 Préfixes et symboles pour les multiples et sous multiples (suite)
Prefixes and symbols for multiples and sub-multiples (cont'd)

Facteur/Factor	Préfixe/Prefix	Symbole/Symbol
10^{-1}	deci	d
10^{-2}	centi	c
10^{-3}	milli	m
10^{-6}	micro	µ
10^{-9}	nano	n
10^{-12}	pico	p
10^{-15}	femto	f
10^{-18}	atto	a

Note.

myria (10^{-4}) *n'est plus utilisé/*is no longer used.

1.5 Désignation des grands nombres/Designation of large numbers

France		USA, Italy, etc.
million	10^6	million
(milliard*)	10^9	billion
billion	10^{12}	trillion
	10^{15}	quadrillion
trillion	10^{18}	quintillion
quatrillion	10^{24}	septillion

*Milliard is not an official denomination, if currently used.
D'un usage courant, le terme milliard n'est pas légal.

II. CONVERSION DES UNITES S.I. ET UNITES ANGLO-SAXONNES/ S.I. UNITS AND UK/US UNITS CONVERSION

Dans les pays anglo-saxons, on utilise le point (.) pour séparer les décimales des unités, la virgule (,) pour séparer les milliers des millions, etc.

In countries other than anglo-saxon, a comma (,) is used to separate decimals from the units, a point (.) to separate thousands from millions, billions, etc.

Symbole/Symbol   *Conversion*

A. Longueur/Length

Symbole/Symbol		Conversion
in (*ou/*or) "	1 inch *(pouce)*	= *0,254 m*
ft (*ou/*or) '	1 foot *(pied)* = 12 in	= *0,3048 m*
yd	1 yard = 3 ft	= *0,9144 m*
mi	1 statute mile = 1,760 yd	= *1,609 km*
m	*1 mètre*..........................approx 1.0936 yd or 39.37 in or 3.281 ft	
km	*1 kilomètre*	= 0.6214 mi

B. Surface

1 in²	1 square inch (sq.in*)	*6,4516 cm²*
ft²	1 square foot (sq.ft*)= 144 in²	*9,2903 dm²*
yd²	1 square yard (sq.yd*)= 9 ft²	*0,83613 m²*
	1 acre = 4,840 yd²	*0,40469 ha*
mile²	1 square mile = 640 acres	*2,5900 km²*

* Note

Abréviations supprimées dans les normes britanniques.
Abbreviations no longer used in British standards.

cm^2	1 *centimètre carré* (square centimetre)	0.1550 in²
m^2	1 *mètre carré* (square metre)	10.764 ft²
dam^2, a	1 *décamètre carré ou are* (square decametre/are)	119.6 yd²
hm^2, ha	1 *hectomètre carré ou hectare* (square hectometre or hectare)	2.471 acres
km^2	1 *kilomètre carré* (square kilometre)	0.3861 mile²

C. *Volume et capacité/* Volume and capacity

in³	1 cubic inch	*16,3871 cm³*
ft³	1 cubic foot = 1,728 in³	*28,317 dm³*
yd³	1 cubic yard = 27 ft³	*0,7646 m³*
UK pt	1 British pint (4 gills)	*0,5683 l*
UK qt	1 British quart (2 pt)	*1,1365 l*
UK gal	1 Imperial gallon (4 qt = 8 pt)	*4,5461 l*
US pt	1 US pint (4 gills)	*0,4732 l*
US qt	1 US quart = 2 pt	*0,9464 l*
US gal	1 US gallon = 4 qt	*3,7854 l*
bbl	1 US barrel = 42 US gal	*158,987 l*
bu	1 US bushel (4 pecks)	*35,2391 l*
	US shipping ton = 40 ft³	*1,13267 m³*
	Registered ton = 100 ft³	*2,83168 m³*
cm^3, ml	1 *centimètre cube, ou millilitre* (cubic centimetre or millilitre)	0.0611 in³
dm^3, l	1 *décimètre cube, ou litre* (cubic decimetre, or litre) *or* *or* *or*	0.0353 ft³ 1.760 UK pt 0.220 UK gal 2.113 US pt 0.264 US gal
m^3, st	1 *mètre cube, ou stère** (cubic metre/stere) or or or or or	35.30 ft³ 1.3079 yd³ 220 UK gal 264 US gal 6.293 US bbl 28.37 US bu

*Note
Pour mesure du bois de chauffe/(à éviter)
For measuring wood as fuel/(to be avoided)

D. *Masse/*Mass

gr	1 grain	*64,799 mg*
oz	1 ounce	*28,350 g*
lb	l pound *(livre)* = 16 oz	*453,592 g*
st	1 stone (British) = 14 lb	*6,350 kg*
qr	1 quarter (British) = 28 lb	*12,701 kg*
cwt	1 hundred weight (British) = 112 lb	*50,802 kg*

sh.cwt	1 short hundred weight (USA) = 100 lb	*43,359 kg*
sh.ton	1 short ton (USA) = 2000 lb	*0,907 t*
kg	*1 kilogramme*	35.274 oz
	or	2.205 lb
t	*1 tonne (metric tonne)*	19.684 cwt
	or	22.046 sh.cwt
	or	1.1025 sh.ton
	or	0.9842 UK ton

E. Vitesse Linéaire/Linear Speed

in/s	inch per second	*91,44 m/h*
ft/s	foot per second	*1,0972 km/h*
yd/s	yard per second	*0,9144 m/s*
mile/h	statute mile per hour	*1,609 km/h*
m/s	*mètre par seconde*	3.280 ft/s
m/h	*mètre par heure*	3.280 ft/h
km/h	*kilomètre par heure*	0.622 mile/h

F. Vitesse de Filtration/ Filtration rate

US gal/ft² min	US gal/min.sq.ft (US gpm/sq.ft)	*2,445 m/h*
UK gal/ft² min	UK gal/min.sq.ft (UK gpm/sq.ft)	*2,936 m/h*
ft/min	cu.ft/min.sq.ft (ft³/ft² min)	*18,29 m/h*
m/h	*Vitesse linéaire/Linear speed)* *1 mètre cube par heure et mètre carré /*cubic metre per hour and square metre	= 0.0547 ft/min (0.409 US gpm/ft²) (0.341 UK gpm/ft²)

G. Masse volumique et concentration/Density and concentration

lb/in³	Pound per cubic inch	*27,6799 g/cm³*
lb/ft³	Pound per cubic foot	*16,0185 kg/m³*
gr/in³	grain per cubic inch	*10,076 g/l*
gr/ft³	grain per cubic foot	*2,296 mg/l*
gr/UK gal	grain per Imperial gallon	*14,25 mg/l*
gr/US gal	grain per US gallon	*17,12 mg/l*
lb/UK gal	pound per Imperial gallon	*99,77 g/l*
lb/US gal	pound per US gallon	*119,3 g/l*
g/cm³	*gramme par cm³ = 1 kg/dm3*	0.036127 lb/in³
or kg/dm³	*kilogramme par dm³ = 1 g/cm³ or*	62.427lb/ft³
mg/l	*milligrammes par litre/*parts per million (ppm)	0.0703 gr/UK gal
or g/m³	*gramme par mètre cube*	0.584gr/US gal 0.4356 gr/ft³

H. Force

| pdl | Poundal *(pied-livre/s²)* | *0,0138 daN* |
| lbf | pound-force *(livre-force)* | *0,448 daN* |

| tonf | ton force (British - 2240 lbf) | *996,402 daN* |
| " | ton force (USA 2000 lbf) | *889,644 daN* |

I. Viscosité / Viscosity

	*Viscosité dynamique/*Dynamic viscosity Poundal second per square foot (= Pound per foot second)	
pdl s/ft²		*1,4882 Pa.s*
in²/s	*Viscosité cinématique/*Kinematic viscosity inch squared per second	*6,452 × 10⁻⁴ m²/s*

J. Energie, Travail, Chaleur /
Energy, Work, Amount of Heat

ft pdl	foot poundal	*0,04214 J*
ft lbf	foot pound-force	*1,356 J*
hp h	horse-power-hour or or	*2,685106 J* *0,746 kWh* *0,641 th*
BTU	British Thermal Unit or or Therm (= 10⁻⁵ BTU) or	*1.055,06 J* *0,293 Wh* *0,252 mth* *105.500 kJ* *25.200 kcal*
J	*joule (= 10⁷ erg = 0,239 cal)* or	23.72 ft pdl 0.737 ft lbf
kJ	*Kilojoule (= 1/3.6 Wh)*	0.3725 × 10⁻³ hph 0.948 BTU
Wh	*Watt heure (= 3.600 J = 0,860 mth)*	3.41 BTU
kWh	*Kilowatt heure (= 3600 KJ)*	1.34 hph
kcal, mth	*Kilocalorie, ou millithermie* *= 1.163 Wh*	3.97 BTU
th	*Thermie (= 10³ Kcal)*	1.56 × 10⁻³ hph

K. Puissance / Power

ft pdl/s	foot poundal per second	*0,04214 W*
ft lbf/s	foot pound-force per second	*1,35582 W*
hp	horse power (= 550 ft lbf/s)	*0,74570 kW*
BTU/h	British Thermal Unit per hour	*0,2931 W* *0,252 mth/h*
BTU/s	British Thermal Unit per second	*1,055 kW* *0,252 mth/s*
kW	kilowatt	*1,341 hp* 0.948 BTU/h
mth/h	*millithermie par heure*	3.968 BTU/h
mth/s	*millithermie par seconde*	3.968 BTU/s

L. Pression, Contrainte/
Pressure, Stress

| lbf/in²
or psi | Pound-force per square inch
or | *6.894,76 Pa*
0,06894 bar/hpz
or daN/cm² |

lbf/ft²	Pound-force per square foot	*47,87 Pa*
ton f/in²	Ton-force per square inch (British)	*154,44 bar*
	Ton-force per square inch (USA)	*137,90 bar*
in H₂O	inch of water *(pouce d'eau)*	*2,49 m bar*
in Hg	inch of mercury *(pouce de mercure)*	*33,86 m bar*
Pa	*pascal (= 1 N/m²)*	*0.0209 lbf/ft²*
bar	*bar (= 1 hpz)*	*14.504 lbf/in²*
atm	*atmosphère*	*14.696 lbf/m²*

M. *Pouvoir calorifique /* Calorific Power

BTU/lb	British Thermal Unit per pound	*2,326 J/g*
	or	*0,556 mth/kg*
BTU/ft³	British Thermal Unit per cubic foot	*37,259 KJ/m³*
	or	*8,901 mth/m³*
kcal/m³	*kilocarie par mètre cube*	
or mth/m³	*ou millithermie par mètre cube*	*0.1124 BTU/ft³*

III. *CORRESPONDANCE D'UNITES/*CORRESPONDENCE OF UNITS

3.1. *Unités de Pression /* Units of Pressure
(Valeur d'une unité de la 1ère colonne / Value of one unit in first column)

	pièze	*bar*	*mm Hg**	*m H₂O*	*Pa*
pascal (Pa)	*0,001*	*0,00001*	*0,0075*	$1,020 \times 10^{-4}$	*1*
pièze	*1*	*0,01*	*7,4975*	*0,10197*	10^3
bar	*100*	*1*	*749,75*	*10,1972*	10^5
atmosphere (atm)	*101,325*	*1,01325*	*760*	*10,3323*	*101.325*
kgf/cm²	*98,066*	*0,98066*	*735,514*	*10*	$9,81 \times 10^4$
mètres de Hg	*133,377*	*1,33377*	*1000*	*13,596*	$1,33 \times 10^5$
mètres de H₂O (4°C)	*9,806*	*0,09807*	*73,551*	*1*	$9,81 \times 10^3$

* Mercure/Mercury

3.2. *Unités d'energie /* Units of Energy
*(Valeur d'une unité de la 1ère colonne/*Value of one unit in first column)

	joule	*kWh*	*kcal ou/or mth*	*hph*	*BTU*
joule	*1*	$27,78 \times 10^{-8}$	238×10^{-6}	$37,25 \times 10^{-8}$	948×10^{-6}
kilowatt/heure	$3,6 \times 10^6$	*1*	*860*	*1,341*	*3 413*
kilocalorie	*4 186*	116×10^{-5}	*1*	156×10^{-5}	*3 968*
Horse power hour	$2,68 \times 10^6$	*0,746*	*641*	*1*	*2 545*
British Thermal Unit	*1 055*	293×10^{-6}	*0,252*	393×10^{-6}	*1*

3.3 *Unités de débit* / Rates of flow
(Valeur d'une unité de la 1ère colonne / Value of one unit in first column)

	m^3/h	m^3/s	l/s	$1\ 000\ m^3/d$	ft^3/s	ft^3/min	U.S. gpm	U.S. mgd	U.K. gpm	U.K. mgd
m^3/h	1	278×10^{-6}	0,2778	0,024	9.81×10^{-3}	0.588	4.403	6.34×10^{-3}	3.667	5.28×10^{-3}
m^3/s	3 600	1	1 000	86,4	35.30	2 118	15 852	22.82	13 198	19.00
l/s	3,6	0,001	1	0,0864	35.3×10^{-3}	2.118	15.85	22.8×10^{-3}	13.198	19×10^{-3}
$1\ 000\ m^3/d$	41,67	$11,6 \times 10^{-3}$	11,575	1	0.4085	24.5	183.47	0.264	152.85	0.220
ft^3/s (= cfs = cusec)	102	$28,3 \times 10^{-3}$	28,317	2,448	1	60	449	0.647	374	0.538
ft^3/min (cfm)	1,70	472×10^{-6}	0,472	0,0408	0.0167	1	7.48	0.0108	6.235	8.98×10^{-3}
U.S. gal/min (U.S. gpm)	0,2271	$6,3 \times 10^{-5}$	0,0631	$5,45 \times 10^{-3}$	2.223×10^{-3}	0.1336	1	1.44×10^{-3}	0.833	1.20×10^{-3}
U.S. mgd	157,7	$43,8 \times 10^{-3}$	43,80	3,785	1.546	92.80	694	1	578	0.832
U.K. gal/min (U.K. gpm)	0,2728	$7,58 \times 10^{-5}$	0,0758	$6,54 \times 10^{-3}$	2.674×10^{-3}	0.1605	1.201	1.73×10^{-3}	1	1.44×10^{-3}
U.K. mgd	189,42	$52,6 \times 10^{-3}$	52,61	4,545	1.857	111.4	834	1.20	694	1

IV. *EVALUATION DES BESOINS EN EAU* / ESTIMATING WATER REQUIREMENTS
*(d'après/*from Deutscher Verband für Gas-und Wasserfachleute. DVGW)

*Quantité/*Quantity

Besoins domestiques	litre/day/hab.	Domestic uses
Boisson et cuisine	3 - 6	Drinking and cooking
Lessive	20 - 40	Laundering
Vaisselle	4 - 6	Washing up
Hygiène corporelle	10 - 15	Personal hygiene
Bain, douche	20 - 40	Bath, shower
Toilette à chasse	20 - 40	Flushing toilet
Entretien de l'habitation	3 - 10	House cleaning
Arrosage des jardins d'agrément	50-10 $1/m^2/d$	Watering of house gardens
Lavage de voiture (chaque) avec seau à la lance	20 - 40 / 100 -200	Car washing (each) with bucket with watering hose

Installations publiques et culturelles / Public and cultural facilities

Hospital, par jour et par lit	250 - 600	Hospital, per bed per day
Bains publics, par visiteur	150 - 180	Public bath, per patron
Piscines publiques par visiteur	150 - 200	Public swimming pool, per patron
Ecoles, par écolier et par jour: sans douches ou piscine avec douches sans piscine avec douches et piscine	10 / 20 / 30 - 50	Schools per student per day: without shower nor sw. pool with shower without sw. pool with shower and sw. pool
Bâtiments publics et bureaux (par employé par jour)	40 - 60	Office and public buildings (per staff per day)
Restaurant, par visiteur	15 - 20	Restaurant, per patron